THE ASHES '79

Other books by David Frith

'My Dear Victorious Stod'
The Archie Jackson Story
The Fast Men
Cricket Gallery (edited)
England versus Australia – A Pictorial History
The Ashes '77 (with Greg Chappell)
The Golden Age of Cricket
Thommo's Tale (in preparation)

THE ASHES '79

by

DAVID FRITH

foreword by BILL O'REILLY

Angus & Robertson Publishers

ANGUS & ROBERTSON PUBLISHERS
London Sydney Melbourne Singapore Manila

First published by Angus and Robertson (UK) Ltd 16 Ship Street, Brighton, in 1979

National Library of Australia
Cataloguing-in-publication data.

Frith, David
The Ashes '79.

ISBN 0 207 14264 5

1. Cricket – Australia. I. Title.

796.35865

Printed in Hong Kong

PHOTOGRAPHS

Between pages 96 and 97

Grateful thanks are due to Patrick Eagar for photographs 2, 8, 9, 10, 11, 12, 13, 15, 16, 17, 18, 19, 20, 21, 22, 23. And to News Ltd and their photographers Ron McKenzie and Peter Bull for photographs 3, 4, 5, 6, 7, 14, 24, 25, 26, 27, 28, 29, 30, 31, 32.

CONTENTS

FOREWORD

by **Bill O'Reilly**, former Australian Test cricketer (taker of 102 wickets against England in 19 Test matches during the 1930s), now cricketer-writer for the *Sydney Morning Herald*.

Consistently in accord with the early confession of his 'bitter sweet schizophrenia of allegiance', my comrade in typewriter tapes, David Frith, sets his inflexible standard for a magnificent tale well told in *The Ashes '79*.

Not only does that phrase prepare the reader for a well-rounded account of a Test series eventually so lopsided that crestfallen Australians find it a subject of infinite embarrassment, but it also sows the seed for satisfying the curiosity it arouses.

Encountering it so early in his tale one anticipates interesting accounts of an Australian side of the author's life which affects him throughout the tour at the appropriate times. There were so many of those opportunities that embarrassment prevents me from pursuing that line any further.

Modesty, I suppose, has been the handicapping force that has made Frith refrain from telling the real meaning behind his use of the word 'allegiance'.

From the age of eleven right up until England repossessed him seventeen years later David Frith was a 'fair dinkum' Australian citizen adequately experienced in the colloquialisms and customs of this far south land.

Firstly, and of course highly unimportantly by comparison with other facts, his primary and secondary education needs were well and truly attended to by the NSW department of public instruction – a period from which he has either benefited or lived down as the case may be in the intervening years.

Paramountly important, however, is the spell-binding fact that Frith, during his youthful residence in our country, showed clear-cut signs that Australia's cricket selectors were ultimately destined to cast appraising eyes over his significant claims to glory.

Were one given the privilege of rummaging through the Frith treasure-chest that safeguards the memory-aids of family history one would be sure to find two faded cricket caps, boy-sized roughly about 6¾ to fit a head not swollen nor seriously affected by an incipient halo.

The more faded cap would bear the designation 'A. W. Green Shield' and the other 'Poidevin-Gray Shield'.

The overwhelming cricket ambition of every gifted Sydney schoolboy dedicated to an all-out attempt to make a name in the game is to be considered good enough to be invited to represent his district in the Green Shield.

With that invitation in his pocket the world belongs to him. He would not change places with the Prime Minister himself.

That is the pinnacle of juvenile cricket ambition in my home town.

Even now the accomplishment impresses me so deeply that I often feel inclined to ask the young heroes for their autographs.

That particular cap represented a pretty good start for young David Frith. But there is more to the story.

That other cap I mentioned is given to the boy who has incredibly accomplished the giddy height of joining the under 21s – a band of highly acclaimed and fully accredited local cricket heroes.

When I was skippering the St George District Club many years ago two of the baby-faced boys of my team, Arthur Morris and Ray Lindwall, both destined to become cricket immortals in the international sphere, were very proud owners of a Green Shield and a Poidevin-Gray cap.

To bring David Frith right into context with this part of the story, he himself was a gifted team-mate of the great Australian batsman Norman O'Neill when the two of them in much more recent times were Green Shield players.

From this you will realise how it is that David Frith handles this story of his with such splendid impartiality – a fact which will go down exceedingly well with the host of Australian readers who will be thankful for even the slightest remissions on their embarrassments.

It will also explain how it is that the author can speak with such splendid authority on so many of the tour's incidents where some highly sophisticated cricket know-how is essential to get the full message across.

Recounting the story of Frith's early cricket performances and ambitions undoubtedly raises the melancholy thought that the game was robbed of a useful player when he turned his back on it.

Fortunately, however, there have been adequate compensations, of which this book, *The Ashes '79*, is an important item to line up with the *England versus Australia*, his pictorial history of the Test matches since 1877, another monumental effort confirming the author's love-affair with cricket.

Our association in the Press boxes throughout Australia has given me an outstanding opportunity to assess the all-round competency of David Frith as a highly-skilled critic conversant with all the intriguing points of cricket-watching.

Indeed, his was the opinion I always sought on the countless occasions I missed the action when concentration flagged in the trying conditions of an unusually hot summer.

Recognising his never-failing reputation as a highly-rated authority in the Press box, it comes to me as a very great pleasure indeed to assure his readers that I regard this work of his as my official history text-book of the Ashes battle of '79.

1. MIKE'S TASK FORCE

It might have been an airfield somewhere in England, 1940: the young men standing in casual clusters, laughing and listening, talking and toasting, yet with a tension about them. Multiple souls joined as a band by their coats of Air Force blue. Any moment the 'scramble' klaxon will surely blare and they will down their drinks and race to the runway. There was something vital to defend; a battle to be won.

But it was only peacetime England, 1978: Heathrow Airport, and sixteen cricketers making the most of the receding minutes with their wives or girlfriends. The battles to be won were on the 'friendly' fields of Brisbane and Perth, Melbourne and Sydney and Adelaide; the prize to be defended: the tiny Ashes urn that has begat so much joy and anguish over almost 100 years. Now, though, there was much more at stake, for even the least serious members of the party knew that this was no ordinary four-month cricket tour.

On the closing page of *The Ashes '77* I felt moved to register a fear that the cricketers who had defected from official cricket to play for Kerry Packer's private World Series might soon be playing for something best described as the ashes of Test cricket. In the absence of a compromise arrangement between the International Cricket Conference and the Packer organisation, could the traditional game retain its hold upon the public and thereby upon a strong financial condition? Or would the entirely commercial World Series concept, with its lurid star attractions and gimmicks, capture the imagination—and with it the gate-money and first place in the television ratings?

The initial season of conflict, 1977–78, offered some clues. The Australian public gave its vote to the competitive Australia-India Test series—both at the gate and in front of the television set. The Packer organisation was said to have lost close on four million dollars.

Now, a year later, the World Series matches were carefully scheduled outside the Australia-England Test match dates. There had been changes in the WSC administrative structure, and, it was claimed, much had been learned from the introductory season. Some of the costs were non-recurring. Confidence within the

WSC camp appeared high, especially when it was expected that Australia's spearhead fast bowler Jeff Thomson, retired from Test cricket for domestic and financial reasons, would be linking up with Dennis Lillee again in the WSC team styled 'Australian XI', with a lighter workload awaiting him and more chance of winning matches than when he was vice-captain of the ill-fated Test side which toured West Indies early in 1978. This all depended, of course, upon 'Thommo's' being able to extricate himself from his Australian Cricket Board contract, which still had a year to run.

Against this screen of fervent confidence were silhouetted the misgivings attending Australia's Test prospects against Mike Brearley's England team. So often Australia had produced, as if from a perpetually well-stocked warehouse, replacements for lost champions. This time, though, not two, not three, but ten or eleven worthy players were needed almost overnight. Peter Toohey, Graeme Wood, Graham Yallop, Steve Rixon—these had all shown their potential in the Caribbean. Craig Serjeant, Gary Cosier and Kim Hughes had proven ability too. But would it be enough? And where were the others coming from, especially a fast attack worth the name? Small wonder England were quoted four-to-one-on to retain the Ashes as the team, the 29th to play one or more Tests in Australia, prepared to fly out.

Not since the star-studded 1958–59 team set out in *Iberia* had England seemed so certain to win. Peter May's nil-four defeat should have served as a warning for all time. That was twenty years ago, when our first-born was due. If a boy, he was to be named Peter; if a girl, May—or so we declared. Adulation sometimes prompts quaint gestures. That boy was now back in his native land, and I made no secret of my eagerness to see him again in Sydney—as well as my father, brother and in-laws. A year ago I was ensconced in Greg Chappell's agitated touring group. Now all my Englishness would doubtless surface, and I was bracing myself for another attack of that bitter-sweet schizophrenia of allegiance that has shadowed me for thirty years.

It was already history that, in Australia's hour of crisis in 1977, Bobby Simpson had emerged from ten years of retirement from the first-class game to lead a depleted Test team against India and on tour in West Indies. At the age of 42 he had made a fine job of the bridging operation. Indeed, he might even have carried on against England and to the 1979 World Cup. His 're-retirement' in September 1978 could have had something to do with the Board's preparedness to name the skipper only Test by Test and not for the entire series. From afar, I had enjoyed his dramatic comeback, and was sorry to see him go—not simply because, for a few months, he had given me a reprieve from being older than anyone currently playing Test cricket, but because I had always admired his neat, businesslike cricket, his stamina and determination in both his main career, which began when he was sixteen, and the postscript. He left as graciously as he had arrived, saying it was time for a younger leader. 'The strains,' he said, 'have been very extensive.'

Certain English players had been enduring burdensome strains too. Mike Brearley, while having led England to eight victories and no losses in thirteen Tests, would not have held his place for his batting alone. Slipping at last from the opening berth to number five, he had put together a competent fifty, which saved the selectors and his most ardent supporters from total embarrassment. But he had yet truly to convince. Over his tactical grasp and his ability to maintain team harmony there was not the slightest doubt. With most of the toils of benefit work behind him, he typically set about remedying his batting technique with indoor net sessions and videotape playbacks during the weeks before departure. The big Archie MacLaren-type backlift was discarded and a slight crouch was introduced.

In truth, there had been no logical alternative as captain, and the erudite Middlesex skipper was appointed on August 28 and given the chance to emulate Len Hutton in not only recapturing The Ashes in a home series but holding them in Australia. No other England captain had done this.

Two-hundred-and-fifty years ago, almost to the day, the greatest of 'Yorkshire captains', James Cook, was born. Like Geoff Boycott, he grew to know a thing or two about Australia. But Boycott, unlike Cook, found himself suddenly stripped of rank. Looking drawn and slightly bewildered still, Boycott stood alone in the departure lounge. A month ago he had been given the news that the county captaincy was to be transferred to John Hampshire, and he had not taken it quietly. On Michael Parkinson's BBC television chat show he had expressed his shock and non-acceptance, saying that his widowed mother, with whom he had always lived, had died two days before the Yorkshire committee—of whose members he had a poor opinion—decided to sack him. The timing, he thought, was cruel. Nobody would have disputed that.

This was no purely domestic issue. The country was split over it, and there must also have been a momentary danger that Boycott would not tour, either because he was too disheartened or because Yorkshire might have referred his outburst to the Test and County Cricket Board on a matter of discipline. But Geoffrey Boycott is nothing if not determinedly loyal, and with the county committee pronouncing on the Monday that their decision stood and that they would not be pursuing the matter of his public protest, here he was on the Tuesday, poised at Heathrow, saying that he wanted to get the first two weeks of the tour over and done with and to 'get his mind settled'. His sole aim was to 'get stuck into it with the boys' and to make runs for England (of whose team, just to add to his misery, he was no longer vice-captain).

Another player with problems, admittedly temporary, was Ian Botham—'Bionic Both'—the young man who had been finding Test cricket much to his liking since his debut little more than a year before. His smart powder-blue blazer did nothing to conceal his bandaged left arm, in a sling, the result of a thrust through a glass door during a farewell party at the weekend. The tendons were unharmed, as were England's Test prospects—for Botham in 1978 was the powerhouse of the Test eleven, taking 54 wickets with an insistent mixture of fast, swinging, cutting and bouncing deliveries, and gathering runs (with three centuries) in the robust manner of a Keith Miller. He was the key figure even in the field, threatening at short leg or in the slips, looking less than the mighty hero only when he donned a crash-helmet.

Memories of the summer, during which England had won five and drawn one of the Test matches against Pakistan and New Zealand, had swiftly been superseded by controversies, one of which was the tour vice-captaincy. Boycott was by-passed, and Bob Willis, the volatile, fun-loving giant, England's principal fast bowler, was awarded the responsibility. In a series when Willis would be looking forward to paying off some of the painful scores of the 1974–75 battles, it seemed likely that he would be needing a rest after each Test, especially when his obvious fatigue late in the 1978 season was borne in mind; who would then lead in the State matches? Not the most easily understood of appointments.

Willis was heading a strong and well-established pace attack. Chris Old, John Lever and Mike Hendrick had 216 Test wickets between them, and Willis himself had 151. They were all about thirty years of age, but knew how to bowl within themselves, and the endurance of Lever, for one, was legendary. This quartet plus Botham gave the selectors an enviable pool from which to choose —an extraordinary depth of bowling skill.

And yet, the Middlesex spin partnership of Phil Edmonds and newcomer John Emburey stood to be a major influence on the series, a prospect which brought a glimmer of anticipation to anyone who had admired the variations and flight of these bowlers, or who might have despaired at the future of this beautiful art. The third spin bowler was Geoff Miller, who retained the selectors' faith when so many felt he had been given sufficient opportunity. His off-spin tended to be flat and his batting hesitant, though he had already played in fourteen Tests. Perhaps we had come to expect instant Test successes in recent times, as served up by Botham, Edmonds, Radley and Gower.

Clive Radley appeared for England for the first time in February 1978, at the age of 33. In his second Test, at Auckland, he made 158, taking only a minute less than Peter Richardson's slowest-ever England Test century (488 minutes). Radley's fierce determination and application were appreciated in inverse proportion to his style, which was apt to be ungainly. But it was mighty effective. Just how effective it would be on bouncier pitches lent itself to speculation. New Zealand's Richard Hadlee had given him some bad moments.

Clearly the most exciting batting 'find' was David Gower, England's youngest Test centurymaker since Denis Compton (1938). An easygoing, personable young fellow, he batted in marked contrast to Radley. Both were fair-haired and both spoke English. There the similarities ended. Radley was squat, gritty, often agitated, busy, grabbing single after single, nudging, pushing, placing the ball to the wrong yet right side of the wicket—a battling boxer among batsmen. Gower was upright, slender, cool, languid, taking easefully-stroked boundaries, driving, sweeping (sometimes riskily), glancing—an ice-skater among batsmen.

This really seemed, at the outset, to have all the makings not only of a superb fielding and catching combination but of a most attractive batting side, so long as the strokemakers prospered. Spectators would be content for Boycott, Radley or Brearley to occupy the crease, always so long as a Gower or Gooch or Randall was at the other end.

One of the most impressive innings in all England-Australia Test history was Derek Randall's 174 in the Centenary match at Melbourne. But little else followed. His confidence slumped, he became jittery—not merely animated—at the crease, and by the summer of '78 the selectors had no option but to 'rest' him. It was good news for all who delight in a touch of vaudeville when his name was included in the team for Australia.

As for Graham Gooch, the hefty cockney who likes to hammer the ball to pulp, he was the latest in the long line of players who have made false starts in Test cricket only to get another chance. He fell to wicked balls from Walker and Thomson to 'bag a pair' at Birmingham in 1975, and was discarded after making 6 and 31 in the following Test. His comback was set up when England needed an opener to replace Packer player Dennis Amiss, when Gooch himself conveniently was making runs for Essex at the top of the order, usually in a wide-brimmed sunhat that gave him a 1920s look. His career yet might follow that of Amiss—all contrasts, ducks and double-centuries. He looked extremely thoughtful as he sat with his parents an hour before flight departure. He and Edmonds were the only players never to have seen Australia: Botham, Emburey and Gower had played club cricket there, and Radley was working for the Packer schoolboy coaching scheme when he received England's SOS from Pakistan the previous winter.

England traditionally have never had any worries in one department—wicketkeeping. Bob Taylor, slipping smoothly into the spot left vacant through Alan Knott's departure to Packer's promised land, became an instant asset, not only for reliable glovework but for his tactical acumen and his mature influence upon team morale.

His deputy for the tour was expected to be Yorkshire's David Bairstow, 27. Failing that, perhaps the Kent colt Paul Downton would be sent on his second tour. Thus, when Roger Tolchard's name was announced it was the one real surprise. Of course, he was a capable 'keeper, even if not the second-best in England; but his true value was intended to be as a spare batsman who was particularly good against spin bowling. This, in a side where the only shred of suspicion lay over its batting reliability, felt like a shrewd choice–though it seems that it prompted John Murray's resignation from the selection committee–that together with the overlooking of Boycott as vice-captain.

The management, too, had been carefully chosen, for there was likely to be more than just the occasional on-the-field problem to overcome. No-one could speak with greater authority from Lord's than immediate past-chairman of the TCCB, Doug Insole, former Essex and England batsman, an establishment man with the common touch. In his time he had batted about as elegantly as the admirable Radley, but he was effective (20,000 runs at just on 40), and he was now confidently expected to withstand some withering Press conferences and conceivably some impromptu and important gatherings of administrators and possibly lawyers (who now seemed to be *de rigueur* at cricket's summit meetings).

His assistant was the trusty Ken Barrington, England's fourth-highest runmaker and now an experienced and popular figure in the field of selection and management. To him were to fall the everyday duties surrounding play and practice, travel and technique. Bernard Thomas once more accompanied the team as physiotherapist and oft-time 'faith healer', and Geoffrey Saulez was there to enter the players' deeds into his well-kept official scorebook.

This was the first major English team since 1881–82 (apart from the Centenary visit) to tour Australia without a Surrey player, the first since 1894–95 to contain none from Kent (who had just won the Sch... Championship and the Benson & Hedges Cup), and Lancashire had to search as far back as 1911–12 to find a team without a representative from their great county. On the other hand, Leicestershire and Essex were not over-accustomed to having two England players on board, nor Derbyshire to having three and Middlesex four.

Another new feature was that the four young players sent to Australia under Whitbread 'scholarships' were on standby should the senior side be unduly disturbed by injuries. Mike Gatting, 21, of Middlesex, had already had a taste of Test cricket, while Chris Tavaré (24, Kent) and Wayne Larkins (25, Northamptonshire) were batsmen who had come close to tour selection. Jonathan Agnew, 18, had played only one match for Leicestershire, but his captain, Ray Illingworth, considered him second only to Willis among Englishmen for sheer speed.

Brearley and his men, then, seen off by old England captains 'Gubby' Allen and George Mann, assembled at the departure point on October 24, ready to board the Qantas Jumbo-jet that would lift them out of an unusually warm English autumn and place them down on a cricket battlefield once known as *Terra Australis Incognita.* No previous English team had gone out to such a tinder-box situation. Would the quality of the home team be so poor that, in the face of commercial competition, an Anglo-Australian series for once would fail to draw an audience or capture the imagination? Would the Australian public become sick of repeated defeat (if it happens) and turn away? Or would the untried local lads rise to a dramatic and emotional counter-attack? Read on, if you will.

The Team:

	County	*Birthdate*	*Tests*
John Michael BREARLEY (OBE) (captain)	Middlesex	28 April 1942	21
Robert George Dylan WILLIS (vice-captain)	Warwickshire	30 May 1949	41
Ian Terrence BOTHAM	Somerset	24 November 1955	11
Geoffrey BOYCOTT	Yorkshire	21 October 1940	74
Phillippe Henri EDMONDS	Middlesex	8 March 1951	13
John Ernest EMBUREY	Middlesex	20 August 1952	1
Graham Alan GOOCH	Essex	23 July 1953	7
David Ivon GOWER	Leicestershire	1 April 1957	6
Michael HENDRICK	Derbyshire	22 October 1948	16
John Kenneth LEVER	Essex	24 February 1949	13
Geoffrey MILLER	Derbyshire	8 September 1952	14
Christopher Middleton OLD	Yorkshire	22 December 1948	40
Clive Thornton RADLEY	Middlesex	13 May 1944	8
Derek William RANDALL	Nottinghamshire	24 February 1951	16
Robert William TAYLOR	Derbyshire	17 July 1941	13
Roger William TOLCHARD	Leicestershire	15 June 1946	4

Manager: D.J. Insole (Essex)
Assistant manager: K.F. Barrington (Surrey)
Physiotherapist: B.W. Thomas
Scorer: G.G.A. Saulez

2. EVENTFUL TREK NORTH

No-one can ever know truly **how** much it hurts to leave family behind for a prolonged absence unless he has experienced it. Four months might as well be twelve. Reassurances are feeble even when uttered in steady voice. Routine is shattered. Nerves are all a'jangle. Suddenly tales of Jeff Thomson's homesickness take on a new meaning. Perhaps one in five cricketers hates every moment he is away from home, and yet the public, unaware, makes no allowances.

In the greyness of early morning the check-in queues nudge slowly forward and the labels go on the baggage. Then, after the long walk in obedience to the direction arrows, the warmth and soft lighting of the Qantas 747B beckon at the end of the corridor. With the seat-belt fastened, reality bursts like a starshell: the adventure is about to unfold.

But not just yet. We reach the runway, pause, and turn back. The message would be disconcerting were it not for the captain's deep nut-brown Australian voice: 'One of our tyres has split, ladies and gen'lemen, but we shouldn't be delayed too long.' The Heathrow puncture men had us aloft two hours later, and as compensation we had free drinks all along the way. Frustration nipped in the tastebud, you might say. Through the clouds into a sunnier place, Europe far below, 570 miles (917 km) covered every hour—and there are eight and a half of them to touchdown at Bombay, steamy, sweaty Bombay at midnight, where the local terminal officials drive the Qantas chief steward to the brink with their indecision. He ought to have exploded, but he shrugged his huge shoulders and grinned. India was probably still in mourning for its recent Test defeat by Pakistan.

Swiftly through the night—chicken fillets in the early hours, a movie, some taped music, half-sleep as the sky lightens over the Cocos Islands. Eight-and-a-half hours more and we are in sunny but windy Perth, where many of the immigrants and visiting relatives alight. Grilled steak for breakfast. That, above all, proves we are Down Under again. The vast unbroken expanse of frothy white cloud makes it seem that Australia has had a bath and nobody has remembered to drain the suds away. But flying from west to east is like going from summer to winter. Melbourne is wet and dark. Sydney is buried under thick cloud. By now I feel very tired, unlikely even to win a wrestling match with Qantas's very first passenger nearly sixty years before, 85-year-old cattleman Alexander Kennedy. Those were the days of wood-and-wire Avro 504Ks and £450 war surplus Bristol BE2e biplanes. How long would this journey have taken them? Like Boycott's runs, we take modern aviation travel for granted.

On the day Qantas was registered as a company, November 16 1920, Wilfred Rhodes and Frank Woolley were bowling MCC to an innings victory over Victoria. Now, as we throttled back over Mascot Airport, Mike Brearley's side were reflecting on their performance against the same State, Phil Edmonds and John Emburey having done the first-innings damage. They were all acclimatised by now. For me there were to be four days of inescapable mental and physical dislocation as the body-clock made its slow adjustment to the dash across the world. Eager family reunion kept the mind off it for a while, but by the fourth day I was at the Number 2 ground at Sydney watching in wonderment as Jeff Thomson and Len Pascoe bowled at a man-size 'bulletproof' plastic shield, the stuff of which batsmen's crash-helmet visors are made. After a few balls delivered at three-quarter pace the shield split, probably because it was fixed rigidly to a base. Soon pieces were dropping out of it, and Pressmen were prepared to admire only from a safe distance. 'Thommo' had just returned from three days' fishing. If he had been match-fit the manufacturers might have been laughed out of business.

Australia's controversial fast bowler was by now in a kind of limbo, the courts having ruled that he could not play for World Series until after his Australian Cricket Board contract expired in four months' time. He was adamant that he would not play in the Tests, and the Board denied that it had tried to tempt him back with an offer of the captaincy. It seemed that World Series would be keeping him in funds in return for public appearances and bowling demonstrations, lending strength to Tony Greig's remarks in an interview with New Zealand's *Cricket Player* magazine. Probed on the matter of a compromise between World Series and Test cricket, he was quoted as saying: 'I really think we need a good battle before we start talking too much about getting together. Let's have a good fight. Let's have it out properly. I don't think we ought to get together too quickly. This has been a big thing for cricket. It is only twelve months old and we may as well have a thoroughly good clean-out before we come together.'

He conceded that Test cricket was needed: 'I have played something like fifty-five Tests, and I would play them all again for nothing—I certainly would play the first twenty for nothing. . . . I do miss it. Test cricket will always be Test cricket, but because of the players, not because of the administrators.'

A visit to the World Series Cricket headquarters in Sydney was an eye-opener. The place was alive with optimism and bright friendliness, and in the merchandising department an astonishing range of products was being prepared for distribution and sale, much of it aimed at the juvenile market. T-shirts, sunhats, brochures, table games, beach-towels, fun-books, ties, posters, miniature bats, overnight bags, prints, cushions, jackets, plastic Dennis Lillee figurines, eyeshades, WSC soap—Father Christmas had no problems this year. But Test cricket might, particularly when the WSC Junior Cricket Foundation was taken into account. This scheme will reach thousands of Australian youngsters in country areas in the hope that a Bradman or McCabe or Walters or O'Reilly might be found.

So far everyone I had spoken to in suburbia thought that Packer cricket, especially in the evening on television, was lively, attractive and easy to follow. People who found Test cricket too complex and too much of an endurance were happy to tune into WSC's entertainment package, and this prompted the thought that the new commercial cricket in Australia was achieving exactly what the John Player League had done in England in bringing a whole new segment of the population to the game—or a freshly-born species of it. These folk were completely disinterested in the vintage flavour of Test cricket, and it seems unlikely that anything more than a slender proportion of them will ever feel like making the transition to the traditional international game—certainly not while it is so severely diluted by 'pirate raids' on its playing ranks.

The latest WSC signing was present at the Thomson/Pascoe 'polycarbonate experiment': Kepler Wessels, the brilliant South African on Sussex's books. He was settling in Australia, taking out citizenship papers, and due to play for the WSC Australian XI, not the Rest of the World. History was moving ahead at breakneck speed.

The Sydney weather was back to full health by the time the England party arrived on November 16. Ian Botham had an energetic net in preparation for his first tour match, and Geoff Boycott, as usual, was last away from practice, his left knee causing him little or no discomfort after his century in Canberra the previous day. He handled my leg-breaks at the nets with consummate ease, needless to say. I didn't even come close to earning the ten dollars he offered for his wicket.

The team looked fit and relaxed, and there was no visual evidence of Clive Radley's injury at Adelaide, when he needed seven stitches after being hit over the eyebrow by a short one from Rodney Hogg.

Hogg went a long way towards gaining a Test cap by taking 6 for 82 in the match—on a slow pitch. The 27-year-old insurance agent had Boycott lbw in both innings, for 62 and 6, and made a large contribution to South Australia's first victory over an English team since March 1925, when 'Dodge' Whysall made a century for Arthur Gilligan's team and Jack Rymill scored 146 for the home side. Clarrie Grimmett, having tormented England with eleven wickets in his first Test match, then diddled out seven more for his adopted State in the second innings.

The effect of this 1978 South Australian win, in the light of the State's lowly rating, was to inspire some Australians to believe that their Test team might have a chance after all. Seldom can there have been so many opportunities for so many unknowns. Three months hence, I was certain, there ought to be several household names who at this moment were known only to their families and friends. John Nash's century put his name among the candidates, if not as a front runner, and it began to seem that whoever could put two centuries together before the team for Brisbane was announced would have a fair chance. Names were being bandied about in profusion as every Sheffield Shield match and every State game against the Englishmen became a Test trial.

The tour was begun at Renmark, where an English combination had last played during Freddie Brown's tour in 1950–51. Radley made 64 and Gooch 47 as the England XI reached 199 for 4 in 160 minutes. Left the same amount of batting time, the South Australian Country XI, 137 for 6, could not be prised out. The touring team's aircraft took off that evening by the light of flares.

At Adelaide, South Australia were 195 for 2 at one point, but Edmonds, Miller, Willis and Lever kept things in check, and one of the more pertinent remarks at the end of the innings of 311 came from Bill O'Reilly when he said that Phil Edmonds reminded him in style and action of the great pre-war slow left-arm bowler Hedley Verity.

Nash, 28, once played for Hampshire Second XI, and his 124 was his second century in just over fifty first-class innings since his 1970–71 debut. Strong on the cut, this physical education teacher, if he had not played his way into Test cricket, had at least done something worth telling his grandchildren about some time in the distant future, when presumably cricket will have become an integrated activity once more.

Chris Old dislocated his left little finger on the first day, but did not have to go far for treatment. Bernard Thomas met him on the field, fixed the problem with a dextrous little twist, patted him on the head, and went back inside to await the call for his next trick. This devolved out of Boycott's knee, but the master batsman passed a fitness test during the match, and went on to give Hogg two magic moments.

David Gower had a fine double of 73 and 50, adding 133 with Boycott in the first innings and stroking five boundaries close together off Hogg in the second. Bob Taylor made five catches and three stumpings in the match, and Mike Brearley got the feel of things with 27 in 100 minutes, saying after the defeat that 'this result has dispelled any lingering feelings that it would be easy for us. It wasn't a disaster as much as a setback, and perhaps has done us good.'

After beating a Victorian Country XI in a one-day match at Leongatha, where John Emburey enjoyed himself with 5 for 10 as the locals collapsed for 59, the side shaped up to Victoria in a match (designated the Sir Robert Menzies Memorial Match) in which rain never allowed a chance of a result. Mike Brearley's long innings, naturally, was vital, both to the team and on a personal level. It lasted 435 minutes and his unbeaten 116 came off 415 balls, only three of which he hit for four. His last hundred had been as long ago as July 20, 1977, against Gloucestershire at Lord's, and since then he had led England to Ashes victory, sustained a broken forearm, and seen almost 500 dawns. Now he must have known a joyous sunset.

Derek Randall (63) was the only other batsman to make a worthwhile score, but with the third day washed out and the fourth reduced to a 2 pm start it became just a practice exercise.

The team headed north-east via Canberra.

In the Federal capital the England XI turned on a spectacular, with Geoff Boycott making 123 not out, Roger Tolchard 108. Their stand amounted to 229, three times what the local side could muster in their innings, in which Bob Willis took 4 for 10, shaking the upper order.

Then came New South Wales, at a Sydney ground now transformed by six enormous grey beanstalks each carrying ninety arclamps. Night cricket! The impending reality was there for all to see. Seventy metres high, the pylons towered from the Hill and every other vantage point, and word went round that Jack Fingleton had sworn never to set foot in his old home ground ever again. To make matters worse, the Brewongle Stand had vanished and the new construction, in its earliest and roughest shape, left a hole at the ground's perimeter as if someone had taken a bite out of a doughnut. The $5.6 million seven-level marvel will be ready by 1980, and until then we all did our best to keep our eyes averted.

After a hearty greeting from Keith Miller, who never forgets a name, I asked the great cricketer if he had enjoyed Packer cricket last year. He went rather pink, took a deep breath, and said '★★★★ Packer cricket!!' I couldn't possibly expect to gather a more forthright view than that wherever I travelled.

The match brought England a resounding victory—perhaps the least they could do, for the NSW side had been in trouble for a number of seasons. The main interest centred on Peter Toohey, and it was clear that the Englishmen were keen to make an early impression on him. Willis and Botham gave him the sort of treatment Lindwall and Miller gave Peter May in 1953, when they wanted him excluded from the Test team. The little man from the bush managed some bold square-cuts but England won the first round clearly, getting him for 23 and 20. Australia could have done with a morale-boosting century from her main hope—who, incidentally, was now working for the old Sydney brewery which happens to bear his name and whose Flag Ale, apart from lending support to the State team, sustained me, rather a few years ago, through my mis-spent youth.

Graham Gooch rehabilitated himself with 66, taking an hour and a quarter over his first five runs and adding 125 with Derek Randall for the second wicket, but Clive Radley failed, moving out of any reckoning for the first Test, and David Gower impressed, as he is bound to do in even a short stay, without making a tall score. The showpiece was Randall.

Randall made a memorable century in his debut match at Melbourne—the Centenary Test—and here he did it again at Sydney. His first appearance there realised 110 runs off 189 balls, with 17 fours, most of them struck with his now-famous nonchalance, and one of them forcing three NSW fieldsmen to climb over the midwicket fence to search for the ball among the stacks of bricks. It was a relief to see the Nottingham marionette at his best again, for the series was going to need him.

Ian Botham was not far short of his best form in this his first outing since his wrist laceration in England. He struck some resounding drives, some high in the air, some electrically over the grass, in a typical half-century, and although his first-innings bowling was unproductive, he took 5 for 51 in the second innings. This was more like what we had come to expect of him. Bob Willis, who led the England XI in this match, said afterwards that 'Both' found it hard going in the first innings. He added: 'There's a good chance he'll take the new ball in the Tests. It's been a very good workout for him.'

NSW failed to avoid the follow-on, making 165 to England's 374, and Willis surprised some by enforcing it. 'The bowlers need practice as much as the batsmen. I certainly needed it.' He said he regarded it as a 'thoroughly professional performance by everyone' and after the disappointment at Adelaide, 'it's picked everyone up.'

From the Australian viewpoint, a new opening batting prospect emerged. John Dyson, head sheathed in a blue crash-helmet, ground out a methodical 67 in three-and-a-half hours, reminding one and all that he had played for Australia and going some way to justifying Bob Simpson's claim that he was second only to Graeme Wood among current Australian openers. Then, in the second innings the State's young captain, lawyer Andrew Hilditch, batted five-and-a-half hours for 93. He looked like making his first century and carrying his bat, but Botham bowled him off his arm. It was the Somerset man's second piece of luck: he had seen a fierce cut by Allan Border rebound off Gooch's leg to be caught by the ever-alert Taylor.

Of the local bowlers, left-arm unorthodox spinner David Hourn was a disappointment, though he confused a couple of England's top batsmen once or twice. The pick of the attack was 20-year-old

Geoff Lawson, another bush lad, from Wagga, who had Boycott caught in the first innings and achieved the near-impossible by being warned twice by umpire Brooks for an excessive number of bouncers in an innings (England's second) whose total length amounted to just five balls. The Yorkshireman finally edged one high over slips to give the England XI a ten-wicket win, tucked his bat under his arm and walked thankfully off.

On the Sunday I called at Marcellin College, Randwick, where those England players not engaged in the NSW match were conducting a coaching class, sponsored by Qantas, for schoolboys in the area. There was an encouraging attendance, and as usual everyone stood too close and took Roger Tolchard's off- and on-drives on the shin, ankle and toe. The enthusiasm of Australian youth was by now quite unquestionable, even if few of them, or their elders, bothered to attend the big match throughout its three fine and one rain-affected days.

Bundaberg had always meant two names to me: Bert Hinkler and Don Tallon. The town also produced singer Gladys Moncrieff. So it was with some anticipation that I boarded the Trans-Australia Airlines 727 for Brisbane, covering the 600-odd miles in hardly more than an hour (how I used to love the day-and-a-half car journey in the old days, when there was time to spare) and transferring to a propeller-driven Fokker Friendship for Bundaberg, enjoying a second breakfast and a conviviality which began with the cabin staff and spread contagiously to the passengers. Fleecy clouds again, mountains like molehills down below, and all the world's cares out of sight. Flying, not marijuana, is the answer.

I found Don Tallon's corner shop, but the old Test wicketkeeper was not in a mood to talk; and I found a nephew of the great aviator Hinkler, of whom Bundaberg is so proud, particularly in this fiftieth anniversary year of his historic flight from England to Australia. This first solo crossing took 'Hustling' Hinkler and his Avro Avian sixteen days, with nineteen stops. When he reached his hometown in triumph his aircraft proceeded along the main street in a glorious celebration journey, and one of the boys helping it on its way was none other than Don Tallon.

Now the town was preparing for the match against Brearley's players, the first English cricket team ever to visit. There were no obvious signs of excitement on the eve of the event, but then the people of Bundaberg go about their business and their pleasure undemonstratively. It's usually far too warm to do otherwise.

That evening, at the century-old Royal Hotel, I made the best of a grilled barramundi and salad and counted my blessings that the Queensland beer strike of many weeks' duration had not prevented the bringing in of supplies from other States. The nineteenth-century structures with their iron lacework balconies were richly atmospheric, and as the sky turned dark behind the war memorial which rises out of the centre of the main street, the statue of the soldier seemed slowly to become a ghost, beckoning the mind away from the affluence and avarice of the 1970s into a time when Anzac bushmen and townsmen gathered to defend their shimmering brown land and also the Mother Country. Wishing that my wife was with me now, I placed a box of Redhead matches just beyond the carnation stems and imagined that the portrait on the box was she.

The morning broke warm and bright, but with the shock news that the young Victorian batsman Paul Melville had died suddenly after a brain haemorrhage. Four months ago I had played in a match with him at Eastbourne and found him to be the happiest of companions that afternoon and evening. English-born, he had shown great promise, and had the loveliest fault any batsman could have: he tried to hit too hard and too often. Such a loss underlines the utter and awful futility of trying to establish a logical set of expectations in life.

The one-day match at Bundaberg's Salter Oval was attended by perhaps 3000 people, many of them youngsters, and resulted in an easy win for the England XI. The day will be remembered mainly for the announcement during the afternoon that Phil Carlson, captaining the Queensland Country XI, had just been named in Australia's twelve for the first Test match. The one real surprise was that Queensland had *three* men in the twelve, Gary Cosier gaining selection and John Maclean being preferred to Steve Rixon. Carlson would be contesting the all-rounder's spot with Trevor Laughlin. The team was: G.M. Wood (WA), G.J. Cosier (Q) (vice-captain), P.M. Toohey (NSW), G.N. Yallop (V) (captain), K.J. Hughes (WA), T.J. Laughlin (V), P.H. Carlson (Q), J.A. Maclean (Q), B. Yardley (WA), R.M. Hogg (SA), A.G. Hurst (V), J.D. Higgs (V). Three—Carlson, Maclean and Hogg—were uncapped, and the others had collected only 55 caps between them, none, apart from Cosier (16), more than eight. This against a total of 298 Test caps in the England party.

The Test was nine days away as the English cricketers circled over the playing area at Bundaberg and landed a mile away. Half an hour later they were exercising under Bernard Thomas's guidance beside the hard, fast wicket which was later to claim some 'heads', Tolchard's the first when attempting to hook Carlson during his dapper 74. Brearley, with a new short haircut and looking very relaxed, made a steady 59, Randall had the crowd in convulsions, and Gooch smacked three sixes off the penultimate over. The real blood and thunder came during the Country innings, however, when opener Scott Ledger, on eight, was struck on the right side of the scalp by a ball from John Lever immediately after being given the benefit of a concerted shout for caught-behind. He was led from the field with blood gushing from the wound, but returned at the fall of a later wicket—only to be floored first ball by one from Hendrick into which he ducked. This time the left side of his scalp copped the impact, and more blood spurted onto his shirt. Now he'd had enough. It so happens that a friend of Ledger's had been rendered quadraplegic by a blow on the head by a cricket ball. Nine out was all out, 127 against 259 for 5 in 35 overs. With three wickets in six balls Lever polished off a match memorable for incident, not least the slip catch by Ipswich player Kevin Maher and the diving left-hand cover catch by Clive Radley. The World Series match coming up at Rockhampton would need to be a good one to justify the claim of a citizen of that town that Bundaberg was unlucky to be getting only the Poms this season.

Cruising over south-east Queensland on a sunny, heavenly afternoon, with the pure, blue Pacific out to the left, reawakened all the old yearnings to be a pilot, even though they must have the odd bad passage, as we know occasional wet or boring cricket days, and mediocre reports. The living map was static three or four miles below, until the rare town or settlement was passed, made starker still in its isolation from our bird's-eye view.

Here was I, just a fortnight back in Australia, and accepting things on the grand scale—the geography, the salaries, the cars, the scope and ambitions. I wondered how difficult it was going to be this time to revert to English values when the time came.

An hour's flight in a TAA Friendship brought us to Brisbane, coming in low over Eagle Farm racecourse, where Ivo Bligh's English team defeated Eighteen of Queensland in 1883. More family reunions, with everyone assuring everyone else how little they'd changed with the years, more stories of recent family delights and disasters, and the ageless dichotomy: which is the reality, the domestic existence or this travelling entertainment called cricket?

Brisbane's Wolloongabba ground is now encircled by concrete stands, and although the capacity has been reduced to around 20,000, it is now well and truly a Test match ground, with the old corrugated-iron shack image now merely an archive vision. Neville Cardus once said that he felt compelled to keep looking through his spectacles for the coming of Tom Mix and the sheriff, and Arthur Mailey once had to communicate with the dressing-room by telegram, enquiring the reason for a player's exit from the field. Half an hour or so later he had his reply: 'Natural causes.' Liaison now is near-perfect, with scorer Bob Spence calling the figures to the Press box as they materialise.

While WSC World XI (42 for 5) were beating WSC West Indies (72) in a fiasco match at Gloucester Park, Perth, Queensland struggled to make 172 against the England XI. David Ogilvie rode his luck to make 43 before taking a stinging blow on the back of the head from a Willis lifter, and from 90 for 1 the State side slipped slowly down the drain, Old, Willis and Botham getting life out of a hard, grassy wicket which was prepared late when the intended strip showed cracks.

The England XI missed three catches, none hard, before lunch. Gooch, fielding away from the slips because of a sore finger, put down a straightforward chance at long leg, and Brearley fluffed one at slip. The most surprising, though, was Bob Taylor's error behind the wicket, stretching up to his right when the ball would have gone—not necessarily comfortably—throat-high to slip.

Phil Carlson disappointed with the bat (1 and 37) but bowled well, giving himself an outside chance of making it into the Test XI, but Gary Cosier, like Toohey in Sydney, missed the chance of a long, sighting innings, falling for only 32 and 0 (played on to a nasty rising ball from Willis).

George Brabon, from Rockhampton, was a popular lad that first evening, having had Boycott caught at slip by Cosier for 6 and winning his team $1000 from a local firm who offered the prize if England's champion were dismissed for less than 20. Others succeeded, however, Gooch making 34. Randall an attractive 66, and the captain, Brearley, 75 not out in three and three-quarter hours, taking the side to 254, a lead of 82. Geoff Dymock's 4 for 46 might have got him into the first Test team if the selectors had been prepared to wait. Apart from that, their wisdom was verified by new wicketkeeper John Maclean, Queensland's captain, as he took five smart catches and now went on to hit 94 and take the match into its fourth day. When Queensland lost Broad and Cosier in the first over of the second innings the prospects were bleak, but Carlson, Ogilvie (sporting a helmet for the first time), Hohns and the skipper stretched things out. The only sour moment came when Max Walters had his spectacles shattered and his forehead gashed by a vicious rising breakback from Willis, the fourth nasty head injury I had seen in as many days. Like Ogilvie before him, Walters was too shaken to resume later.

The touring side moved cautiously and professionally to their six-wicket victory, Gooch again getting out after making a steady start, and Boycott seeming more himself with a 60 that occupied four hours, with three fours across the slow outfield. Gower failed again, and looked thoroughly fed up, but Randall enjoyed himself for two hours making 47, just missing his fourth half-century in a row, and Mike Brearley survived some awkward bowling from ex-Victorian left-arm quickie Len Balcam to reach 38 as the winning run was made. Geoff Miller saw it through with 22 but looked no more convincing than before.

Graham Whyte, the Queensland off-spinner, aroused some interest with his control and sharp spin, and at times he justified, and had, a crowded array of close catchers. But the tourists got home for their second win against a State side and seemed to be moving into gear at just the right rate. Willis had looked hostile and sharp, and Botham and Old moved the ball about, the former taking his customary five wickets in Queensland's second innings. With Radley out of the reckoning, if only *pro tem*, all the major batsmen had had the feel of longish innings, and if there was any serious worry it would have concerned the fielding and catching—something new for England XIs of recent vintage.

After the match, Brearley said that the pitch was 'not dangerous, but a bit unpredictable'. Asked about the bouncers bowled at him, he replied that he didn't enjoy them too much, but added ominously, 'Nor did they!' He was concerned at the massive number of no-balls by his bowlers (37), but put it down to their stretching a little as they reached top pace. The England captain had his bat destroyed by vandals over the weekend, but he finished the match with a first-class average on tour so far of 140.50, and felt ready for Australia.

Australia, for its part, was still unsure of itself. The newspapers carried pictures of Jeff Thomson aboard his fishing boat, and quoted him as having said that he wanted to play for Australia after all. But the Queensland selectors had ignored him for the England XI match, and the Test match door seemed shut and bolted too. Places in both teams were reserved for the wholehearted.

There was anxiety when word got round that two of the Australian Test team were not willing to sign their contracts and the statutory declarations which forbade them from signing for any other cricket organisation simultaneously. Eventually it came down to Graeme Wood, but on November 28 he did sign, after his lawyer had agreed to the alteration of the commitment from *two* years to *one* year. Hughes and Yardley (who had passed a fitness test) flew eastwards without him, but there were sighs when it was established that Wood, the brilliant left-hander, was soon to follow.

Attention now turned to the World Series. Benson & Hedges had been advertising their sponsorship of the Australia-England Test series, but there was no way they could compete with Channel 9's heavy promotion of its own product. On the evening of Monday, November 27, I sat and watched a television programme which was billed as a summary of the introductory season of Packer cricket, 1977–78. It amounted to an hour-long commercial, some of it hypnotic—Lillee pinging Greig on the helmet, Hookes's jaw fractured, Hookes hitting Roberts for six upon his comeback, staggering catches by Laird, Julien, Knott and Barlow—and some of it far-fetched—'Greigy himself, the ultimate competitor and master batsman', 'The world's best cricketers playing the world's best cricket for Australia's television audiences', and Richie Benaud repeatedly saying 'Great shot'.

The montage of dismissal after dismissal made it seem like the fastest game on earth, not the slowest, as legions of antagonists have always claimed. There seemed little point in trying to find a purpose and meaning for it all. The closing statement by the bass-baritone voice-over left us all thinking. 'A great summer for World Series Cricket,' quoth the bass-baritone, 'but this is just the beginning.'

Twenty-four hours later the lights went on. Not just a few bulbs here and there, but 540 of the dazzlers, turning the nocturnal Sydney Cricket Ground into a vast and brilliant pool of brightness, and prompting a local architect to monitor the effect half a mile away in South Paddington. 'The lights,' he said, 'are an environmental disaster.'

Few of the 44,377 present (plus about 7000 who squeezed their way in when the gates were thrown open) would have cared about the outside world. The frenzy was audible and visible, and sent the WSC people into raptures. Missing, though, was a takings figure, which lent weight to the belief that many complimentary tickets were in circulation.

I have been used to watching floodlit Rugby League and Soccer and boxing late at night, but cricket after dark seems about as natural as going to church on a Tuesday. And besides, I am surely not alone in feeling too tired to get excited—over sport anyway—at ten or eleven at night. The nausea I felt this evening I put down to fatigue, for the cricket had its moments. If I'm prejudiced at all, perhaps it is in favour of playing cricket in God's sunshine.

WSC Australia won their International Cup match against WSC West Indies, their first limited-overs victory over that particular opposition, and Dennis Lillee was back in business, collecting the match award of $500. There was something very baseball about it—the hard-hats and visors, the constant background roar, the players' voices through the ground microphones, and the glare coming in from all angles. The white ball, while new, was easily seen and therefore seemed to be travelling more slowly, and the glimpses of the black sightscreen made it seem like a photographic negative. The commentators' overkill and the commercials after each over and fall of wicket made it seem more than ever like a telecast of Mets v Red Sox.

Here we were, resisting bed's beckoning, and instead being sold hamburgers, deodorant, cars, hi-fis, tyres, air conditioners, *Playboy* magazines, mortgages, soft drinks, canned fruit, refrigerators, weed-cutters, diamonds, security locks, cassettes, hotel accommodation, and tomorrow night's movie. For those in doubt, animated diagrams showed what a yorker was, and a bouncer, and a good-length ball, with Fred Trueman explaining in the kindliest of tones.

Two chaps ran round the perimeter carrying an Australian flag, and were pelted with beer-cans, and when shortly afterwards Ian

Chappell was given out caught at the wicket there was a chorus of booing. Few if any police were present. Perhaps there was no room for them. A friend told me that at the end of the game, when hordes ran over the field, a man was seen urinating on the pitch.

David Hookes batted in a hard-hat without face visor, but Ian Redpath wore the lot, and looked like a lanky construction worker striding off for a night's work. Joel Garner, the ball a mere marble in his huge hand, yorked him for 1. After 32 overs the white ball needed servicing by the umpires, but a few minutes later it was all over, and the fireworks burst upon the sky, commemorating a weighty move forward by Kerry Packer's World Series Cricket. Worcester spectators who sat through Ian Davis's four-and-three-quarter-hour innings of 83 during the 1977 tour would have rubbed their eyes at the slender batsman's bold strokeplay here, and Lancashire supporters would have been asking why Colin Croft, the West Indian giant, had not shown such fire while bowling for the county. The stimuli of big prizemoney and a large, noisy crowd had much to do with it.

I watched more the following night, when WSC Australia beat the World XI in a match aborted by rain. This time only 20,000 were at the ground, and the following day I could not remember a single detail of the play.

When I turned in at last, bleary-eyed, I was yearning for the smell of mown grass.

3. THE FIRST TEST MATCH

BRISBANE, DECEMBER 1, 2, 3, 5, 6

First day

The first noise at dawn was heavy rain upon the metal roof, but the radio weather forecast brought solace. The clouds were to blow out to sea. Even so, they had a long way to go when the first Test match began at 11 am. Not one piece of blue sky showed.

Never before had I felt such an inclination to banish all outside considerations and to focus sharply on the match about to unfold. All the threats and distractions of past months had to be shut out, and even reflections on past battles in this grand old saga seemed inappropriate, notwithstanding the fact that Brisbane was anxious to celebrate fifty years of Test cricket. The first of its Tests, played at the Exhibition Ground over at Albion, was won by England by 675 runs. This 1978 contest was expected to last less than the allotted fived days, and nothing like the same aggregate of runs was considered likely. The pitches here had been helping the bowlers, and there was not any reliable depth to the batting of either side. While the odds against Australia had lessened, still it was felt that England's bowling was more penetrative and varied. It could be a good toss to lose.

England's team was as expected: J.M. Brearley, G. Boycott, G.A. Gooch, D.W. Randall, D.I. Gower, G. Miller, I.T. Botham, R.W. Taylor, C.M. Old, P.H. Edmonds, R.G.D. Willis, with J.K. Lever twelfth man. Miller seemed rather lucky to make it, but it was clear that he had been part of the plan for some time. Astonishingly, only Willis survived from the last England team to play at Brisbane, in the Lillee-Thomson massacre of 1974, and none of Ian Chappell's team was now playing for Australia.

Phil Carlson was made twelfth man for Australia, and before an encouragingly large crowd, building up all the time, Graham Yallop, using a specially-minted coin handed him by a parachutist, won his first toss for Australia and batted, pursuing the confident line he had taken at the Press conference two days before when he said his team would win by six Tests to nil—this with no discernible sign of tongue in cheek, and almost as ill-advised as Greig's 1976 'grovel' gaff, which the West Indians punished so painfully hard. Discretion might have been advisable, on the opening morning if not at the Press conference. No batsman could have relished the prospect of facing Willis, Old and Botham on a green-tinged pitch under a threatening sky, even though the pitch was uncovered overnight and had not sweated. But Yallop's decision to bat was apparently supported by the selectors.

It was none of these bowlers, however, that drew first blood. Graeme Wood took a single, and Gary Cosier another. Then Wood played gently square on the off side and called for a run. Gower swooped in, underarmed a direct hit on the stumps from almost side-on, and Cosier was very narrowly beaten. One down for two, the crowd buzzing, and Australia's Viking-like vice-captain moving slowly from the field, left to the comforts of his newly-announced contract for half-a-million dollars spread over ten years, an arrangement aimed at keeping him for Queensland and Australian Test cricket.

Peter Toohey, Benson & Hedges' Man of the Match twelve months ago when he made 82 and 57 against India on this ground in his maiden Test, never seemed comfortable. He made his first run against England with a push to midwicket, and then, after jack-knifing out of the way of a sharp breakback, to the third ball of Willis's second over he played forward and ... simply missed. The ball came back, as most of Willis's do, through the gap and clipped the top of the off stump. Australia two down for five, and Yallop, Australia's 36th Test captain, made his confident way to the crease, wearing a tasteful green helmet with visor. The six men in England's slips cordon crouched alongside wicketkeeper Taylor, and Willis pounded in again, firing down a bouncer that had fond memories of 1974–75 written all over it. The batsman coolly ducked.

After five overs the umpires inspected the ball, but apparently allowed it to pass for further use. Willis and Old would not have wanted it changed, for it was moving nicely, especially off the pitch. It was gradually becoming routine for one or two balls to beat the edge each over. Willis reverted from around the wicket to over for the left-handers, but Old plugged away from the conventional side, cutting the ball from right to left, if anything a more lethal package for the left-hander than the right-. One of these at last touched Wood's edge and Taylor caught it with ease.

After 63 balls Australia were staggering at 14 for 3, and all the gloomy forecasts seemed vividly three-dimensional.

Kim Hughes joined Yallop, who, after the noon drinks break, edged Old high between first and second slip, escaping at the hands of Gooch. The suffering bowler soon had worse to contend with: diving at fourth slip to an uppish edge by Hughes off Willis, he took the flying ball on the little finger of his left hand and had to go off to hospital for an X-ray, his figures thus far 6-1-7-1. Botham, who was surely bound to relish the conditions, took over from the pavilion end.

Yallop was the next to go, nicking Willis to Gooch knee-high at second slip, allowing him to make partial amends, and Australia were 22 for 4. Recovery became more remote a likelihood when Hughes, having made four runs in 24 minutes, fell to Botham's fourth ball, drawn tentatively forward and getting a fine edge to Taylor. This brought in local idol John Maclean, who would have made a formidable tag-wrestling pair with his partner, the beefy Trevor Laughlin (known as 'Super'). Maclean was given a memorable welcome by the crowd, and soon a beautiful juvenile chorus of 'Come on, Australia' floated across the ground. It was as poignant in its way as the singing of the passengers as *Titanic* went down.

Australia's horrible day moved on. Laughlin, the third left-hander in his side's top six, hooked Willis, somewhat tucked-up, and substitute John Lever ran in and took the catch low at long leg. Six down for 26, and the light questionable.

At 23 minutes to one, after 97 minutes' play, there occurred something which the crowd, particularly the younger section, appreciated no end: the first four was hit. It was not a convincing stroke, but from the edge of Maclean's bat the ball flew through to the third-man boundary off Willis, and there was noisy acclaim.

As the lunch interval approached, the incidents mounted up. Umpire O'Connell was merciful to a wide ball from Botham, who was now bending his outswinger almost as much as his inswinger. Bruce Yardley, always a willing pounder, slashed Willis almost for four, Randall chasing and backheeling, and while the Press box was abustle with research for Australia's lowest at Brisbane (58 in 1936–37, if the 32 for 7 declared in 1950–51 be disregarded), Maclean edged Willis for one to reach double-figures, a notable performance in itself this tense and steamy morning. Yardley then ducked helplessly before Willis and was hit somewhere not painfully enough to stop him taking off for a leg-bye, and when

Botham pitched one well up he smacked it through the vacant mid-off area for four.

Five minutes before lunch Bob Willis was rested after a gallant spell of ten overs in which he had taken 3 for 28 and proved that his stamina was beyond question. In the humid conditions, a two-hour spell would have been beyond him four years ago—quite apart from the fact that the opposition would have been at least a little sterner. Gooch sent down the last over before the interval, taken at 48 for 6 off 21 overs. Every second or third person one passed during the break had a stunned look.

The first ball after lunch was a lifter from Botham, and Yardley just saved his facial features in time, spooning a four almost over the 'keeper's head and bringing up 52 in 121 minutes. Two balls later he edged to Gooch, but the difficult, low catch to his left was grassed, and it remained for the Willis-Taylor combination to account for the unorthodox Western Australian as he drove without quite getting there. The stand of 27 had taken the score to 53 for 7, and the earthquake had become a tremor; but the light was just as dubious as Australia's future, and the umpires talked as Yardley departed and Rodney Hogg, unrecognisable in a white crash-helmet, came on.

Hogg stirred things up a bit. Before long he was picking up an outswinger from Botham and placing it through extra cover for four, and after Maclean had square-driven the same bowler for three, Hogg lofted him straight for four. Next came a back-cut four off Willis, and a cut over slips to the boundary yet again, to reach 20. The crash-helmet was obviously inspiring delusions of personal safety, and Willis felt compelled to put this to the test, for after a lovely Hogg square-cut for four, the big Englishman peppered him with several bouncers and drew a warning from umpire French which had Brearley, in his deerstalker-style sunhat, trotting up for a brief conference.

Australia were going to make the hundred; this was now a comforting certainty for the large, animated crowd. Maclean had shown the power of his square-drive, and Hogg played the same stroke with style and ease when the ball was on the up. The Test debutants were becoming heroes by the minute.

When Hogg twice called for replacement gloves it began to seem that the tactical advice from the dressing-room was being overdone, but without question he was having problems with his helmet. Several times he borrowed the umpire's handkerchief to wipe perspiration from his face. But it was all worth it. Maclean swung into one hook at Botham that missed and another next ball that brought him four, and Hogg was suddenly in trouble when he ducked a Willis bouncer and left his bat raised. The ball hit it and ballooned over slips for a single, and at the end of the over Willis left the field—to boos and cheers.

The weather forecast was rapidly coming true. The batsmen shed their sweaters, shadows attached themselves to the players, and the bat was no longer being beaten ball after ball. With every over the question loomed larger: Should Australia have batted?

Botham switched ends to take over from Willis with the Clem Jones Stand behind him, and Old resumed at the other. Willis had drawn breath with figures of 14-2-44-4.

There followed some frustration for England. Several lbw shouts were turned down, and Maclean would have been run out if Gower's throw had hit at the bowler's end. Then Maclean played involuntarily at a ball from Old and was caught by Botham low down at second slip—but it was a no-ball, the old curse returned. Drinks were gratefully taken at 99 for 7, Maclean 25 and Hogg 28, and soon the hundred came up, clapped with relief, as Hogg scrambled a single in the 33rd over. For 188 minutes now Australia had been on the rack.

Next came the fifty stand for this eighth wicket, posted in 65 minutes, followed by a juicy cover-drive by the ever-more-commanding Hogg off an increasingly-frustrated Botham. Today, on the whole, the Somerset man was keeping the ball well up, in ideal conditions, but the harvest was absent ... until Hogg edged him and was swallowed up by Taylor behind the wicket, and Hurst went the same way four balls later, giving the 'keeper, (wearing Bertie Oldfield gloves some twelve years old) his fifth catch (a record for England in Australia) and drawing from the aggrieved batsman a baleful glare towards the umpire. Maclean continued to get his all behind the ball, setting his bat and both legs up like a three-part partition, and Higgs scored a run, something he failed to do throughout the 1975 tour of England. But Australia, playing with badges on their shirts and sweaters, were done for now, and the dispatch of the alliterative nine, ten and eleven, Hogg, Hurst and Higgs, was completed when Old bowled the Victorian leg-spinner—Australia all out for 116 at a quarter past three, Willis (4 for 44), Old (2 for 24) and Botham (3 for 40) having completed the demolition in 37.7 overs. Maclean's staunch, unbeaten 33 took 133 minutes, leaving Hogg as the unlikely top-scorer with 36. Only nine boundaries had been hit. It was now to be seen if Australia's pace attack could extract as much life from the pitch and induce as much indecisive strokeplay as we had seen during the past four hours.

The weather still hadn't made up its mind as England began their reply after tea, Boycott, sleeves rolled high on his biceps, facing Alan Hurst. Gooch took two to midwicket from Hogg's first ball, and during a good, lively first over the South Australian fast man, who has a crouching, raking run-up rather like Alan Ward's, hit his thigh-pad, raising a big shout when the ball was caught at gully, and then beat the outside edge for Maclean and company to yell loudly yet again.

When Hurst whistled one past Boycott's cap and beat him next ball it was clear that the battle was not—yet at any rate—to be too one-sided. Hogg struck the first blow. He forced Gooch to edge towards gully, where Laughlin just failed to dive far enough forward, and then he got one through Gooch's defence, seemingly hitting only the thigh-pad, and this time Laughlin took the ball cleanly and umpire O'Connell gave the batsman out, to his emphatic disapproval. It was the fifth ball of debutant Hogg's second over, and as Gooch plodded off in his moulded pads, which resembled a pair of white skate-boards tied to his large legs, I saw—for the moment anyway—my long-odds hopes of the Victoria Sporting Club champagne prize for the first century by England go with him.

Derek Randall played and missed at his first ball from Hogg, and skipped off towards square leg to avoid any likely suspicion of an edge. Soon Boycott had made his first run, and Hogg, who had twice fallen over in his followthrough, was rested with figures of 3-2-2-1.

Hurst then bowled a most eventful over to Randall. A model hook for four opened his score, but Hurst found the edge twice and brought another back and came close to getting an lbw decision as the batsman offered no stroke. A yorker on the boot gave rise to a shrieked appeal and had Randall hopping out of his crease and then diving frantically back to safety like a jaywalker evading a runaway ten-ton truck. To complete the excitement Randall hooked another four, airily and nowhere near as comfortably as the previous one.

Laughlin took over from the pavilion end, bowling at such a pace that old-time wicketkeepers might have stood up to him.

Randall, ever ready, gloried in another boundary, this time pulled square, a stroke of complete command.

Hogg returned at the opposite end now, and both batsmen played frequently to slip as the light dimmed sufficiently for the umpires to consult, and after drinks, taken at five-to-five, England 33 for 1, Boycott 12, Randall 18, Yallop decided to introduce Yardley's off-spin. The deeply-tanned Western Australian gave the ball a lot of air and his second delivery, a full-toss, was swung by Randall heartily for four and had Cosier at backward short leg signalling for protective gear of some sort. There was no need. After one further ball the umpires led the players off in the evening gloom.

They were not off for long, and when they returned, Australia secured the wicket they wanted. Boycott thick-edged Hogg to Hughes at the finer gully position and England were 38 for 2; the spectators sprawled on the hill and swaying in front of the stands cheered up visibly. This gave Hogg Boycott's wicket three times in as many meetings, and marked the high point in an amazing spell in which he conceded no runs between his very first delivery, which Gooch hit for two, and his 46th.

Randall now restored English spirits in a Yardley over, though it brought its moments of discomfort. He swept the off-spinner for a wholesome four, but then edged just short of Yallop. Then came a sweet hit high over the long-on boundary for six, followed by an unseemly sight as Wood, helmeted, crashed into him from short leg in a pointless effort to gather a rebound. Randall jigged his shoulders, went for a little walk, and carried on his job of steering the ship.

His partner was Bob Taylor, surprisingly sent in to keep the nightwatch with three-quarters of an hour remaining. He looked sound enough, though he was once hit on the body as he ducked into a short one from Hogg, but Randall kept things moving with a pulled boundary off Hogg to raise the fifty in 112 minutes, and a pleasant on-drive also for four. Soon after, the umpires again checked the light, and their offer to go off was readily accepted by the England batsmen. At 60 for 2 they could be content—but only to a point. Rodney Hogg had had a splendid first day in Test cricket with a top score 36 and 2 for 8 off seven overs, while Bob Willis, in an ABC interview at the end of the day, expressed the view that England had a long way to go. He also told viewers that the captains had agreed that only he and Jim Higgs were to be exempt from bouncers. Bigheartedly, he didn't really agree with any exemptions, though it was to be remembered that Hogg was also considered a protected species, umpire French having warned Willis after a bouncer.

England's vice-captain displayed his skinned and sore left foot—a problem which arises only in Australia. But he had not let it come between him and a very fine performance earlier in the day. It would not have amused Australians to learn that Dennis Lillee had been an inspiration. 'When I saw him bowling so well in the Centenary Test last year after his injuries, I said to myself I can do that.' He said he had been through a lot of work since the middle of the 1976 season, since when he had not missed a Test match.

This particular match looked like developing into something quite as eventful as any of the others. The 14,026 paying customers (only slightly down on the first-day crowd four years previously) had plenty to talk about as they wound their way home in the warm, darkening evening.

Second day

A welcome piece of news at the start of the day was that there is to be an anniversary Test match in England in 1980 to mark a hundred years of England-Australia Test cricket★. As this Brisbane match progressed it became clear that it would be one of those still being talked about during the 1980 celebrations, for the morning session this Saturday, before another large crowd, was in stark contrast to the day before, when six Australian wickets fell for 48 runs. Now, still with a heavy atmosphere pressing down on sweating players and spectators (Maclean's shirt was stuck to his broad back ten minutes after the start), England added just thirty runs in the morning session in an hour and a half. At six minutes to eleven there was a sudden shower, but the pitch was soon draped in a tarpaulin and play resumed half an hour later, with Bob Taylor, in blue crash-helmet, playing straight most of the time and adding altogether no more than eight runs to his overnight two.

★*The following week, when I met him at the Melbourne WSC 'Supertest', Richie Benaud was wondering whether* all *former Test players might be invited to the celebrations, as in the 1977 Melbourne Centenary. He seemed to expect a degree of discrimination. I dismissed his anxiety, perhaps a little too breezily, with the suggestion that by 1980 the 'war' would be over.*

Randall kept his head down, and obviously relished being back as England's number three after falling from grace for so many months. He reached his half-century with a single to long leg off Hurst, having been in for 113 minutes, but was soon missed when he fended off a lifter from Hogg, Yallop juggling as he fell and spilling a fairly straightforward catch. He continued to rotate his slips fieldsmen, and was next seen himself at mid-on, a practice hardly to be commended.

The crowd's patience was being tested as the Englishmen played well within themselves. Laughlin took over from Hurst at the Jones Stand end and began a respectable spell of good-length medium-pace bowling, but there was nowhere near the menace in the air of twenty-four hours ago. Once Laughlin came close to having Randall leg-before when he perpetrated his familiar failing of walking right in front of a full-length ball—and missing it. Umpire French, of the luxuriant head of hair, was unimpressed by the shout.

All around the stands and grassy banks the colourfully-dressed spectators became restive, and only fast bowler Hogg was able to sooth their discomfort. Every once in a while he beat the bat, and by the time he was relieved close on the interval he had figures of 2 for 26 off 14 overs. The break for rain had come at the right time for a man who, because of a slight asthmatic condition, preferred short spells of bowling.

Randall's stand with Taylor passed 50 in 104 minutes, and by lunch England were solidly on 90 for 2 in 39 overs, with Randall 62 in just over three hours and Taylor on 10 in just on two. Yallop had not seen fit to try either of his spinners, when surely it would have been worth looking at them, if only briefly. This, following his defensive decision to bat after winning the toss, set him miles apart from his not-so-distant-in-time predecessor Ian Chappell.

After lunch the sun broke through. It was still very hot and humid, and the play remained slow. Tactically it might have been preferable for Taylor to have hit out or got out, but he stayed, prodding, resisting, nudging, while his Nottingham partner tried for the occasional full-power shot. Randall inside-edged Cosier to long leg for four, and was soon having fun and games at Cosier's expense as he signalled a wide to the crowd on the hill after a non-swinger had shot through almost over the return crease. The next ball was straight and Randall gave the bowler the thumbs-up after playing it. When Cosier switched to around the wicket, Randall flicked him off his toes for four to bring up the hundred in 229 minutes, off 44 overs. Hurst replaced Laughlin.

The tempo was languid, and in the Press-box (where it was hard to digest that John Woodcock was not writing for *The Times* because there was, for the moment at least, no *Times* to write for) there was a readiness to create hilarity—so much so that the banter brought forth gusts of laughter, and the 'inmates' had to be warned that soon the players themselves would be looking up here for their entertainment. It soon passed, for the match came alive.

The first breakthrough came with a magnificent catch at gully by Laughlin to dismiss Randall. It was a firm stroke, front-foot to a ball well pitched up, but 'Super' flew to his left, like Superman himself, and caught the ball in his left hand. His team-mates mobbed him, and Hurst, with his first wicket, looked very pleased. Randall swung his bat dolefully as he walked away, having batted 220 minutes for his 75, with ten fours and a six, perhaps his most important innings in twenty months, since his memorable Centenary effort. The third-wicket stand had lasted 146 minutes while producing just 73 runs.

England's captain, Mike Brearley, was booed, presumably for the preceding go-slow, but he was soon crouching over his bat, threatening to consolidate the position. An edged four gave his side the lead.

Averaging 140 on the tour, Brearley could have been said to be heading for a fall, and sure enough it came when he was six. He glanced Hogg hip-high and Maclean, though nursing a sore hand and a niggling hamstring, had no great difficulty in pouching his first Test catch.

No sooner had David Gower arrived, looking worldly with his blond curls concealed under a helmet, than Taylor's self-sacrificing vigil came to a close. Leg-before to a full-length ball from the bounding, bustling Hurst for a 170-minute innings of 20, he was generously applauded by most of the Australians as he made his neat way off. England now were 120 for 5, having lost three wickets for nine, and the match had been transformed. It was a glad development for the spectators in more ways than one, for it now brought Gower and Botham (also helmeted) together, with the guarantee that while they lasted there would be no protest at the scoring rate or any absence of strokes.

Botham was into it straightaway, slashing and driving with the full swing of his bulging shoulders. One thrashing hit through gully was too hard for a vaulting Laughlin to hold, but there followed a glorious, copybook cover-drive for three off the tiring Hogg, fielded by Toohey in a wide stetson sunhat, the throw dropping over the 'keeper's bails. Gower made his first runs against Australia with a straightish drive for two off Hurst, and repeated the stroke for three against Hogg, after which the fast bowler was unlucky not to get Botham when an attempted hook sent the ball, via his blue helmet, some distance into the air, only for Maclean, no sprinter, to fail by a couple of yards to reach it as it crashed to earth.

Laughlin, the stock bowler, came on for Hurst and had a full-toss punished for three by Gower through cover, but Yardley, taking over from Hogg at the pavilion end, twice beat him in his first over, a maiden, watched by a crouching, helmeted Wood at short leg.

A French-cut by Botham drew cries of exasperation from some of the watchers under the trees and in front of the Queensland Cricketers' Club, that preserve of friendliness and good humour. The members' forebearance was tested by some untidy wicketkeeping by Maclean though, as he allowed two byes off Laughlin ('Oh, Macca!') and four off Yardley, and just failed to pick up a sizzling edge by his right boot off Botham.

Boundaries were no longer rare. Botham cut Yardley to the third-man fence, and Gower cut Laughlin uppishly through the gully region for four more. Next over, Yardley, off his longish run, got no further joy out of Botham, who lofted him twice, a sighter for two then a stronger blow to the fence just under the sightscreen. The fifty came in 57 minutes just before tea, and Australia had one final chance to break this dangerous stand when Botham clubbed Yardley to long-on, Higgs sprawling desperately forward but failing to collect the catch. The very next ball was bowled by Higgs himself, called up at long last for the final over of the second session of play. As always when a leg-spinner is called into the attack, people stopped what they were doing. The Victorian approached slowly, dropped his right arm by his thigh, turned side-on and wheeled down a tidy over. At tea England were nearer to poise once more at 176 for 5, Gower 20, Botham 30. The innings was already five-and-a-half hours old, but it was unmistakably a battle royal, no over limits, no conjured-up teams, no razzamataz. The gruelling attrition was behind us now, for a time at least, and Botham and his graceful partner Gower were moving into overdrive.

A handful of proud Englishmen took the huge risk of carrying a large Union Jack across the base of the hill on the west side, and were pelted with beer-cans. But they survived their passage, brave and smiling, just as the batsmen were untroubled by the new ball. Hogg and Hurst gave them enough room to put their cuts and drives to good use—eleven runs came from Hogg's first over—and a pull for three by Gower brought up the 200 in six hours. Botham swung the next from Hurst violently for four, and after Gower had maintained parity of a sort with a perfect square-cut to the fence, Botham, who now looked as fit as he could ever have been, pulled a ball from Hogg that was barely short of a length through to the midwicket boundary, one bounce only. It was very entertaining cricket.

For the moment, we had had our fun. Botham, one short of his fifty, swung into a hook shot off another short ball from Hogg and Maclean took the fine touch. The stand had been worth 95 in 101 minutes, and soon the other half was dispatched too. Gower, having been close to lbw to Hurst, played a square-cut that was pure Sobers, but in trying to repeat the stroke he edged and became the third victim not only of Hurst but of 'keeper Maclean, who took the catch in squatting position.

At 219 for 7, the lead 103, Phil Edmonds, with cap but no helmet, joined Geoff Miller, whose larger-than-life namesake, Keith, beamed benevolently down at that moment from the television room onto the ground where he made his Test debut unbelievably 32 years ago.

Thousands of others were beaming shortly when Edmonds, with only a single to his name, hooked at Hogg and could scarcely believe his eyes when Maclean leapt to his left and took the second great catch of the day, one-handed. It gave Hogg a deserved fifth wicket, Maclean his fourth catch, and put England in some sort of check at 226 for 8.

Old, the sixth of England's ten batsmen on view thus far to wear a crash-helmet, might have been bowled twice in Hogg's first over to him, once when he played no stroke and once when he did. As the evening clouds took over, Rodney Hogg bowled valiantly on, into his 22nd over, his 23rd, his 24th of the innings, still getting lift and some right-to-left movement. Eventually he was rested, with figures of 24-7-70-5, and Alan Hurst bowled from the pavilion end for the first time, to an unimpressive Old, who clipped him along the ground through slips for four and doubtless felt healthier for it.

Higgs came on, stuck, as before, with a left-hander to bowl at, as when Gower was in. Old made no real attempt to savage him, and with Miller merely content to keep the ball out, the evening stole gently up on the Gabba. Miller brought the 250 up (440 minutes) with a wristy square-cut off Hurst and followed it with a similar shot for three, but with five minutes to go the umpires decided the light was too poor, and play ended with England 257 for 8, 141 ahead, Miller 19, Old 17.

The Benson & Hedges television advertising theme for this series was based, and most attractively, upon Roman gladiators engaged in mortal combat. The crowd of 11,157 this day had seen a hard-fought contest in which Australia were just managing to stay alive. The Sunday would be the crunch day, when early dismissal of the last two England wickets and an Australian second-innings total of around 400 would ensure some kind of climax.

Third day

Australia's stocks slumped further in the Sunday pre-lunch session. Old, who unleashed some telling shots in front of the wicket, and Miller extended the ninth-wicket stand to 40, Miller making his best score of the tour so far (27) before Hogg trapped him lbw as he played across the line. Willis then stayed in, often one-handed, for three-quarters of an hour for eight runs as England's total grew to 286 in 507 minutes. Maclean caught him, his fifth catch, winning the side another $2500 on top of the same sum awarded the players for Hogg's mighty performance (6 for 74) of five or more wickets. The money may have gone some way towards easing the pain as England tightened the vice.

The deficit was 170 as Australia began their second innings at a quarter past twelve, and disaster lost no time in landing. Willis stomped in from the pavilion (Vulture Street) end and launched a full-length inswinger. Cosier played hesitantly forward, and his off stump was hit. One down for none. Worse followed.

Toohey, to an offside field of six slips and gullies and a cover, all in sunhats, survived only seven balls. He inside-edged a single to square leg off Willis, and then faced Botham with the new ball. The first delivery he drove, the second hit him on the pads, and the third, swinging in, found him leg-before as he played forward. Two for two, the match surely destined to be finished tonight. Not only that, but the worst fears of a washout Test series were beginning to materialise, like the early signs of a developing photographic print as the chemical paper floats in the processing tray. The emerging picture might conceivably have an embroidered pattern of the letters WSC around the border.

The left-handers, Wood and Yallop, saw Australia to the lunch break, though the Western Australian was hit on the pads by Willis dangerously close to the fatal line. Brearley brought Edmonds in close at point, but Wood struck Botham for two twos through point, the second off a no-ball, and then succeeded in finding the fence with a crouching pull that raced down to the Wilson Stand. Brearley gave Botham, Old and Miller consecutive overs from the Jones Stand end, Miller getting little turn and conceding four to Yallop from a full-toss, and at lunch Australia tottered at 20 for 2.

Graeme Wood, looking more like Greg Chappell the longer one watched him, despite his left-handedness, had a narrow escape right after lunch, popping one off the splice against Willis and seeing Edmonds, only two yards away on the off side, lunge forward a split-second too late for the catch.

Perspiration continued to seep from every pore, and the wonderment persisted: how could this overheated place produce so many men with 56-inch waistlines? The beer and iced drinks were being consumed as fast as the barmen could supply them, and global considerations were non-existent.

The wicket began to look more like a Brisbane wicket, the match more like a Test, as Yallop and Wood kept out of trouble and picked off runs. The captain off-drove Old for two, two, and three, Randall running himself into a lather, and after Miller had failed to gather at midwicket with the batsmen hesitating in mid-pitch, Yallop (19) had an eventful over against Bob Willis. He flicked at a no-ball and was nicely caught at first slip by Brearley in front of his face, and next ball swung hard into a hook and appeared to glove the ball to Taylor. But the deep-throated appeal was turned down by umpire O'Connell. Yallop restored his coolness with a straight four past a diving Randall.

While Willis fired them in with a field consisting of a silly point, a point, gully, three slips, and extra cover, with a long leg and wide mid-on, Chris Old had a more conventional field. He also had his first success of the innings, for with the fourth ball of his fifth over he brought one back at Wood, who had just survived an lbw shout, and this time the bowler—perhaps luckily—got the verdict.

Wood, neat in his slim-fit shirt, had batted for 87 minutes for his 19, and though time had elapsed, the runs were still in short supply, the deficit still burdensome.

Kim Hughes, with golden sweatbands on his wrists, glanced his first ball for two to raise the fifty, and soon began to look the part. He and his captain looked for runs and were alert for the quick single, with Yallop spotting anything slightly short and ducking or pulling—something he did effectively twice within a few minutes, for four each time. If ever a 'captain's innings' was called for, now was the time.

Hughes sometimes unleashed exciting strokes, as when he hooked Botham almost for six, following up with another powerful hit to the square-leg fence from a ball in line with off stump. This took him to 15, with Yallop having moved on to 43. Australia's highest score so far.

A delightful square-cut took him to 48, but in the same over Aussie hearts were in Aussie throats as Hughes was struck on the pads by Botham, who was using the width of the crease well. Yallop nudged Miller through gully for a single to reach his half-century in 130 minutes (five fours), and Hughes battened down for the rest of the over, with a model forward defensive block. This was not, after all, going to be a three-day match. Which led to further anxieties for some, since a national airline stoppage was threatened for tomorrow night, and there might be no easy escape from this city afterwards.

The batsmen stole a cheeky run, and Gower's return was taken by Randall at the stumps for a lightning piece of work—though Hughes had made his ground. Randall gave his team-mate a fatherly pat on the head for his effort.

Ten minutes before tea, after Hughes had played a bad pull stroke off Miller to a ball too far up, Yallop, who looked increasingly more secure as well as theatrical in mannerism, followed a crunching square-cut for four with another for two, also off Botham, to raise the hundred, and the fifty partnership as well, in the 29th over.

Miller was now getting the occasional ball to bounce and spin, and so Edmonds was called into the attack five minutes before the interval, bowling over the wicket to Yallop with a deep square leg and Old on the line at wide long-on. It was a quiet over, one after which the players could decorously exit for tea. At 102 for 3, Australia were still 68 behind, but Yallop's possible debut century was a matter of some personal interest, and Hughes was looking good.

Soon after the interval Hughes picked up a Willis bouncer and hooked it for six with the noise of a branch breaking. A quick two followed, taking him to 29. At 30 he got into difficulties with a Willis lifter which brushed his shoulder as he ducked, and umpire Dick French signalled no-ball, byes, and a boundary, though it seemed that the batsman had been taking evasive action as he was hit. Not long after, Hughes got his revenge by stepping inside a ball just short of a length and cutting it upwards, deep to the unguarded third-man boundary. He looked heavier and stronger than when he was in England in 1977, when he surprisingly failed to make a century and scored only a tortured single in his sole Test innings.

A chance for a breakthrough came when Yallop was 64. He drove at Willis, got a fast edge, and Gooch, at second slip ahead of Brearley at first, threw his considerable bulk to the right and lost both his sunhat and the ball. He was having a nightmare match.

Willis vacated the pavilion end in favour of Botham, but was soon running hard after a Hughes pull for three. A neat sweep by the same batsman hit the boundary boards near the dressing-rooms. Yallop, of the broad beam, seemed happy to keep an end going, while the sunbronzed creatures on the scoreboard hill noisily amused themselves and the policemen kept themselves in a secure nucleus. The players maintained concentration even through the worst of it, when the clouds of beer-cans raining down, apparently harmlessly, were upstaged by a 44-gallon drum. A wrestling match ensued, and someone set light to a tee-shirt. My mother-in-law and sister-in-law, both watching their first Test match, must have felt they were wiser to watch most of their cricket in the safety of their lounge-rooms out in Ipswich.

Edmonds came on after drinks, Miller having bowled a tidy spell of 7-2-11-0 since tea, and his curling flight and away-spin made a refreshing change from the predominance of pace bowling travelling towards the pads and thigh. The fourth-wicket partnership hung on 99 for a longish time, but at last Yallop placed Edmonds to mid-on for a single and the valuable three-figure landmark arrived in 158 minutes. Soon the 150 was posted, in the not unusual time of 252 minutes. With Old on at the pavilion end, the umpires had a cautionary look at the light, which was obviously going to get no better.

By now Yallop was 74 and Hughes, bat vertical as a plumb-bob,

47. He went to his half-century when Edmonds overpitched slightly, the cover-drive speeding to the fence just before the umpires offered the light. Off they came. Australia, seven wickets in hand, needed thirteen runs to make England bat again, and, much against the morning expectations, the match might now run into the fifth day on Wednesday. Tomorrow's rest day would be welcomed by sweating players and journalists alike.

So ended a day of intense competition, watched by 12,250, when Australia were down the drain at 12.20 pm, but back in the match by the close, with England not having taken a wicket in almost three hours' play—a day to be remembered for the first show of defiance by a maligned Australian team. Mr Packer may indeed have been clapping his hands with delight at the trend of the match, but so were thousands of spectators who relished the competition and were glad to demonstrate their loyalty to the old contest, which had launched every great name known to English and Australian cricket.

Two of those names from the recent past were in the news this day. Colin Cowdrey's marital problems were prominently spread up front in the newspapers, and elsewhere we were told of Tony Greig's new home in Vaucluse, a 'bargain' at $275,000, a residence 'for life'. Kerry Packer's right-hand man had just been appointed managing director of a new enterprise, an insurance broking company, and it was reassuring to read his acknowledgement of his good fortune over the years, even to his recall of his maiden first-class century in 1965, when he might have been lucky with an umpire's decision before he had made a run. Life had moved on for him in these thirteen years.

Fourth day

The rest day was well chosen. It rained in torrents and the skies were grey as prison linen. But the Tuesday dawned bright and sultry, and with hopes high, Australia's not-out batsmen, Yallop and Hughes, made their way to the middle, with 13 overs to go before the new ball. Miller began the bowling from the pavilion end, Botham from the other.

Miller was giving the ball plenty of air and getting a distinct curl with the breeze. Yallop took three from a drive which hit the stumps and brushed umpire French as he skipped to his left, and soon a poor, wide ball somehow went through Taylor for three byes. Botham ran through his considerable repertoire, giving Hughes a bouncer and hitting Yallop on the shoulder when he ducked to one that failed to climb. The appeal was turned down.

When Hughes tucked Miller past Edmonds at short leg for two runs, the overall scores were level, and the small crowd showed its appreciation. A sumptuous off-drive to the boundary off Botham by Hughes followed, and just before the new ball became due, Brearley tried Edmonds, whom Yallop swept fine for four. Immediately 65 overs had been bowled, England took the new ball, with Australia 188 for 3 and their captain making determined progress in singles. Another compact off-drive for four by Hughes off Botham—now at the pavilion end—was further testimony to the soundness of the pitch, and when drinks were taken Australia were 197 for 3, 27 ahead, with Yallop 91, Hughes 70.

The 150 partnership came with a Hughes nudge through slip for one, and when Yallop next did the same thing, the 200 was posted, in 327 minutes. Gower now made the first of several fine saves at gully, but Yallop found another gap with a pleasant straight-drive to take him to 96. The ball was 'kept rolling' when Taylor surprisingly allowed a low-bouncing ball from Willis through for four byes after Hughes had aimed a big pull at it as it passed outside off. Meanwhile Yallop tiptoed towards his historic hundred, 96, 97, 98.

Hughes took a short one on the shoulder from Botham, who switched to around the wicket for left-handed Yallop. The captain tucked him behind square for another single to reach 99. Australia held its breath.

Eleven Australians so far had made hundreds in their first Test matches against England, and there were some good names in the list: Bannerman, Burke, Greg Chappell (the most recent, eight years ago), Collins, Duff, Graham, Hartigan, Harvey, Jackson, Ponsford, and Walters. Only Herbie Collins had been captain at the time, but he had led Australia previously. Thus, when Graham Yallop pushed Old's first ball to midwicket at 12.25 pm and Gooch fumbled, the hurried single gave him a momentous century. It was his second in Tests and his tenth in first-class cricket; it had taken him frve-and-a-half hours and included eight fours, with luck definably coming his way only at 19, when he was caught from a no-ball and then given the benefit of a thunderous appeal for caught-behind, and at 64, when Gooch put him down at slip. His staunch performance must have secured his position and the captaincy probably for the series. It was Ray Robinson, that revered connoisseur of matters relating to the Australian captaincy, who pointed out that Yallop was the fifth player to make a century in his first match as Australian leader, following Billy Murdoch, Harry Trott, Lindsay Hassett, and Greg Chappell. His satisfaction must have been all the greater when he thought back to the mean reception he received at the hands of some of the 1975–76 Test team when he made his debut. Willis, whose left foot was giving him a lot of trouble, battled on at a steady pace from the Vulture Street end, suffering in the hallowed 'bloody-sock' tradition of Tate, Larwood and Bedser, and after Yallop had dashed a thrilling two, Old hitting the stumps with his throw, the big Warwickshire man captured his second wicket at last. Yallop played him straight back, unhurriedly, but the bowler took the ball in his right hand as casually as he would have patted a dog. The stand, which was the salvation of the match—and of the embryo Test series—was worth 170 (the best for Australia's fourth wicket against England at Brisbane) and had occupied 266 minutes. Hughes, Australia's remaining big hope, was on 75.

Any thoughts of a new stand of large proportions were soon snuffed out when Laughlin, having clipped Old for three and then seen Hughes make one of his very rare false strokes, Willis passing the bat, was himself trapped lbw by Old. It was a near-full-toss on the leg stump, and at last umpire Max O'Connell felt justified in raising his finger. It was a second reversal hard to bear for Australia so close to the lunch break.

Resuming at 232 for 4, Hughes 78, Maclean 2, Australia consolidated. Graham Yallop said, after his dismissal, that he was looking for a lead of at least 200, and felt that would take some getting on a pitch with a few cracks in it and keeping a little low, helping the spinners. (It was noticeable how little work Edmonds was being given.) He also said that the century gave him immense pleasure, since he had had to convince himself that Brisbane was not his hoodoo ground. His highest score here previously was only 35.

Ian Botham toiled on, finding wickets much harder to come by than in the majority of his Test appearances. The batsmen took runs off him with fair frequency, and numerous were his gestures of self-admonishment, most of all when the flat-footed Maclean crunched him away for runs.

Hughes took three runs from an unusual half-pull off Old, raising the 250 in 412 minutes, and a single took him to 90. Maclean took some more runs off Botham with a cruiserweight's hook-stroke, and it took Miller, reintroduced at the pavilion end, to make the next breakthrough. A big outfloater tempted Maclean to sweep, and he became the fourth lbw victim of the six wickets so far.

Hughes, showing untypical restraint, moved through the nineties. A sweep off Miller took him to 99, and after Yardley had stretched and unravelled the rest of the over, Hughes faced Old. The first four balls were played carefully out on the off side, the next to mid-on, the next to gully. Then he received the one he wanted, on leg stump. He glanced it, there was no-one in close, and he ran two to take him to 101, his maiden Test century, fulfilling at last all the high promise shown since he made a hundred on his first-class debut three years earlier. He had been in for 369 minutes, hitting seven fours and a six from the 295 balls received, and anyone betting on two Australians making centuries when the second-innings score stood at 49 for 3 on Sunday would have deserved large winnings.

Yardley swung extravagantly into a back-cut for four off Old, and Miller's interesting spell of flighted, curling deliveries ('He must have been reading the *Daily Express*,' said that paper's cricket expert, Jim Laker) was interrupted by a pulsating six, two steps down the cricket track and over the dog-track at long-on. When he took two after stepping out again and placing Edmonds to leg, the 300 came up, in the 100th over. England's next chance came when Yardley prodded out at Edmonds and the ball flew to hit Gooch, at silly point, hard on the chest. The rebound reached the batsman, giving the fieldsman no chance of recovery. This situation was just what England, way-out favourites, had feared.

At tea Australia were 303 for 6, 133 ahead, with Hughes 117 and his State team-mate Yardley 11.

Yardley went soon after tea, caught left-handed by Brearley at slip off Miller, the batsman waiting for the umpires to confirm with each other that the ball had not touched the ground, while the England captain trotted a wide semi-circle, the ball held aloft. Hogg came in, this time without a helmet, and Hughes knew that a great deal still depended on him, with only the three Hs to support him. Willis strove for the final breakthrough, but continually spared his left foot in delivery and followthrough. Brearley played the containing game, trying to keep Hughes from the strike. When he did, Gooch took his crash-helmet from the umpire and went in at close square short leg to Hogg. Hogg held on—even took a two 'against the spin' off Miller and a leg-bye from a thump in the back by Willis. Singles to a wide-set field were refused, but Hogg once gave Miller the full treatment with a towering drive to the untenanted long-off fence, and generally looked good enough for a Test number nine.

Botham, with 1 for 85 to his name, replaced Willis, and Hughes opened up, missing a few times, getting four to long leg. 'Both' was getting dangerously close to a Test century of another kind: 1 for 91 at the end of the over.

Willis, all guts, surprised by appearing at the opposite end, and troubled Hogg with short-of-a-length balls that hit him or passed him at waist level, but the open-featured Australian pleased himself with a big drive for three, and it was clear that Willis had little left to offer.

The ideal last day was going to see England needing something just over 200, and the prospect drew nearer as Botham bowled Hogg, having been spoken to by umpire O'Connell for bowling him a bouncer. The bowler put a lot of effort into that ball, and a lot of feeling subsequently into an upward sweep of his fist—which might just have had a finger or two pointing from it.

Hurst lasted two balls. Botham, truly stirred, flashed a full-toss through him, hitting the off stump some way from the ground and sending it towards fine leg. The Victorian fast bowler thus bagged a pair.

Higgs may have been the 'rabbit', but it was the 24-year-old hero Kim Hughes who was the last to go. He tried to pick Willis up over the top of midwicket, but the tall Edmonds calmly rose to full height and took the catch in his left hand. So after all, England needed as few as—or as many as, thinking back to Sunday—170 in 345 minutes plus 15 overs, and had three-quarters of an hour to get into their task this evening.

The first over went well for them. Hogg hit Boycott's pads first ball, but there followed a two, four byes, a no-ball when he switched to around the wicket, and two through slips—nine off the over. Hurst bowled a series of big outswingers and then one that came back a shade. The ball made a noise like a kettle-drum on Gooch's pads, and the fieldsmen made a noise like so many Afghan warriors; but umpire French was unmoved. He usually is.

Gooch was twenty-five minutes getting his first runs, but survival was of capital importance. As the sun slide away beyond the city it seemed that the wicket was anticipating a night's rest, for many a ball kept low, reaching Maclean first bounce. The one to watch was the one pitched on the line of the stumps.

To three short legs, one of them Carlson, substituting for Wood, who had a stomach upset, Yardley bowled the final over of the day, and a wholly watchful Boycott kept out six balls, Gooch two. Sixteen runs had been made, and with all day tomorrow to make another 154, all wickets standing, England were set to go one-up. The only reservation was that on Friday the match was thought to be all over by Sunday evening, but it wasn't. This series was not as predictable as expected—as if we didn't know.

After play, Graham Yallop spoke of his stand with Hughes and how they had helped each other maintain concentration. 'It's the best I've ever seen Kim concentrate,' he said. Australia were a lot better side than their first-innings 116 suggested, and they had been out to make amends. Looking to the final day, Australia were 'not out of it by any means'.

With the final interview involving Kim Hughes, a day which had begun with a visit to my old hero Ray Lindwall (back and shoulder not too good, but business at his florist shop brisk enough most days—he was just off to a funeral) ended with a few relaxed words with Australia's latest idol. The fair-haired Western Australian said he had lost a stone and a quarter since his unfortunate West Indies tour, and was 'a little bit older than last year'. His fitness and concentration had improved, as well as his sense of responsibility. He had never batted longer than five hours before, and his highest Test score was a puny 28 before this admirable showing. When asked about the quality of the opposition, he replied: 'They didn't serve up much tripe.' Arthur Mailey would have grinned from ear to ear.

Fifth day

A most pleasant evening at the home of Australia's premier cricket book collector, Pat Mullins, together with Aub and Pearl Yallop, the proud parents, set up the final day nicely. Most conversations revealed morsels of hope within an overall acceptance that England must win.

Hurst came perilously near to getting Boycott lbw second ball of the day, but in the next over, from Hogg, Australia got the early breakthrough they needed when Hogg's first ball found Gooch's edge and Yardley made an extremely good catch at third slip, taking it low to his left as he fell.

Before a smattering of people, Randall, all breezy and confident, reached out and hit his first ball for two, then hooked a single, but Boycott fended off a lifting ball from Hogg with head averted, and the Australians crowded in as if it was only a matter of time.

But there was to be no immediate bowling breakthrough. It came from a run-out. Randall played Hurst between the cover fieldsmen and took off. Boycott got up steam, but not enough, and Toohey's throw was perfect, hitting the leg stump. Mike Coward, the Adelaide journalist, recalling the 1977 Trent Bridge disaster when Boycott caused Randall's downfall to a run-out, dubbed it 'The Nottingham Revenge'.

Derek Randall had off-driven Hurst for four and hooked the next ball, a bumper, straight to the square-leg fielder (along the ground). Now extra responsibility fell upon him, but he continued to go for his strokes. When Yardley came on at the Jones Stand end for Hogg he swept him for four past the helmeted Wood, and looked loose and free against the bouncing, spinning ball. Hurst bothered him twice with big lbw shouts, but umpire French shook his head. When, after drinks, Randall attempted a big leg hit at Yardley from outside off stump, he earned a scathing glare from the bowler.

The fifty came up in 110 minutes when Randall's on-drive got past a spreadeagled Hogg, and Brearley, wearing one of the more 'conventional' helmets in place of his skull-cap, swept Yardley for four and reached even further across to sweep for one. When Randall late-cut for three, eight valuable runs had come in four balls. After a respectable spell (6-2-14-0) Hurst gave way to Laughlin, whose three overs before lunch were to cost only six runs without offering a threat to England's security.

At 12.30 pm Higgs took over at the pavilion end, and immediately began to spin sharply from leg on the dry, worn wicket, with a canny loop through the air. His first over was a maiden and he beat Randall with the sixth ball.

Brearley, after sweeping at Yardley a number of times, tried to cut a ball that kept low, and Maclean took the under-edge catch not far from the ground. So with just a quarter of an hour to go till lunch England were 74 for 3, with only all-rounders to come. Gower, the new batsman, sighted the ball for a while, then pulled Higgs hard and high to midwicket, where the ball bounced over the boundary fieldsman. At lunch England were 82 for 3, 88 runs from victory.

England's most exciting pair of batsmen got on with the job afterwards, running hard in the heat for threes and twos as the grassy outfield slowed all but the hardest hits. Gower might have been caught straightaway when a mis-hit pull popped up near Yardley close in, but the fieldsman was busy taking evasive action. Randall swept Higgs for four, but edged Yardley fractionally short of Yallop at slip. Inevitability took a grasp on the afternoon.

The spinners toiled on, but the hundred came up after three hours, from a Yardley no-ball, and Randall went past 50 with a sweep to the fence off Yardley, a disciplined but attractive half-century that had taken 139 minutes. Yallop tried Cosier, whom Gower soon cut hard and wide of the captain at slip, and a beautiful off-drive by the left-hander off Higgs, who now bowled from around the wicket, raised the fifty partnership in even time. During Cosier's next over the ugly mountain of byes for the match was swelled by four more when Maclean was obscured by Randall from a legside ball, and as the total moved into the 130s Yallop had a final throw of the dice by calling up Hogg. There was nothing in the pitch for a pace bowler, and with the batsmen in total command, except when they lost their respective headgear in running between wickets, drinks were taken at 146 for 3. At this point Gower called for his helmet, presumably to get further used to it. Soon he was pull-driving Higgs for a four which might have been a six, until the umpire consulted the fieldsman.

Gower almost went when he cover-drove Higgs without quite getting to the pitch, but Wood, diving bravely forward, failed to gather the catch. A crisp square-cut for three followed.

Hogg bowled round the wicket, and David Gower, England's greatest discovery of 1978, awaited the honour of hitting the winnings runs in his first Australian Test match. A long-hop cleared his diving shoulder-blades; he played back down the pitch; he edged fast and low to Maclean, who made a smart left-handed stop; and then he cracked a half-volley behind point and ran a quick two. England were home, by seven wickets, for their first victory at Brisbane since 1936.

It was not unexpected. It was not even close. Neither was it a humiliation. It was more of a struggle than had seemed likely, either before the series began or after two days' play, and Graham Yallop reminded his audience at the award presentation that there were five Tests to go. He said later that he regarded England's batting as having weaknesses. It had to be admitted that in this match Boycott, Gooch and Brearley made little impression, but Randall, the Man of the Match, was a treat, and Gower was well on the way to working himself out of a bad patch. Botham and Miller made marks as batsmen too, and if Botham had to fight for wickets, Miller had probably never bowled as well in a Test match.

Willis worked bravely and Old adequately. Only Edmonds failed to make an impression among the bowlers. Brearley should have been fairly happy—and was. It was his ninth win in fourteen matches as captain (five draws), and as he sipped his champagne in the blinding Queensland sunshine, he paid his tributes to the vanquished. Hogg 'bowled well', Hughes 'played beautifully'—the innings of the match—and he thought this very young Australian side would improve as the series went on.

Yallop, looking ahead, said his side wanted some good starts to the innings. And looking back, he said that it had been a good toss to lose. That was probably as close as he would ever get to saying that it might have been better after all if England had batted first.

Soon after the popular Randall had acknowledged his match prize with a strangled little speech further garbled by the acoustics, the Australian team for the second Test became known. South Australian opener Rick Darling, back in the runs, and Queensland left-arm medium-pacer Geoff Dymock replaced Laughlin and Higgs from the Brisbane twelve. Thus Australia tightened up their batting and bowling in a defensive double switch. They had shown they were not to be written off, and the message was being hoisted all over the land: 'Australia Expects'. The conundrum was that Signalman Roome, who hoisted Nelson's historic 1805 battle cry, deserted ship soon after the Battle of Trafalgar.

FIRST TEST MATCH

Brisbane, December 1, 2, 3, 5, 6, 1978

AUSTRALIA

			Mins	Fours			Mins	Fours
G.M. Wood	c Taylor b Old	**7**	45	0	(2) lbw b Old	**19**	87	1
G.J. Cosier	run out	**1**	4	0	(1) b Willis	**0**	1	0
P.M. Toohey	b Willis	**1**	9	0	lbw b Botham	**1**	7	0
*G.N. Yallop	c Gooch b Willis	**7**	60	0	c & b Willis	**102**	344	8
K.J. Hughes	c Taylor b Botham	**4**	34	0	c Edmonds b Willis	**129**	476	8*
T.J. Laughlin	c sub (Lever) b Willis	**2**	9	0	lbw b Old	**5**	13	0
†J.A. Maclean	not out	**33**	133	2	lbw b Miller	**15**	59	1
B. Yardley	c Taylor b Willis	**17**	38	2	c Brearley b Miller	**16**	79	1
R.M. Hogg	c Taylor b Botham	**36**	79	5	b Botham	**16**	42	1
A.G. Hurst	c Taylor b Botham	**0**	4	0	b Botham	**0**	2	0
J.D. Higgs	b Old	**1**	6	0	not out	**0**	5	0
Extras (1 lb, 6 nb)		**7**			(9 b, 5 lb, 22 nb)	**36**		
		116				**339**	*plus 2 sixes	

Fall: 2, 5, 14, 22, 24, 26, 53, 113, 113. 0, 2, 49, 219, 228, 261, 310, 339, 339.

Bowling: Willis 14–2–44–4, Old 9.7–1–24–2, Botham 12–1–40–3, Gooch 1–0–1–0, Edmonds 1–1–0–0.

Second innings: Willis 27.6–3–69–3, Botham 26–5–95–3, Old 17–1–60–2, Miller 34–12–52–2, Edmonds 12–1–27–0.

ENGLAND

			Mins	Fours			Mins	Fours
G. Boycott	c Hughes b Hogg	**13**	93	1	run out	**16**	98	0
G.A. Gooch	c Laughlin b Hogg	**2**	20	0	c Yardley b Hogg	**2**	53	0
D.W. Randall	c Laughlin b Hurst	**75**	220	10*	not out	**74**	209	5
†R.W. Taylor	lbw b Hurst	**20**	170	0				
*J.M. Brearley	c Maclean b Hogg	**6**	19	1	(4) c Maclean b Yardley	**13**	55	1
D. I. Gower	c Maclean b Hurst	**44**	110	5	(5) not out	**48**	109	4
I.T. Botham	c Maclean b Hogg	**49**	101	5				
G. Miller	lbw b Hogg	**27**	92	1				
P.H. Edmonds	c Maclean b Hogg	**1**	16	0				
C.M. Old	not out	**29**	113	2				
R.G.S. Willis	c Maclean b Hurst	**8**	44	1				
Extras (7 b, 4 lb, 1 nb)		**12**			(12 b, 3 lb, 2 nb)	**17**		
		286	*plus 1 six		3 wickets	**170**		

Fall: 2, 38, 111, 120, 120, 215, 219, 226, 266. 16, 37, 74.

Bowling: Hurst 27.4–6–93–4, Hogg 28–8–74–6, Laughlin 22–6–54–0, Yardley 7–1–34–0, Cosier 5–1–10–0, Higgs 6–2–9–0.

Second innings: Hogg 12.5–2–35–1, Hurst 10–4–17–0, Yardley 13–1–41–1, Laughlin 3–0–6–0, Higgs 12–1–43–0, Cosier 3–0–11–0.

Toss won by Australia.

Umpires: R.A. French & M.G. O'Connell.

*Captain †Wicketkeeper

ENGLAND WON BY SEVEN WICKETS

4. JOURNEY INTO PACKERLAND

As the Englishmen went west, I went to Melbourne to see the first World Series 'Supertest' (or 'Superficialtest' as Bill O'Reilly referred to it) of the summer, feeling the need to take on-the-spot soundings rather than be subjected to the limitations of television coverage. It was rather like going to the zoo to see rare and exotic species, and the only two other British Pressmen who went along on the first day probably regarded it the same way.

The England XI match in Perth against Western Australia was over in two days and a bit, the touring side winning by 140 runs after bowling the Sheffield Shield champions out for 52 (their lowest ever against an international side) and 78. Brearley's men mustered 144 and 126.

There was apparently nothing dangerous about the pitch, though it was moist, but the overcast conditions made the ball swing, and in the third innings Bruce Yardley took 5 for 54, three falling to bat-pad catches by Geoff Marsh. The batting all round came in for some harsh criticism, only Roger Tolchard (61 not out, to put him in line for a Test place), Phil Edmonds (21 and 27), John Emburey (22), and Yardley (38 not out) passing 20. Fast bowler Terry Alderman, who three or four years ago had been regarded as the 'new Lillee', took five English wickets, Wayne Clark only three when a handful in each innings would have projected him back into the Test selectors' thoughts, and medium-pacer Porter five. For the England XI, the irrepressible Botham took 4 for 16 and 4 for 37 and Mike Hendrick reminded everyone that he was still around by taking 5 for 11 and 3 for 23.

Geoff Boycott was in the news again, but not for any runs he might have made. He is supposed to have said something disagreeable to umpire Don Weser after Kim Hughes was given the benefit of an lbw appeal off Botham's bowling. England's senior batsman later apologised, but life seemed to be getting on top of him, for in Harrogate the members of Yorkshire CCC voted against his reinstatement as county captain. The margin (4826 to 2602) was decisive, as, to a lesser extent, was that in favour of retaining the general committee (4422 to 3067). The resolution calling for the resignation of the cricket sub-committee was defeated 4216 to 3346. So all was well, or reasonably so, with the county of Yorkshire; but not so for her most famous son of the 'seventies. After the Western Australia match his tour first-class figures stood at 198 runs at 19.80. Quite apart from the fact that he would not now be mounting any real attack on Wally Hammond's Australian tour aggregate record, it seemed a question of whether he would bother to stay in English cricket, or even for the remainder of the tour. When asked, World Series 'Godfather' Kerry Packer said that although feelers had been put out to Boycott recently he was not certain in his own mind that the Englishman was worth signing. The bad run continued with a run-out at 29 (in 101 minutes) when the England XI (208 for 3) were on their way to a winning total against a WA Country XI (all out 139) at Albany. Graham Gooch got the feel of runs again with 112 in 140 minutes, with ten fours and four sixes, making sure of retention in the Test side.

Elsewhere, the headlines had taken in such matters as a century by Yallop in the NSW-Victoria match—in which David Hourn, the sometimes wayward left-arm spinner, showed some wizardry with 9 for 77 in Victoria's first innings. This, and Higgs's persistent skill, gave the impression that Australia had the material to unbalance England, but lacked the nerve to use it.

Brisbane to Melbourne via Sydney is 1514 kilometres, or 946 miles. But I was growing tired of multiplying every distance and road-speed by five and dividing by eight. Dollars per litre, too, takes some working out into pence per gallon. Suffice to say that petrol is a great deal cheaper, so vive le difference.

The TAA T-jet cruised over valleys where the early settlers beat their expectant tracks and over hills like the stubbly backs of wild boars, always with the tempting blue Pacific miles to the left. The shadow of the aircraft was printed flickeringly and dramatically on the patchwork of immaculate white cloud beneath, until we came in over Sydney's western suburbs for the most breathtaking view I have ever had of the town where I did most of my growing up. Just time to ring my surprised son, then onwards into the near-frozen southern State. Melbourne's coolness after Brisbane's mugginess took some absorbing—as did the theft of my sportscoat from the hotel. Worse followed. After Day One of the World Series match I booked to Perth. Then *The Guardian* asked for more, so I cancelled the booking. By now there was a fresh outbreak of industrial action at Tullamarine Airport, and my suitcase went missing for thirty-six hours. How the TAA staff kept their cool during the chaos I shall never know. The thought of never seeing my belongings again quite spoiled Days Two and Three. But it all came right in the end.

It came right, too, for the WSC World XI, made up of Englishmen, Pakistanis, and South Africans. They beat the WSC Australians by 102 runs in the opening 'Supertest', winning $11,000 prizemoney, with Western Province, Burnley and Sussex fast-bowling giant Garth Le Roux taking the $1000 Man of the Match award.

Kerry Packer had a happy match. He beamed almost throughout, from the moment he knew that the first-day crowd had built up to the respectable figure of 18,884 (a year previously it could have been counted with ease, and quickly) until he gave me a farewell ribbing about my overnight bag, which bore the Benson & Hedges Test match sponsorship stamp. 'Bet it doesn't last to the end of the season!' he chortled.

Just as at Brisbane I had had an overwhelming desire to study the match in its isolation, to blinker out cricket's troubles for the moment, so at VFL Park, a long way out of Melbourne, I wanted to assess the quality of the cricket, and to find out at long last whether it meant anything to me. It did.

Although the organisers have grown used to the terraces being bare at the 1.30 pm start, filling towards evening, when the floodlights go on, the emptiness distracted me. No matter how good the play, if the theatre is less than one-tenth full the question is bound to arise: What are we doing here?

In time, this was almost overcome. So was the objection to brightly-coloured caps. Why not? Schoolboys and English club cricketers wear crimson, purple, green, puce, and cerise—sometimes all at once! There was also the matter of musical themes over the loudspeaker when the teams took the field, something about which the management was still thinking hard. The gladiatorial theme when the World XI came out of the tunnel was quite stirring, but the theme for the home players, 'C'mon, Aussie, c'mon', jarred. It jarred every time. But an hour later some of us would shamefully catch ourselves humming it, and there was no question about the appeal to the youngsters on the terraces (and the audience was pronouncedly young).

While the quality of the play was there for analysis, so was that of the crowd. It was raucous at times, and it threw things and got drunk. Two male streakers ran across the field. There were ten arrests on the first day/evening. But it would have been wrong to object to this as a defect peculiar to WSC performances. It is an unhappily familiar feature of cricket and other sports in many parts of the world. The trouble came later in the day. So thin was the attendance before tea that I heard one of the camera crew exclaim that everything was 'going great' except that they hadn't used the ground cameras yet—'No crowd!'

The shrewder spectators brought blankets for the last few hours, having paid four-and-a-half dollars for a seven-and-a-half-hour day, the last portion of which, in Melbourne before Christmas, can be chilly and windy. They were fiercely partisan, noisy, and keen to communicate with their players, and the players made unusual efforts to oblige, whether on the boundary, in the dugout, or along the vast concrete corridors and staircases. Rod Marsh was positively eager to give autographs, backed up with a pat on the head and that whimsical smile. He told me he thought that a World Series Australians and West Indians match at Melbourne Cricket Ground would produce attendances of 100,000.

The crowd, which totalled 59,180 over the four days at VFL Park (compared with the 43,532 who watched the five days of the Brisbane Test), had its patience tested by a dreadfully sluggish pitch that might have been made of cork. The ball went through slowly and low. The run rate throughout was around thirty per hour. Yet the slow handclaps were sparing—perhaps the biggest surprise of the entire event.

Greg Chappell, in yellow cap and yellow shoes, bestowed some charming touches on the final stages of the match, driving with all his peculiar elegance in the same kind of lost cause he knew as Australian captain in England in 1977. He made 81. Kepler Wessels, the 'instant Australian', struck well for a time in his 46, but Underwood had a stranglehold on the home batsmen almost all the final day, taking 4 for 59 off 37 overs. Imran Khan swept away the last four wickets to hasten the end.

Le Roux, with a bit of Andy Roberts in his delivery action, made a big impression, taking over from Tony Greig as the crowd's villain. He was booed when he batted and when he bowled, his chief sins being the demolition of the Australians in the Sydney one-day match and his dismissal of folkhero Lillee here. He enjoyed being the big, bad man. As for Greig, whose form had been appalling (94 runs in 14 innings in New Zealand and Australia), he dropped himself, made Asif Iqbal captain, and went off to the concrete practice pitch to face the automatic bowling machine, which was fed by team manager Mike Denness. When Greig did appear as twelfth man, taking out sweaters or for a brief spell of fielding, he too was heartily booed.

Dennis Amiss failed twice (0 and 6), but to Gilmour both times, not Lillee. Javed Miandad, surely now the finest fielder in the world, topped the World XI's first innings with 59, made painstakingly in four-and-a-quarter hours, and Majid Khan batted with great patience in the second in making 77 in over six hours. Mike Procter gracefully applied some muscle in his 66, actually reaching the elusive boundary nine times, while the Australian XI's first innings was saved by Ian Chappell, 48.

Le Roux's 5 for 39 off 25.5 six-ball overs put paid to the home side's first innings after Lillee had taken bowling honours for the Australian XI. I had not seen Lillee in action since the Centenary Test, since when he had come under the guidance of a pre-war Australian professional sprint champion—who also happened to be the father of Austin Robertson, one of the founders of World Series Cricket. Lillee's approach was now more disciplined, like a long-jumper's, the ball held steadily by his lowest rib. The raw speed was no longer evident, but the guile and menace, backed by the unearthly chorus from the terraces, made it an ordeal for all but the finest temperament opposed to him.

Again, the white ball showed up well, although when well-used it was harder to see from afar than the traditional red one. Junior model white balls were given free to the first five hundred schoolchildren passing through the turnstiles on the second day—more smart marketing.

What were the other outstanding impressions, the major differences between WSC and any other cricket I had ever watched? Well, I had never seen a motorised buggy delivering the drinks before. Sarfraz Nawaz drove expertly, though on one occasion the vehicle had to be push-started to get it off. The worst time for batsmen and fielders is twilight, when the floodlights have not quite made their presence felt because the eye searches for the receding natural light. The intervals—half an hour at 3.30 pm (tea) and an hour at six (dinner)—came strange at first. It was strange, too, to contemplate the Chappell involvement. At one point Greg and Ian were fielding, Trevor was driving out the drinks buggy, and father Martin was one of the official scorers. It was assumed that Mrs Chappell senior was charged with the job of laundering the equipment.

Crash-helmets may make identification hard at times, but it gradually dawned that they are accepted, little more than a year after their controversial introduction. It now gave an odd feeling to see a batsman without one. Majid seemed very brave, and Lillee seemed complacent, virtually saying 'I'm a number eleven, and no-one bounces them at me.'

Sir Garfield Sobers, in this environment, prompted a double-take or two, and the umpires' blue jackets invited approval or otherwise. Actually, they looked quite classy. Everyone seemed to be taking it all very seriously, and the only moments of hilarity were provided quite involuntarily by Clive Rice, who often fell flat on his face as he delivered the ball—and once did so while beginning his run-up.

The whole scene was backed by the Dandenong Ranges, which I had last seen as a lad. A lyrebird made an appearance that afternoon. Worlds away.

There was a chance to talk with Andrew Caro, the diminutive English-born managing director of WSC, and to Tony Greig, who never tires of answering questions and engaging in verbal wrestling matches. Caro hoped that an 'accommodation' might result in the early months of 1979, but did not anticipate that it would. He said he was always ready to negotiate. He thought that the success or otherwise of the Australia-England series would point the way. Like Greig, he saw World Series as being an area for innovation.

Tony Greig, agreeing that he had put on a few pounds (fifteen stone now), wrapped his legs around several plastic chairs in the dugout and expressed his continuing bitterness at the uncompromising attitude of Lord's and Melbourne. With passion, he said he wanted World Series to get stronger still so that when a settlement was reached it would not imperil WSC people.

He was not prepared to go into the matter of how WSC could retain public interest when the top players had all been restored to Test cricket, except that night cricket must remain an attraction.

He spoke of Boycott, saying that he had given him a lot of help and had even offered him the England vice-captaincy while he was in the wilderness. 'We could have won the Centenary Test with him, but it would have disturbed team morale to have brought him in.' He said he would never forget how Boycott was missing for thirty Tests, 'when we needed him'.

After waving agitatedly through the window at Asif's field-placing, he became even more intense as he expanded his insurance broking plans. It would be a big shake-up for the industry. There was a lot of money to be made in Australia. 'I love work,' he said, 'I thrive on it.'

Had I enjoyed it? asked the taxi-driver. Apart from the over-long schedule and the unnaturalness of it all late at night, yes, almost as much as the Test match, I replied. But the pleasure from neither was as great as it would have been with all the best players available. Once more I cursed the circumstances that had led to cricket's broken skull.

Talking of skulls, Ned Kelly's was stolen from the museum cell at Old Melbourne Jail the day I visited it. The loss was discovered at 4 pm, but the grisly exhibit was missing a couple of hours earlier when I was gazing at the chilling death-masks of some of Australia's nineteenth-century offenders. Perhaps the same person who appropriated my jacket felt the need to embellish it with a celebrated crown.

Such is life, as Kelly said when he stood on the gallows platform.

5. THE SECOND TEST MATCH

PERTH, DECEMBER 15, 16, 17, 19, 20

First day

Smooth flight, avoiding random thunderstorms, to Perth via Adelaide over pale brown, dry country, after a trying three-hour delay at Melbourne airport because of an industrial dispute. The weather became clearer the further the TAA T-jet flew westward. One way and another I was glad to see the back of Melbourne, after the theft and the lousy weather and the fatigue induced by the marathon VFL Park days and evenings. A few hours in the air—when we eventually got off—was revitalising, the tiredness at journey's end being the result of a long day with frustration at the start. Jet-lag, so it is said, cannot creep up after only four hours' flying!

Eating delectable kiwifruits and drinking local port, I was transported over the Lofties into Adelaide, across the blue-green Gulf St Vincent, the brown-fawn Yorke Peninsula, Spencer Gulf, the Great Australian Bight—the map of Australia steadily moving under us from east to west, pushing the clock back three hours, with the tantalising knowledge that one's loved ones were a couple of thousand miles less further away.

We stopped, of course, at the edge of the Indian Ocean, where Perth sits, flat and bright. (Car number-plates proclaim Queensland to be the Sunshine State, Victoria the Garden State, and Western Australia the State of Excitement). We came down through a fairyland mountain range of flossy white cloud. How sad it was that MCC, of necessity, used to deprive their players of aerial travel before the war. A copy of Harold Larwood's 1932–33 tour contract hangs in the Cricketers Bar of the Windsor Hotel in Melbourne. Clause 6 reads: *The said Harold Larwood shall not travel by air during the tour, nor engage in aeronautics, aviation or racing of any kind.* History records that this did not stop England's great fast bowler from indulging himself extensively in the missile business during that Bodyline series. Thoughts now turned to England's 1978 warhead, Bob Willis. Would his damaged left foot be all right for the second Test?

It was. Well enough, at any rate, with the blisters drained and a foam-robber cradle for his battered little toe. Willis was named in a group of fourteen from whom the eleven were chosen on the morning of the match, and the changes from the Brisbane Test were John Lever and Mike Hendrick in place of Chris Old, whose back was troubling him, and Phil Edmonds, who became twelfth man. Australia left out Carlson again.

The parachutists dropped from the overcast sky to within a few yards of the pitch, the captains tossed with the airborne coin, and the yellow and gold balloons went up to signify that Australia had choice of innings. Graham Yallop did what he should have done at Brisbane: invited England to bat. This time, though, the pitch looked good and there seemed little humidity in the air. It was a defensive measure, but less so than if Yallop had put England in in the first Test.

Hogg began proceedings from the Causeway end, to Boycott, and Hurst bowled to Gooch from the pavilion end. A little movement in the air and off the wicket had both batsmen tentative, and when the ball was dug in it quite naturally lifted steeply.

England's first reversal quickly came. To the first ball of Hogg's third over Gooch got a touch and Maclean took a straightforward catch. One down for three. Randall came in, all twitches, running on the spot between balls, looking ready to smash a double-century before lunch. Alas, third ball he went into a hook, a stroke he usually plays in such a positive, accomplished manner, but he mistimed and sent a lob to square leg, where Wood ran after it and managed to hold it. Two down for three, last man 0, and the two seniors together as Brearley came out sooner than he would have hoped.

A fighting session ensued. The bat was beaten often, and appeals rent the skies. Ones and twos were scrambled, but a boundary seemed as likely to turn up as a snowstorm. Boycott did his jack-knifing parry outside off stump, bowing quickly into the stroke and unbending with a 'there, I've handled that one OK' sort of finality. Brearley, back in his 1977 cranium-and-temple-guard, crouched defiantly, taking much of the bowling high on the bat.

Hogg was relieved with figures of 2 for 0 off four overs, and Hurst was brought in downwind while Dymock persevered, left-arm fast-medium, at the other end. Brearley edged him just short of Hughes at second slip, and when he drove him for two, it was the first score from the bat in 22 minutes. The crowd, which filled the ground only to about a third of its capacity, took it all in quietly.

Just before drinks, taken at 10 for 2, Hurst flung the ball towards the stumps in disgust after several appeals had been turned down. Unfortunately, the ball hit Brearley's pad, and it looked a petulant act.

After 18 overs, at the hour-and-a-half mark, England were 21 for 2, and five runs later Hogg took over from Dymock at the pavilion end. The first run off his bowling brought an ironic cheer, but after a two-over spell he rested again (6-5-1-2) and Yardley was tried for the final over before lunch, in the hope that he would do what he did in similar circumstances in the State match against the Englishmen: dismiss Boycott. With three short legs and a silly mid-off, he tossed the ball up and got some bounce, but the over was negotiated safely, and England went in at 30 for 2 off 24 overs, Boycott 17, Brearley 9. It was the sort of scoreline Australia might have expected in Brisbane if they had put England in. Instead, they themselves had been 48 for 6 at the interval.

Batting seemed easier after lunch. Brearley and Boycott picked up runs at both ends, though it was still another ten minutes, i.e. after 130 minutes of play, that the first boundary came. Brearley, having been very ill at ease with a short one from Hogg which he could only spoon back up the pitch, edged Dymock over third slip to the caramel-coloured picket fence.

England's captain was out soon afterwards. Dymock slanted one across him and he got the touch, as he tried to cut, for Maclean to bag his eighth catch in sixteen England wickets to have fallen since he won his long-awaited Test cap. This made it 41 for 3, and Yallop's gamble had paid off well thus far.

Gower, in helmet, was quickly into runs, but difficulties were soon arising. He took his eye off a short one from Hogg and was thumped in the neck. Next ball he struck to midwicket for two, and after Hogg had been warned for running onto the pitch, Gower brought up the fifty with a high edge past Yardley. The innings was 153 minutes old.

Boycott was thriving on his protracted life at the crease, even though he was falling further and further below a run per over. But this was the pattern foreseen all along: an anchor at one end, a strokeplayer at the other. Gower grew in confidence, cover-driving Hurst to the boundary beyond the grasp even of Darling, and Boycott picked up four runs—though not yet a boundary—when his quickly-run two for a leg-glance was doubled when Hogg's throw went through a couple of fielders at the bowler's end. Shortly afterwards Gower put Cosier away for two lovely fours, one pulled, one cut, and left Boycott's score of 33 behind.

There was a stir when Boycott, having hooked Hurst with good control for two, was put right off balance by another short ball, half-evading and half-hooking. The 'keeper, slips and bowler seemed certain it was a catch, but umpire Tom Brooks, back in partnership in the old firm of Bailhache and Brooks, would have none of it. Minds were taken off it by another gorgeous cover-drive by Gower, this time off Yardley. Only the slow outfield, top-dressed with sand, stopped the four.

Yallop continued to swing his bowling around. Hogg came up for his fourth spell, and bowled at a fair velocity, with the occasional sharp bouncer, and Yardley looked good, causing Boycott to mistime his quicker ball and to put a legside push into the air soon after tea (taken at 102 for 3), Yardley uttering a deep and desperate groan. As the afternoon wore on, still almost totally unlit by direct sunlight, a tinge of frustration crept into the Australian ranks. The tinge became a wide stain when Hogg whacked Boycott on the pads with an inducker. It was extremely close to lbw, but not close enough. Hogg expended further energy jumping up and down several times in his appeal.

Gower's fifty came when he stroked Yardley through cover for three, the milestone reached in just under two hours, but he was almost lost ten minutes later when he played the same bowler backward of point and took off for a run. Hughes gathered and returned the ball, and Gower, sent back by Boycott, dived to safety as Maclean obscured the umpire. The early breakthrough was archive stuff now, and it was not apparent just where the next wicket would come from.

At last Geoff Boycott, England's troubled champion, reached his fifty. He did so with an untypical stroke, a whipping glance to a floater from Yardley outside his legs. They ran three, and he raised his bat calmly as the crowd whistled, clapped, and even booed. When Dymock was reintroduced, he played him with a broad bat and redoubled concentration. Not for him the anxiety of having hit no boundary yet. Not for him that thing known only to ordinary mortals—fatigue. He had been in 278 minutes for his fifty, and was probably still well short of halfway to his aim.

Gower was perilously close to lbw to Yardley, bowling around the wicket, and when he attempted an ill-judged pull against an offside delivery from Dymock he was lucky that the ball soared well beyond slips. He had posted the century stand (152 minutes) with a handsome on-drive to the boundary off the lanky Yardley. An elegant back-cut off Dymock took him to 76, but failed to silence the beery mob at the Causeway end. It was a mild surprise to hear the 'alcohol boys' among the crowd of 7883 here in clean, wholesome, fresh Perth. But then is there a ground anywhere that has no visit from them, and would the scene be the same without them?

Perth is the sunniest of Australia's State capitals, with almost eight hours of sunshine per day on average. At last it decided to keep up its average, along with Boycott's, in a delightful evening as the new ball was taken and used well by Hogg and Hurst. Hogg nearly took a return catch from a lazy push by Gower, and, switching to around the stumps, he beat him a couple of times. At the end of the over Boycott walked down for a lengthy chat with his young partner.

The pitch, made of soil from the Margaret River area, was playing well. It was faster than any other in Australia, if not as fast as it used to be. But it played true and the bounce was to be trusted. Gower left several balls from Hogg alone in the knowledge that they would clear the bails. It made the bowler irritable, and he sometimes paused at the end of his followthrough. But he could only turn and walk back, polishing the ball in his left groin and swinging his right arm across rather than beside his body.

Gower took two twos off Hurst to reach 82, but at 5.45 pm there was doubt as to whether he could make his century before stumps, even though he was now dominating the strike, something Boycott would not have resented. Off Hogg, for some reason operating around the wicket and therefore risking another warning for running down the track, Gower got two balls just where he wanted them, and hit them both hard to the distant point boundary to go to 91. A single, then a heartily-struck off-drive for three off Hurst, Darling sprinting, took him to 95. Boycott dutifully made a single, and Gower sent a cut screaming through gully for two more. That took him to the threshhold, and a half-volley from Hurst let him in to one of cricket's greatest prizes—a century against Australia. He on-drove with such perfect timing that he was able to remove his helmet at the bowler's end, revealing his mass of lambswool, as the generous applause broke out. He had been in for

213 minutes and this was his ninth four, as sweet as any. As throughout 1978, his form may have been dubious between Test matches, but when the big occasion came he was up to it. He had enjoyed spasmodic good fortune, but only the Australian slips men seemed to have resented it. Many of the spectators would have seen him during his club cricket days in Perth, which lent a special charm to the innings.

At the other end, Boycott saw it safely through to the close in one of the most extraordinary of innings, played on the first anniversary, as it happened, of Mudassar Nazar's world record slowest Test hundred (557 minutes). He made 17 before lunch, 19 more before tea, and a runaway 27 in the final session. His only four had been all run, and he hit two threes. Most of us go to a psychiatrist or to the bar when we are troubled. 'Boycs' goes to the batting crease.

Second day

Resuming at 190 for 3, Boycott 63, Gower 101, England set about building a good total. It had rained heavily during the night but a wild wind and warm sun dealt with any surface moisture. The nocturnal downpour had trapped me at a bus-stop with 'King Wally', a full Umbalgarri aborigine and allegedly chief of his tribe. He came from Wyndham and was whitehaired with age. He was craving a drink, but my coins would cover only a beer, whereas he demanded port—a bottle, not a glass. His black, watery eyes turned to me with a hostility that suddenly gave way to crinkling good humour. He told me he could fly an aeroplane, which I doubted, and that he had a father who was even older than he, which I did not. He certainly was not the unhappiest person I met all day.

Hurst, one of cricket's moodier operators, began with a wide, but Hogg seemed bent on testing the Gower helmet again. At the centurymaker and at Boycott he shot parabolic and flat bouncers, and the runs were slow in coming, as before. Only nine runs had been added in just over half an hour when England's fourth-wicket stand was broken.

Gower played inside a ball from Hogg, now bowling round the wicket, and his off stump was hit as the ball went from left to right. The Leicestershire man held his bat at the present-arms as he walked off to warm applause, his 102 having taken four hours and eight minutes, with nine boundaries. He was very disappointed at having failed to carry on productively, but the century had increased his stature and shown yet again that he is a man for the big occasion.

With Botham in at number six, Boycott continued on his barely-perceptible way. I walked round the ground, so few were the incidents, and the mystic opener looked the same from all angles. 'They've been here about three-quarters of an hour, Basil,' said one exasperated man to his companion, 'and they've only put on thirteen flamin' runs!'

The wind was still blowing the top half-inch of beer out of the plastic beakers as England reached 200 with a two by Boycott to midwicket off Dymock, the rate virtually a run every two minutes, and the first boundary of the day was still a long time coming. The session was 72 minutes old before Botham crashed Dymock to the midwicket boundary flags. Another pull brought him three more runs, but any prospect of things igniting faded with Botham's dismissal. Hurst brought one back at him and he was lbw for 11.

The longest hundred in England-Australia Tests was Woolmer's at The Oval in 396 minutes. Boycott was already well past this time, and there was the matter of whether anyone had ever made a Test century without a boundary hit. But all this speculation drifted off in the breeze as the House of Boycott fell. The lively Hurst, in his 18th over, cut another ball back, and umpire Brooks's finger gave the signal the Australians and the spectators were desperate to see. Boycott, who had ground out his 77 in seven-and-a-half hours, his only four having been all run, had given a quaint answer to his critics. Self-denial for this Yorkshireman has never been a painful process, and if it was this time taken to new extremes, it had made certain of England's survival beyond the tricky first hour or two into a situation of some comfort. If he was tired, it showed only in his refusal to acknowledge the applause that saw him in.

Australia had now taken three wickets for 34 runs in the hour and a half of the morning, and a fast inside-edge by Taylor off Hurst almost made it four as Maclean's left glove came close to gathering it. Yardley was called up as lunch approached, breaking the long sequence of pace, and with the wind threatening to lift the flapping galvanised-iron roof off the old stand which houses the open Press enclosure, the adjournment came at 242 for 6, Miller and Taylor both eight.

Three byes came from Yardley's first ball at 1.40 pm, and soon a full-toss gave Miller the chance to wade in with a meaty drive for four. Hogg, at the pavilion end, continued to show fine stamina, and indirectly got Taylor out. The wicketkeeper edged a very fast delivery to Maclean's right, but the Queenslander could not hold it. It would have dropped short of Cosier at slip. Then, at the other end, Taylor surprised by swiping at Yardley, and Hurst took an easy catch at midwicket. That was 253 for 7.

Lever made his intentions plain, swishing at Yardley, but Geoff Miller seemed to grow a size larger hereabouts, after surviving a frantic, prolonged shout for caught-behind off a hook off Hogg. The bowler had to be soothed by vice-captain Cosier, who walked across like a helmeted knight. Miller actually took two boundaries from the remainder of the over, a pirouette hook and a masterly back-cut.

Three byes displeased the WACA crowd, many of whom feel they have Australia's next 'keeper in their midst in Kevin Wright, but a slow yorker from Hurst which Miller only just defied tickled their fancy. The valuable eighth-wicket stand prospered.

When it had reached 42, Lever went, caught easily by Cosier at first slip as he fished at Hurst, and five runs later, at 300, Miller, having batted quite soundly for almost two-and-a-half hours for his 40, had his defence broken by Hogg. There followed twenty-two minutes of frustration and gentle farce as Willis and Hendrick pushed and swished, Willis giving the impression, by the way in which he stretched preposterously far forward one-handed, that his right hand was insured for ten thousand.

Hogg finished it, beyond the usual time for the tea interval, having Willis caught off a spooned drive which everyone left for the captain to catch. It gave Rodney Hogg half of England's wickets in an innings for the second time in two Test matches (6 for 74 at Brisbane), just reward for a wholehearted assault.

England's 309 had taken seven minutes over ten hours, 117.5 overs, and was a perfect, attritional answer to being sent in from a side in possession of The Ashes. Australia would now have to bat with assurance and some speed, though there was no expectation that the pitch would break up. In other words, England held the trumps, Australia had the headache.

Brearley sprang something of a surprise at the start of the Australian innings. Lever was given the new ball from the pavilion end, with the breeze aiding his inswinger (awayswinger to Wood), and Botham bowled opposite. Wood took three through point off Botham, but Darling, in white helmet, swayed inside a bouncer, adhering to the advice of pre-war fast bowler Tim Wall ('Don't think of hooking until you are 100. Then forget about it.'). Then he forgot the advice and swung another very fine for two. The first setback came from the second ball of Lever's second over.

The ball had been moving sharply away from Wood, but Lever now made one cut back at him, and he was hit on the pads moments before Lever disappeared into an excited throng of team-mates. He had struck an important blow, and Australia had missed the good start Yallop had demanded.

Hughes, one of the heroes of Brisbane, came in and soon saw a grotesque bouncer from Botham to Darling called 'wide'. After three overs each, Lever and Botham made way for Willis and Hendrick, Willis, having gratefully accepted an extra day and a half of rest, now wearing a special sponge-rubber pad in his left boot to spare his pummelled little toe. He was soon testing the batsmen with bouncers, and a short ball outside off got the full treatment from Hughes, a crisp square-cut that the crowd loved. At 34, however, Australia's second loss occurred. Willis pitched a top-speed delivery well up to Hughes, who played for the customary off-cut. The ball went straight on and broke the stump at the base. For a time it seemed that Western Australia's top mining experts would be needed to extricate the snapped-off point.

Four runs later Australia experienced another shockwave when another ball of some speed burst through Yallop, sending Willis on a euphoric dance out to square leg. The Australian captain had made only three, and at 38 for 3 the side was on the skids. Peter Toohey came in, the man with the greatest potential but in the most horrible form. He heartened himself with a solid straight-drive off Willis for three, but Hendrick bowled to him wastefully outside off, and he repeatedly pulled his bat inside his front pad in his characteristic way. When a Willis bouncer whistled overhead he resembled Doug Walters as he ducked, leaving his bat aloft like a periscope. The last quarter-hour must have stretched out like an eternity.

Rick Darling, from the Murray River town of Waikerie, the third by that surname to play against England, did not survive it. In the most tragic manner he was run out off the penultimate ball of the day. He had started to look at home, driving Willis handsomely for three and Botham for four. But Miller came on for the last over and Toohey, facing the seventh ball, turned it through the leg-trap. Darling began the run, turned too late as Botham darted after the ball and threw it close to the bowler's stumps. Miller broke the wicket with Darling lying full-stretch, desolate, dusty, and out. Australia, watched by a lamenting crowd of 8791, had descended into darkness again, and at 60 for 4 a stupendous recovery was needed.

Third day

I thought my own misfortunes were being added to when fire engines descended upon Hay Street last evening. The fire caused thousands of dollarsworth of damage, but it was in the adjacent block. My hotel was spared. Australia's innings, though, was soon burning once more. Toohey took a neat four from a leg-glance off Willis, and Cosier, bareheaded, hooked the same bowler for two; but he looked flatfooted against Miller's flighted stuff. As the likelihood of his dismissal at that end was being considered, he fell at the other. Willis bowled a ball of fullish length and Cosier went for the drive. The thick edge flew fast to Gooch at fourth slip, and the catch was accepted with comfort and joy. Australia 78 for 5.

One run later Maclean went, sweeping at Miller and gloving the ball in a dolly-catch to Gooch, who thus took his second catch within three minutes. Australia now 79 for 6, and the follow-on figure of 109 being discussed. Yardley started with a single to mid-on and a three off Willis from a square-drive, all exuberance and elbows. For Willis, Miller stood at short leg for Toohey and third man for Yardley, who wore a white helmet and, at number eight, might conceivably be spared any bouncers. The grimness of the situation was relieved when Randall tossed the ball high over Miller's head, drawing some catcalls from the outer to which he responded by flexing his bicep—the old joke, fresh laughter.

John Lever replaced Willis after the drinks pause, Willis having built his figures up to 13-2-32-3, and the first ball was a big inswinger. Soon Yardley was clubbing ferociously wide of Randall at cover, but the fielder brought the house down with a reflex full-length dive to bring off a left-handed save.

At 99, Hendrick came on from the pavilion end, and Toohey ran the first ball away to bring the hundred up. But next ball Yardley got a faint touch and was caught behind. It was at this point that I could not rid my mind of thoughts of Greg and Ian Chappell,

Lillee, Thomson, and company, the men who had played themselves out of Test consideration, taking with them the heart and relentless soul of the side. Here in Perth, four years ago, Australia had put England in and won by nine wickets, Walters and Ross Edwards making centuries, Greg Chappell making 62 and taking seven catches. Forecasts were now turning to reality. Australia, under Graham Yallop, were not up to it, but there were men on the other side of the continent who could have made a contest of it. I felt like asking my friend King Wally to put a spell on all who act in such a way as to prevent a settlement of this calamitous split.

And yet ... and yet. There was a more immediate problem threatening: the airline dispute was now into an ugly phase. Aircraft might be grounded until after the Melbourne Test, and there was much discussion in the Press-box as to means of crossing from Perth—hitch-hiking, coastal tramp, Qantas via Singapore, bicycle!

As always, cricket sheltered against fear. Hendrick rhythmically rolled in, Hogg dabbed to gully, the movement was repeated twice, and then Hogg found the gap for four. Botham took Miller's place (1 for 17 off 73 balls today) and beat Hogg repeatedly before switching to around the stumps. A Hogg slog off Hendrick brought three runs to wipe out the follow-on possibility, a much more stylish off-drive brought him four more just before lunch, which was taken at 121 for 7, with the neat little Toohey 35 and Hogg 13.

It took 23 minutes after the interval for the first new run to be made. Willis and Miller kept at their task, and Toohey made no noticeable effort to collar either of them. Hogg again showed his worth, preferring the off side, until Willis got one through him which Taylor caught. Umpire Brooks gave the catch, but Hogg was indignant, pointing to his thigh.

A while afterwards Toohey gave the crowd something to remember with a flashing cut off Willis that scorched to the fence at an angle of forty-five degrees, and after another quiet period, with Dymock holding an end, Toohey reached his first half-century off English bowling, just after half-past-two. Miller was bowling to him with a scattered field, but he steered backward of point and ran two. He had been in for 205 minutes and had hit two fours.

The rest was understandably tedious. Dymock gave us a thrilling moment when he chopped down on a slower ball from Botham and shouldered away the high rebound. If he had used his hand we should have had a rarity on *our* hands. His cover-driving, too, was of an unexpectedly high order.

When Lever, who had bowled only five overs in the innings so far, came on for the 63rd over, Toohey twice straight-drove him with clean timing, for three and four, wakening many a nodder-off, and when Botham dropped one short the Toohey hook created the biggest cheer of the match, exceeded only next ball, which he hit even harder to the same place. Yet again Botham dug one in, and Toohey pulled straighter, for two, to reach 74 and the depths of his doubting public's hearts. The last ball of the over was yet another bouncer—or long-hop, depending on one's reflexes—and Toohey banged that away to the rope as well, bringing up the fifty stand and taking his toll off the over to fifteen. The total had now rocketed to 180, the deficit down to 129. Then, at 185, the stand of 57 was terminated as Hendrick with the new ball bowled Dymock, and after Hurst had evoked amused admiration with a square-driven four, and then had his off stump touched without disturbance to a bail, he became Taylor's third victim and Willis's fifth. With 190 to England's 309, and with fourteen hours to play, Australia were in a hole. To escape, they would need all the ingenuity shown by the Anzacs at Gallipoli, when they set up self-firing rifles operated by water dripping into tin-cans.

England began their second innings after tea, Boycott and Gooch facing Hogg and Dymock, and the pitch near-perfect. For Gooch, transformed into a 'modern' now that the crash-helmet concealed his 1920s hairstyle and moustache, Hogg had a man in very close either side, but there was no real discomfort for either batsman, until Boycott took a lifter from Hogg on the side of the head and acquired four leg-byes. Soon afterwards there was a near-hysterical shout for caught-behind against Boycott off Dymock, and the Australian fieldsmen were horrified at the rejection by Tom Brooks—whom many of the agitated lager-drinkers called names, including 'Tom the Pom'.

A male streaker ran on and hurdled the stumps (he was fined $100, the magistrate telling him the sun had probably fried his brain) and a scrap broke out at the Causeway end, but the England openers focussed on their job, and after 66 minutes Gooch hooked Hurst for the first four of the innings, and his first of the series—this in his fourth innings. He knew he needed seventy or a hundred here and now to hold his place.

Riskless, tough Test match batting carried England nearer and nearer to invincibility as the swarms of seagulls spread out all over the outfield. The Australians tried. How they tried. But Boycott got his head over the ball as if England were in trouble, and Gooch relished the overdue longish innings. As the crowd, which had numbered 9802 at its peak, began to drift away, Hogg, looking very lethargic, had a bowl, but shortly afterwards left the field, and Yardley took the Causeway end, getting some bounce and turn. He also got a huge surprise when, with ten minutes of the day's play left, he was hoisted for four through long-on by Gooch, who cracked two more twos in the over. He survived the rush of blood, and England went to the rest day 58 without loss, an overall lead of 177. The need from King Wally now was a productive rain dance.

Fourth day

Mike Brearley, at a Press conference on the rest day, said he was looking for a lead of 400 towards the end of the fourth day, but he felt slight regret at having only one spin bowler at his disposal. I asked him what had been the topic of conversation when he and the umpires were in mid-pitch conference on the previous day, and he explained that the last three tailenders on each side were, by agreement of the captains, to be spared bouncers. But when Geoff Dymock had been in for an hour, the England skipper asked if perhaps he might now be allowed to receive the occasional short one. This the umpires were prepared to allow, though permission was withdrawn when the new ball was taken.

Brearley had something to say on the slow outfield, not the first dead surface on this tour. He thought it 'a great pity' that groundsmen felt the need to make them green and pretty, for some really good shots which normally would have reached the boundary did not do so. The thick grass also helped retain the shine on the ball, which was against the interests of spin bowlers. 'It's amazing the difference it makes to the game all round,' he said.

The Tuesday pre-lunch session went well for England. It probably helped the cause when Boycott went, lbw to Hogg after eight minutes without addition to the overnight score. It was the fifth time in six encounters that the South Australia fast man had got him, and in a total time at the crease in this match of nine hours 36 minutes Boycott had failed to hit a boundary.

Randall avoided a 'pair' with a quickly-scuttled single and was soon opening his angular shoulders with a square-drive to the flags off Hogg. Gooch seemed more himself too, cutting Dymock fine for four and then repeating the shot off Hogg. When a difficult ball found the edge it dropped just short of Hughes at second slip, but there was not the faintest indecision about a hook through square leg off Hogg. Meanwhile, Randall was bolting off at every opportunity, and once only narrowly avoided being run out at the bowler's end. When Gooch was hit on the pad, apparently right in front of middle and off, Hogg did a prolonged jig as he implored the umpire to raise his finger, prompting Randall to mock him. The bowler had the answer next ball, however, hitting Gooch's pads so hard that the ball rolled back the full length of the pitch. He was out for 43, and the Australians were jubilant.

Better things followed. Brearley got a beauty from Hogg first ball and nicked to Maclean. It was 93 for 3 as he received a consoling pat from Randall as he walked sadly away.

The hundred came up in the 35th over, and Randall continued to go for his shots—and some that might have been borrowed from a village rustic. Twice he smeared the ball along the ground from outside off to long-on, and an attempted hook off Dymock sent the ball soaring over wicketkeeper Maclean's head for four. With Gower finding gaps in the field, England's two star attractions were shaping to carry out team requirements to perfection at the same time as they gave the crowd a good time.

The introduction of spin broke the stand of 42. Randall (45) tried to sweep Yardley from off the line of the stumps, and appeared to get the ball on the lower forearm. It spooned to Cosier behind the 'keeper and Randall skipped pavilionwards, seeming to stop on his way as if in reconsideration. But he was out, even if he had given himself out, and England were 135 for 4, 254 ahead.

By lunch, with Botham lashing out, and the attendance building up to 4698, England had 150 up, but six minutes after the interval Gower was severely bothered by a lifting ball from Hogg, turning his head away and taking it on the bat-handle, from where it flew towards square leg. The next ball was fractionally outside off and he stepped away to cut. He edged to Maclean instead, and a vital wicket had gone. The first-innings centurymaker had made only a dozen this time.

Botham, three inches taller in his beacon-like helmet, laid into Hogg, clipping him for four wide of the slips and bashing him back over his head. Soon after Hogg had crashed to the ground in his followthrough, Botham hit him for four again, this time a succulent pull. Then, in attempting to put Yardley over the top, he gave a high catch to Wood at deep mid-off, and England were 176 for 6, with Lever joining Miller. These two kept the runs coming, Miller once swivelling neatly to hook Hogg for four, and the 200 came up in five-and-a-quarter hours in the 57th over.

Lever then went, thick-edging Hurst to Maclean, and Taylor entered with Randall as his runner. The Nottingham joker may have been the fastest runner in the side, but I'm not sure he would be my choice, for he usually has enough problems negotiating his own comings and goings between wickets, without taking on those of two partners. Taylor was clearly inconvenienced by his right groin strain, but he dropped anchor, and with 'One-armed Willis' stretching out at the other end, England regained some of her poise with tea approaching (and some dark clouds in the west) and the lead past 320. Immediately the new ball became due Yallop took it, bringing Hogg on from the Causeway end after Yardley's long spell there. A quick dispatch of the last two wickets was essential.

The first, Taylor, soon went. He edged Hogg low to Maclean's right and a very capable catch was completed. It was only when Taylor reached the benches in front of the pavilion that it was realised that his runner, Randall, was still in the middle. He needed coaxing from the field.

Hogg, with ten wickets under his belt in the match now, bowled perhaps the fastest ball of the match to Willis, hitting him painfully on the thigh, but it was Dymock who finished it off, bowling Hendrick when England had made 208 in six hours, taking the overall lead to 327. Australia had five minutes under eight hours to make the runs, and had to be given some chance, even though the run rate throughout had been little more than a run every two minutes. The requirement called for one-and-a-half runs every two minutes.

After half an hour of the Australian innings, it was all academic. 'Cacka' Darling had hooked Willis for four and been hit agonisingly in the box, by a no-ball, necessitating a long delay, before Lever made one lift at him. He leapt up, took his right hand off the bat and threw back his head in a horrible contortion, a spasm of revulsion. Boycott took a child's catch at midwicket. Minutes later the light began to go, and the umpires offered it to Wood and Hughes, who quickly accepted. Then, at 4.45 pm the rain came—

and kept on coming. Torrent after torrent, pounding the iron roofs, collecting in pools on the square, turning the spread tarpaulin into a shallow swimming-pool. The tall white figures of cricketers were replaced by the strutting masses of seagulls. At 5.10 pm the umpires, in raincoats, made their formal way to the middle, looked briefly about them, and called it off for the day. It was the first time rain had interrupted a Perth Test match.

With a requirement of 317 in six hours, Australia could be written off, whereas, so long as the weather righted itself well before morning, England had every chance of going two-up. That would be a nice present for Christmas for all the folks at home. For, unrealistic as it seemed, the festive season was upon us. The calendar, the carols in the shops and the decorations in the hotel said so.

Fifth day

December 20 dawned hot and blue, the rain long gone, the field dry. Fishing or surfing would have been ideal activities. At the WACA ground there was just time to wish Bill O'Reilly a happy birthday—I couldn't do so to my son, who had to celebrate his twentieth alone at the other end of the continent, probably hoping for a long-odds Australian victory to top off the day—before the action started. There was no instant England breakthrough, and Hughes's scrumptious four cut square off Willis gave local supporters some heart. But Lever soon had the ball jumping off the same spot that spelt Rick Darling's downfall. Hughes managed to parry it. The spoilsport outfield turned several would-be boundary shots into threes.

Graeme Wood is a neat, stylish, well-balanced batsman, whose chief weakness often seems to be his judging of a run and his calling. 'Yeah, no, no!' he barked at his State team-mate Hughes, and the nuggety man had to flee for safety. If the runs were to be made, these two looked the best pair to make them.

But Hughes was not going to do a 'Brisbane'. On 12, he tried to cut Willis and Gooch took the slip catch with a slap of the palms. Two down for 36, and almost three as Yallop parried his first ball from Willis, which could have gone anywhere.

Botham came on at the pavilion end and had his loosener hooked to the boundary by Wood, and another boundary came by irregular means when Willis bumped one over the heads of everybody and four wides were called. The asking rate was rising by the over, yet Australia's batsmen had to bat as naturally as possible, for excessive caution could lead to trouble. As it was, the spot at the Causeway end was a hazard—in the mind and occasionally in reality.

Almost an hour had elapsed before the fifty was raised, Wood pulling a Botham no-ball for four, but at 28 the young left-hander had a sizable chunk of luck. He failed to hit a short one from Botham with the meat of the bat, and the ball steepled to Boycott's territory at squarish midwicket. He waited and waited, edging ever closer to the descent path. The ball thumped to earth.

At 57 for 2 Hendrick came on in place of Willis, and beat Wood with his first ball. The Derbyshire man looked loose and powerful, the rhythm right, and in his second over he had Australia on the run. The third ball almost eluded Yallop's bat—but not quite—and was taken by Taylor down the leg side. Fifty-eight for 3. Then a shock to dumbfound Australia: Toohey's first-ball assassination. Hendrick found the outside edge, and Taylor did it again. The little man, hero of the first innings, was back in the horrors. And back in the pavilion.

Cosier staved off the hat-trick, and was soon making his first runs, a two through mid-on that had Miller casting aside his helmet as he gave chase. Soon Hendrick had a split-second chance to make his figures 3 for 2 as Cosier punched back a sharp catch to his left hand, but it failed to stick, and Australia breathed again. Cosier was to give them frequent cause to tighten in their seats.

The next scare came from Wood. He played an ungainly stroke off Botham that sent the ball high towards midwicket, where Lever left it for Boycott. Again, the ball rushed through his grasping hands, this time with the ironic postscript that another chance came his way almost immediately, which he held. But it was a no-ball.

A strong pull for four by Cosier in the final over before lunch took Australia to 80 for 4, still needing 248. Expectations were low, but the fight for survival could yet take people's mind off the heat ... and the continuing airline crisis. Were we or were we not to be on our way to Adelaide and Melbourne by air, or perhaps by train across the seemingly endless Nullarbor. Down the afternoon the Australian batsmen had to negotiate a Nullarbor of their own.

Wood, wearing cap rather than helmet and with his sleeves buttoned at the wrist, ran to his fifty in 170 minutes, soon after being hit in the belly by Botham, whom he immediately repaid with a pull to the boundary. Cosier continued to live dangerously, pushing one just past Lever at silly point, then, after the hundred was up, edging Botham to the fence between third and fourth slips. There were gasps as he capped it all with a daring upper-cut—the only word for it—which landed fifty or sixty yards from the bat in the empty mid-on area and brought him two runs to raise the fifty stand after 73 minutes.

At half-past-two, Miller came on for the first time, and bowled a maiden which incorporated an urgent appeal for catch or stumping by Taylor. At the other end, backed by the impressive police headquarters complex, Willis pounded in, showing great stamina, and let Cosier have a bouncer. The batsman responded with an upward chop that sent the ball soaring over slips and into the third-man guttering. At drinks he was 36, Wood 58, Australia 125 for 4, having added 45 runs in the hour.

Refreshed, Cosier played a much more convincing shot, a firm drive along the ground, beating three fieldsmen on its way until the fourth arrested it in the outfield as they ran three. When Miller bowled, things looked even better—Wood whisking a half-volley away for three and Cosier striking a most attractive four through mid-off. But then England came back. Miller floated one temptingly up to Cosier, three short of his half-century, and he went into a hearty sweep and was adjudged lbw. He took a long time to get up from his kneeling position, and slapped his pads viciously all the way off. This made it 141 for 5, and it was a matter of whether Wood could carry it through almost alone.

Lever came on at the Causeway end and put paid to any chance of that. His second ball went through to Taylor as Wood played tentatively at it, and the appeal, less than usually loud, was answered, after a dramatic delay, in the affirmative by Tom Brooks, who, during the lunch break, had announced his impending retirement from umpiring after 24 Test matches. This dismissal of Wood was one of his least popular decisions. The batsman was frozen for some while with disbelief, but there was to be no reconsideration. He had batted for just on four hours for his 64 and had found the boundary three times, asserting at last his right to open for Australia and showing that he could discipline himself in the best traditions.

Without addition, Maclean was caught at slip by Brearley off Miller's non-turner, and Australia were 143 for 7. Four runs later

Hogg was bowled by the off-spinner. And with 151 on the board Yardley went to the catch of the match, Botham plucking the ball out of the air as it sped past him low and to the left. 'Prone slips the youth, yet glories in his fall; with arm extended shows the captive ball.' James Love had seen it all in his verse of 1744.

The fall of the ninth wicket meant the postponement of the tea break, but not for long. Dymock swept Miller for four, and at 3.44 pm England won as Hurst was bowled by Lever, who in 24 balls had taken 3 for 11. Miller's three wickets had been taken without cost in 23 balls, giving him his best Test figures of 3 for 21. It was England's first Test victory at Perth, though admittedly they had played only two Tests there previously, and it was the first time since the 1936–37 series that they had won both the first two Tests of a series against Australia. 'Gubby' Allen's side then lost the next three, but it was next to impossible to perceive of such a thing happening this time. The last six wickets had been swept aside for 20 runs as if England could control the match at will whenever there was a need, and if proof of dominance were needed, Australia's four totals in the series now read 116, 339, 190 and 161. None of these innings was played on a pitch of less than good quality, and in none of them had the score been higher than 58 when the third wicket fell. There was growing depression among Australian supporters.

One player at least gave them hope and pride, and this was Rodney Hogg, the outstanding discovery of the season. His 10 for 122 in this Test gave him series figures of 17 wickets at 13.59 apiece, tremendous bowling, especially when it was considered that fourteen of his victims came from the upper ranks and that he had not had the best of luck throughout. Four of the adjudicators for the Benson & Hedges Man of the Match award (Brian Bearshaw, Ken Casellas, Frank Tyson and John Yarwood) voted for Hogg, who was accorded a grand ovation when he shuffled forward to receive his cheque and medallion and to mutter a few indecipherable words. The fifth judge, myself, gave his vote to David Gower, and the more I pondered it the more I felt he should have had it, for in a match almost bankrupt of batting flair Gower's century illuminated the first day at least. He may have needed the cloud cover of Boycott's innings to aid his assault, but he did all that could have been asked of him and brought to the match some Test-class strokeplay and spirit.

For the rest: Boycott won few friends but had the personal

satisfaction that derives from almost ten hours at the crease; Gooch and Randall both rehabilitated themselves in the second innings; Brearley had the customary contradiction of a further Test victory alongside batting failure; Botham at last came away from a Test with no wickets and few runs; Miller began to look like a Test all-rounder; Taylor weathered his strained groin and maintained his high standards; Lever grabbed his opportunity when it finally presented itself; Willis continued as the chief wrecker; and Hendrick did all that was asked of him.

For Australia, Wood showed himself to be an opening batsman in the best Test tradition—except when he allowed himself an outburst to the Press afterwards concerning his controversial dismissal (he later wrote an apology through the WACA); Darling, Hughes and Yallop gave little when it was needed, and Toohey, though registering some runs at last in the first innings, was a crucial failure in the second; Cosier, when it seemed he had scrambled enough second-innings runs to hold his place, was dropped for the third Test, the vice-captaincy being filled by Maclean; Yardley bowled reasonably well without looking a match-winner; Maclean looked cumbersome but pouched six catches; Hogg was admirable, Dymock almost adequate, and Hurst aggressive still without realising his potential (he took a hat-trick in the Gillette Cup semi-final against Western Australia which followed the Test match).

Messrs Harvey, Loxton and Ridings dropped Carlson as well as Cosier from the twelve, bringing in NSW left-hand all-rounder Allan Border after his two recent Sheffield Shield centuries, and restoring Jim Higgs to the side on his home ground. There was no panic, nor was there room for it, for it was not as if there were vast ranks of ready replacements for the men who had failed so far. The commitment to them had been made, and the lucky ones who were about to play for Australia for the third consecutive time this series came closer to the bonus of $6000 for next season, one of the stipulations in the new Board contracts which would enable the Board to have a firmer hold over its players. (A player will lose the bonus if—apart from injury—he is omitted from three or more consecutive Tests of the eight this season).

The captains were both in mellow mood after the match in Perth. Graham Yallop, said by several who were close to the camp to be less than universally popular with his team, refused to be drawn when Tom Prior of the Melbourne *Sun* teased him with the remark that there had been eleven dubious umpiring decisions in the match. Any comments? No!

Yallop confessed only to being disappointed—not disheartened. He felt he had the players to make a comeback in the remaining Tests, but reiterated that it was the poor starts to the innings that made the job so hard. One recognisable gain was former milkman Rodney Hogg, the 'find of the series'. He asked, rhetorically, 'Had any of you heard of him last year?'

Questioned on his decision to put England in to bat, he said he had no regrets, and when Mike Brearley was asked if he would have done the same thing, he said he would. He was in accord with Yallop too in not entering into discussion on the standard of umpiring. In fact he gave the questioner a gentle ticking-off for raising it.

He thought England had rendered a great effort in bowling Australia out twice in bright sunshine on a good pitch, though there was a time, when catches were going to grass, when he felt England might not win. He regarded the Perth pitch as a 'good cricket wicket, with a bit of bounce and taking a bit of spin'.

The final day's attendance came through: a modest 4493, taking the match total to 35,667, less than half that of the 1974–75 Perth attendance of 75,196, and a day or so later a set of figures on television-viewing in the previous weeks came through from the Roy Morgan research organisation. It claimed that 22 per cent of Melbourne sets were tuned to World Series matches and only 10 per cent to the first Test match at Brisbane. These compared with 40 per cent tuned to the Melbourne Cup on November 7.

There was still some way to go before conclusions of any real value could be reached, but the need by Test cricket for a closely-fought Australia-England series had been starved during the five sunny days in Perth, and Christmas this year was going to be a time for reflection as well as worship and celebration.

I saw the English cricketers off from their Perth hotel, as sartorially smart a bunch of travelling sportsmen as one could wish to see, and then I enjoyed my last stomach-swelling smorgasbord meal at the Miss Maud hotel before packing for the midnight flight to Melbourne, missing the three-day match against South Australia. The tailend of the industrial troubles meant a ninety-minute delay at departure, and a 4 am (7 am local time) touchdown in

Melbourne, where the fierce dawn light tortured the eyes.

The England XI finished the Adelaide match nine wickets down with the scores level, Miller and Boycott (in at number eleven) managing a draw when any of the four results might have materialised. The match, which featured three declarations, was, especially in its latter stages, played in free-and-easy fashion, Gower taking a pink parasol with him as he performed twelfth-man duties and Miller and Emburey trotting from the field with physio Bernard Thomas a laughing passenger on the stretcher when it was not needed by Brearley, who had been hit in the midriff. Randall at one stage was wearing two sweaters in the heat—because his wife had told him it was snowing in Nottingham. When batting he not only danced and whistled but muttered 'Come on, Slumberland, let's have you!' when Peter Sleep was on his way in to bowl. He made another pair of forties; it was becoming a habit. He was also, it seemed, the latest Englishmen to sign for an Australian club, Wanneroo in Perth being the lucky team.

When Boycott hit a four in this South Australia match it was the first time he had reached the boundary in an unbelievable 857 minutes at the crease. Even allowing for slow outfields and a negative approach at least equal to that of Scotton or Hanif or Bailey or Mackay, this was a staggering 'achievement'. For over fourteen hours the Yorkshireman had not even edged hard enough to find the boundary. It was trancelike, paralytic to a tragic degree at this time in cricket history, when the established game needed to be at its shiny best.

Emburey again did all that was asked of him, taking 5 for 67 in the second innings, but Edmonds failed to take a wicket in the match, conceding over 100 runs. Gooch (20 and 64) had the distinction of being stumped in both innings, the Tolchard returned yet another lively knock, 72 in an hour. Radley, the forgotten man, scored 60, and Miller, growing every match, finished 68 not out at the climax.

A nice little throwback was the appearance of David Johnston as a new-ball bowler. His father was the famous Bill Johnston, third member of the great 1948 Australian fast attack headed by Lindwall and Miller. The new generation secured 3 for 44 in the second innings.

Christmas Eve saw itself out with flashing lightning, heavy thunder and torrential rain that made the arrival in Melbourne of the English party a somewhat tricky operation. Candles by Candlelight in the city was not the smooth and joyous event it was intended to be either.

On Christmas morning we were invited to drinks with the team, and handshakes and good wishes all round helped absorb the sadness at the many separations, the split families. Then fellowship and warmth turned to hilarity as the cricketers donned their fancy dress costumes, each having to find something corresponding to a letter of the alphabet. Bob Taylor looked utterly magnificent as the Earl of Derby, Derek Randall, coping with the letter Q, passable as the Queen. Ken Barrington was presumed to be General Amin. Graham Gooch was an impressive Zorro. Ian Botham became a rampaging gorilla. Geoff Boycott wore a towel. David Gower took an easy way out by becoming a cowboy. Bob Willis was topical as an umpire, complete with white stick. Clive Radley was a Red Indian squaw. Most of the others in this very private party were not so easily identifiable, but all had fun, and the rest of us were left to our own nectar and ambrosia.

Boxing Day was to have brought us to the first Benson & Hedges Gold Cup one-day international, but heavy rains had rendered the ground unplayable, and a late start was ruled out for fear of the Test pitch being damaged. The match was rescheduled for some time in the New Year.

So Christmas in Melbourne was extended for us workers, and in keeping with the rest of the so-called civilised world we lolled about and drank our squash and discussed cricket and other things. A few strokes in the pool passed as exercise, and the occasional glimpse of people like Arthur Ashe and Sue Barker and Ken Rosewall, here for the Australian Tennis Championships, served as a reminder that there was an outside world. Tomorrow the mails would start to flow again, and perhaps the loneliness would abate.

The three days leading up to the Melbourne Test were warm but there was rain most nights, and outdoor practice was restricted. Nevertheless, Mike Brearley was tempted to try out the MCG turf, and the young Leicestershire fast bowler Jonathan Agnew, playing the season for Essendon, started to whirl a few down off a short run. His second ball lifted horribly and cracked the England captain below the brim of his protective cap, gashing his right eyebrow. Six stitches had to be inserted. Concern for his Test availability was shortlived, but he was angry with himself for exposing himself to the risk, and for the anguish caused to Agnew, whose shock was noticeable. Australian captain Graham Yallop, who was about to leave the ground in his high-powered car (number plate GY 100), was one of those who went to Brearley's assistance.

Meanwhile the England twelve was announced, Emburey coming in for Edmonds, and it was made known that Brearley would open with Boycott, Gooch moving down the order, where he would feel more at home. It seemed that either Lever or Emburey would be twelfth man, and that the pitch would be anything but totally dry, even if there was no further rain.

The media worked at drumming up interest, though no-one seemed to have much conviction in any belief that Australia could come back strongly into the series. World Series matches continued to be televised day and night, but their audience was not swelling. Neither did public interest seem to be mounting. If it had gone as far as it was going to go, it was still insufficient to ensure profitable continuity. It would be some months before the 1978–79 attendances, receipts, profits and losses would be assessed—for both circuits—and it was to be hoped that this time the figures would be dependable and illuminating.

The year of the earthquake, 1977, had been followed by twelve more turbulent months. A few days hence we should be into 1979. Everyone—or almost everyone—had had enough of the conflict. The New Year had to herald a solution. If, in addition, the South African problem could be resolved, cricket would emerge as just about the greatest game on earth.

But it was a lot to hope for, and almost certainly too much.

SECOND TEST MATCH

Perth, December 15, 16, 17, 19, 20

ENGLAND

			Mins	Fours			Mins	Fours
G. Boycott	lbw b Hurst	**77**	449	1*	lbw b Hogg	**23**	127	0
G.A. Gooch	c Maclean b Hogg	**1**	21	0	lbw b Hogg	**43**	172	5
D.W. Randall	c Wood b Hogg	**0**	3	0	c Cosier b Yardley	**45**	91	3
*J.M. Brearley	c Maclean b Dymock	**17**	115	1	c Maclean b Hogg	**0**	1	0
D.I. Gower	b Hogg	**102**	248	9	c Maclean b Hogg	**12**	69	0
I.T. Botham	lbw b Hurst	**11**	45	1	c Wood b Yardley	**30**	53	4
G. Miller	b Hogg	**40**	144	4	c Toohey b Yardley	**25**	80	3
†R.W. Taylor	c Hurst b Yardley	**12**	51	1	(9)c Maclean b Hogg	**2**	36	0
J.K. Lever	c Cosier b Hurst	**14**	61	0	(8)c Maclean b Hurst	**10**	47	0
R.G.D. Willis	c Yallop b Hogg	**2**	42	0	not out	**3**	38	0
M. Hendrick	not out	**7**	22	1	b Dymock	**1**	5	0
Extras (6 b, 9 lb, 3 w, 8 nb)		**26**			(6 lb, 8 nb)	**14**		
		309		*all run		**208**		

Fall: 3, 3, 41, 199, 219, 224, 253, 295, 300. 58, 93, 93, 135, 151, 176, 201, 201, 206.

Bowling: Hogg 30.5-9-65-5, Dymock 34-4-72-1, Hurst 26-7-70-3, Yardley 23-1-62-1, Cosier 4-2-14-0.

Second innings: Hogg 17-2-57-5, Dymock 16.3-2-53-1, Hurst 17-5-43-1, Yardley 16-1-41-3.

AUSTRALIA

			Mins	Fours			Mins	Fours
G.M. Wood	lbw b Lever	**5**	11	0	(2)c Taylor b Lever	**64**	237	3
W.M. Darling	run out	**25**	111	1	(1)c Boycott b Lever	**5**	13	1
K.J. Hughes	b Willis	**16**	43	1	c Gooch b Willis	**12**	54	1
*G.N. Yallop	b Willis	**3**	21	0	c Taylor b Hendrick	**3**	43	0
P.M. Toohey	not out	**81**	268	6	c Taylor b Hendrick	**0**	1	0
G.J. Cosier	c Gooch b Willis	**4**	32	0	lbw b Miller	**47**	110	4
†J.A. Maclean	c Gooch b Miller	**0**	3	0	c Brearley b Miller	**1**	19	0
B. Yardley	c Taylor b Hendrick	**12**	45	0	c Botham b Lever	**7**	26	1
R.M. Hogg	c Taylor b Willis	**18**	67	2	b Miller	**0**	10	0
G. Dymock	b Hendrick	**11**	79	0	not out	**6**	14	1
A.G. Hurst	c Taylor b Willis	**5**	6	1	b Lever	**5**	6	0
Extras (7 lb, 1 w, 2 nb)		**10**			(3 lb, 4 w, 4 nb)	**11**		
		190				**161**		

Fall: 8, 34, 38, 60, 78, 79, 100, 128, 185. 8, 36, 58, 58, 141, 143, 143, 147, 151.

Bowling: Lever 7-0-20-1, Botham 11-2-46-0, Willis 18.5-5-44-5, Hendrick 14-1-39-2, Miller 16-6-31-1.

Second innings: Willis 12-1-36-1, Lever 8.1-2-28-4, Botham 11-1-54-0, Hendrick 8-3-11-2, Miller 7-4-21-3.

Toss won by Australia. Umpires: R.C. Bailhache & T.F. Brooks.

*Captain †Wicketkeeper

ENGLAND WON BY 166 RUNS.

6. THE THIRD TEST MATCH

MELBOURNE, DECEMBER 29, 30, JANUARY 1, 2, 3

First day

The threatened rain was nowhere to be seen, the sky was blue, and the crowd wending its way across the park was sizable and eager on the opening morning. Well before lunch the great ground was heavy with people, and for the first time in the series it felt like a Test match, an occasion.

For the ninth time in nine matches this season Graham Yallop won the toss, and although the decision to bat on a pitch into which Ken Barrington's famous penknife had sunk with ease the previous day was anything but automatic, Australia's skipper did the conventional thing—and this time got away with it. The pre-lunch session would obviously be the tricky passage, but with the ball seaming and lifting, though not violently, Australia's youthful openers, Wood and Darling, launched into their task confidently.

England has omitted Lever, banking on a three-man pace attack and two off-spinners, while Yardley was left out of Australia's eleven in favour of Higgs. The only other change from Perth was Border for Cosier.

Australia's team meeting, where the chief objective was to retrieve morale and to consolidate support for the captain (Ian Chappell exploded in the *Age*: 'You don't ask for respect. You go out there and earn it.'), seemed to have changed their luck as well as attitude. Wood and Darling sometimes played and missed, but the edges of the bats remained untouched, and soon the gaps in the field were being exploited. The outfield was almost as slow as in the two previous Tests, and the square was dark and patchy, treacherous underfoot to sprightly fielders such as Randall, who had one spectacular slide in the opening session.

Willis's first ball hit Wood's pads and the over was a maiden, but Botham, operating from the pavilion end, conceded a single to Darling first ball and a nice four to a Wood square-drive. Gower claimed a catch in the gully, but umpire French was not interested. When Willis let a bouncer go it climbed relatively slowly, but another had Darling falling over backwards towards point, his white helmet flying off. He soon regained his composure, running daringly between wickets and, like Wood, pulling his bat out of danger when the need arose. The crowd responded to this best of beginnings, and loved a hook by Wood off Willis that not even the heavy outfield could prevent from reaching the fence.

Darling, who moves into many of his strokes in such a way that his right foot finishes well in front of the left, played well off his legs, like his partner, and once back-cut Willis with all the aplomb imaginable for three runs. Always, though, there was the fear that the running would let them down. Darling should have been run out when stranded halfway down the pitch as Randall gathered the ball, but nobody was up at the stumps and the throw, for once, missed.

After Darling had played an on-the-trot off-drive for three of Hendrick there was a further mix-up next ball as Wood had to get quickly into reverse and dive back when a direct hit underarm by Hendrick would have had him out. Again nobody had time to get up to the stumps. Australia's tension was relieved by a bold hook for four by Darling off a Willis no-ball.

Drinks were taken out after 11 overs, when Australia were 47 without loss, Wood 21, Darling 20, and Botham, who had been replaced by Hendrick, came on at the other end in place of Willis, who had had the unusual experience of starting the match with eight wicketless overs (0 for 27). Botham, irrespective of his tour contract, had allowed his name to appear above a combative article in the latest edition of the *Sporting Globe*—a deliberately provocative piece in which he asserted that England would win all six Tests and that 'I've got something to show you lot in Bay 16 at the weekend.' Bay 16 is one of the noisier parts of the Southern Stand.

The red rag had the desired effect in that the bulls roared, but only at Botham's impassioned appeal for lbw or caught-behind. Darling pulled him for three to raise the fifty after 71 minutes, and a fine leg-glance of perfect touch brought four off Hendrick. At 12.25 pm Brearley tried some spin, Emburey coming on at the pavilion end for his first bowl in an Australian Test, and the over was played quietly, both sides treating it as exploratory. The only real scare came a few minutes later when Wood came out of his ground to play Emburey and only just got back as Botham at silly point hurled the ball at the stumps.

The opening stand was just what the Australian captain, and the public, had yearned for, and it was being constructed out of conditions short of ideal. Willis, Hendrick and Botham were all making the ball lift and cut, and most observers must have felt that something like 60 for 4 would be a likely lunch scoreline. So confidently were Darling and Wood going about their business that visions of a fat score were emerging. But for all the boldness and skill, one thing was to let Australia down: the appalling judgment in running.

Darling's downfall was exclusively Darling's fault. Wood drove to deepish mid-on, Boycott, and tentatively started a run. But Rick Darling bolted. He was halfway down the pitch before he knew he was on his own, and his forlorn return mission had no chance as Emburey took the throw and flicked the bails off. A tragic but hardly surprising end to another budding innings. The South Australian's share of the stand of 65 was 33.

Australia needed to settle down again, to win the battle against panicky running as much as the tussle with the bounding ball. But worse followed. Hughes, one of the Brisbane heroes in defeat and possibly the finest batsman in the side, played at his first ball, pitched on the ideal spot by Botham, and was given out caught behind by Taylor. The ball seemed not to have deviated, but there must have been a noise, for umpire O'Connell was in no doubt. Hughes, for his part, was temporarily paralysed with horror, but eventually took those first unhappy, reluctant steps towards the pavilion.

That made it 65 for 2, and there must have been a feeling out on the terraces that it had all been too good to last. But there was no further setback for Australia before lunch, and a hooked boundary by Wood and a straight-driven four by Yallop off Emburey brought roars of appreciation. The interval came after 23 overs had yielded 88 runs, and the worst could be said to have been negotiated. The left-handers Wood and Yallop looked as secure as any Australian batsmen had been during the series, outside the Hughes-Yallop partnership at Brisbane, and with the sun still beaming down, the afternoon could yet be Australia's.

Miller began the afternoon from the pavilion end, with three men in a line in the covers and a short cover, and Hendrick rolled in from the far end. England's first opportunity soon came. The Derbyshire fast man found the edge of Yallop's bat and a relatively easy catch flew just to the right of Brearley at first slip. He went for it with both hands, but spilt it, and at the end of the over Hendrick could only turn away and gaze into the distance as he put his sweater back on.

After Yallop had confidently straight-driven Miller for four, Wood brought the hundred up with a controlled nudge through the slips off Hendrick in the 29th over, but the next ball lifted sharply and gave him a painful knock on the bottom hand.

While Wood kept himself in check, Yallop began to chalk up the runs. A cut off the suffering Hendrick soared over slips and raced to the fence, and then he turned to Miller and hoisted him for four after a length-destroying pace down the pitch. This made the score 111 for 2, but the time-honoured statistical hazard was soon passed as the captain crunched another of his straight-drives away for two. The fifty stand came in just over the hour.

Emburey took over from Miller, but it was Botham, the darling of the Southern Stand, who struck next. Yallop, 41, committed himself to a big drive but edged between first and second slip, who were slightly staggered in formation. Hendrick, at second, dived to his right and brought off a thrilling catch, and Australia were swaying again at 126 for 3, Wood 44 and defying all as in the second innings at Perth.

Soon after drinks, a drive by Wood brought three runs that had to be reduced to two, Toohey having 'fouled' Boycott at the bowler's end when Gooch's return came in at the completion of two runs. Then came Wood's well-earned fifty as he stepped away and cut Emburey for a couple. He had been in for 194 minutes and had faced 136 balls, and his stature had grown still further. This time his determination to go on to the hundred must have been all-consuming.

Peter Toohey, with three failures behind him in four Test innings, scrambled a single to leave the dreaded zero behind him, and had to endure a tight cordon in the field. His frustration showed in several wild swishes at the off-spinners, but he held on, earning the gratitude of the Southern Stand boys with a sweep shot hard into Botham's thigh. The fieldsman went down in such agony that one thought of Sid Barnes in 1948. But the beefy Somerset battler was soon on his feet again, even if his next over, his twelfth, was to cost ten runs, including Toohey's first boundary, a glance to raise the 150, and a cut for three off his 'slinger'.

This all came after Wood had survived his first chance, a snap caught-and-bowled to the right hand of Botham, bowling around the wicket. The batsman was 53 at the time, and looking more like a left-handed Greg Chappell with every over.

Into the sixties he went, as the crowd kept building up, reviving memories of the Centenary Test attendances. A game pull-drive off Emburey, who was getting little from the pitch, brought him another boundary as the haven of tea drew near, but there was just one further flutter before the interval. Toohey, on 15, edged Botham to the unhappy Brearley at slip and the low catch eluded his grasp. It was the third definable chance of the day, all of them expensive to some degree.

Just before tea, taken at 166 for 3, with Wood 65 and Toohey 19, Botham had shown that there were still possibilities in this pitch by bringing one from wide of Wood's off stump well back, to be taken by Taylor to his right. But on the whole the wicket was behaving itself, and there could be no questioning that Yallop had done the right thing in batting.

Wood took another boundary off Botham, half steered, half played involuntarily, to third man, and when he went for his sweep shot, the speeding ball was cut off at square leg by none other than Brearley, who had taken himself from slip, where Gooch now planted his giant feet. The fifty stand, the third of the innings, came after 65 minutes. But yet again, the pint was destined not to become a quart. The end for Toohey came sensationally.

He hit Miller into the gap between midwicket and mid-on. The ball had a very good chance of penetrating the widish gap and bouncing through for four. Then along came Derek Randall, making enough ground to get within diving distance of the ball, and he flung himself full-length to his left and took it close to earth. Not for the first time the thought occurred: what a grand baseballer he would have made. One of the British flags draped over the boundary fence was accompanied by the statement Randall is God, and certainly on this ground of happy memories for him the claim is only slightly farfetched.

Allan Border, small and dark, came in now for his first innings in Test cricket, with successes behind him for his Sydney club Mosman, for East Lancashire in the English Northern league, and for New South Wales. He swung his arms and looked skywards for the bright light, and proceeded to have an uncomfortable baptism in cricket at the top plane. Having jabbed his third ball through point for a single, he had to wait a while for his next runs,

1. England's assistant manager, Ken Barrington, gets some help packing his duty-free purchases. Chris Old, centre, was due for partial eclipse during the 1978-79 tour, but Bob Taylor was to make an outstanding impression as wicketkeeper and, unexpectedly, batsman

2. The England touring party at Sydney: front row, from left: Bernard Thomas (physiotherapist), Geoff Boycott, Bob Willis, Mike Brearley (captain), Doug Insole (manager), Bob Taylor, Chris Old, Ken Barrington (assistant manager). Back row, from left: Derek Randall, Clive Radley, John Lever, Geoff Miller, Ian Botham, Phil Edmonds, Mike Hendrick, John Emburey, Graham Gooch, David Gower, Roger Tolchard, Geoffrey Saulez (scorer)

3. Peter Toohey looks wistfully at the stumps after he is bowled by Bob Willis for 1 at Brisbane. Toohey was to have a disappointing series, finding the tag 'the next Doug Walters' difficult to live with

4. Derek Randall started the series well at Brisbane. Here he is caught for a first-innings 75 which he followed up with 74 not out in the second

5. Leading Australia for the first time, Graham Yallop scored a second-innings century at Brisbane that put his side back into the match. He was the twelfth Australian to score a hundred in his first Test against England. Here he takes a short ball from Ian Botham on the body

6. Kim Hughes scored 129 in his second-innings partnership of 170 with Graham Yallop at Brisbane. Had he been able to score as heavily in later matches, the series could possibly have been more closely fought

7. Geoff Boycott is run out at Brisbane. Derek Randall was his batting partner at the time, and it was a reversal of the incident at Nottingham during the 1977 series

8. Batting down the order at number four, Mike Brearley made a reasonable start at Perth, but a delighted Geoff Dymock eventually had him caught behind for 17

9. David Gower gave crowds throughout Australia exhibitions of his classical batting style, and at Perth he posted his first century against Australia

10. Bob Willis puts his usual wholehearted effort into a delivery at Perth. After this Test he took fewer wickets than expected — Mike Hendrick taking over his role of main strike bowler — but he was always a threat to the Australian batsmen

11. Peter Toohey punishes Geoff Miller during his one effective innings of the series, 81 not out at Perth

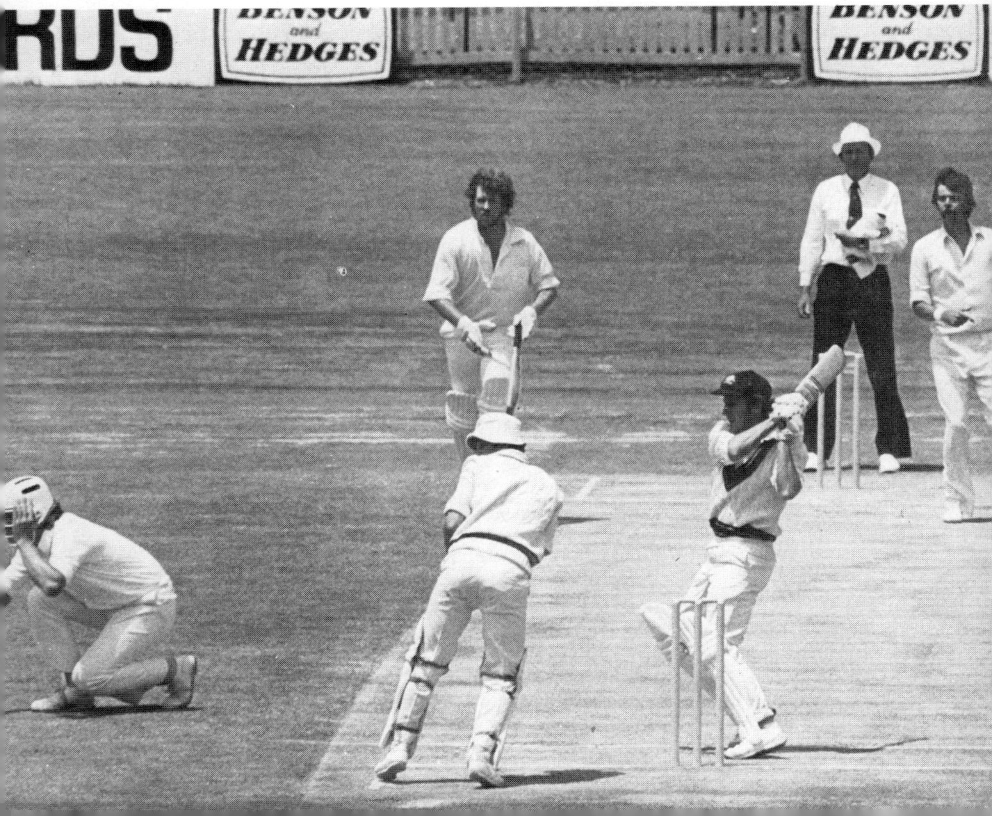

12. *John Maclean, Australia's wicketkeeper for the first four Tests, found his firm-footed approach to the English spinners fatal, and Geoff Miller dismissed him twice at Perth, here for a first innings duck*

13. *Umpire Tom Brooks, who shortly before had announced his retirement, appears unimpressed by Bob Willis's and John Lever's dance of delight after his 'out' verdict against Graeme Wood, caught behind for a second-innings 64*

14. Bob Willis's views on umpires are easily gauged by his blind man's stick and faceless countenance — a playful rather than cruel send-up for the England team's Christmas Day fancy-dress party. 'Her Majesty' Derek Randall keeps him company

15. Australia's win at Melbourne revitalised the series for a while, and was brought about by far more disciplined batting, notably a fine hundred by Graeme Wood, who hooks this ball from Ian Botham with much relish during his 390-minute marathon innings

16. Uncapped at the beginning of the series, Rodney Hogg's impact was nothing less than phenomenal. He took 41 wickets, troubled all the batsmen — particularly Geoff Boycott, whom he dismissed 6 times on the tour — and the crowd's soccer-style chant 'Hoggy, Hoggy' became as familiar as it had been for Dennis Lillee in his day

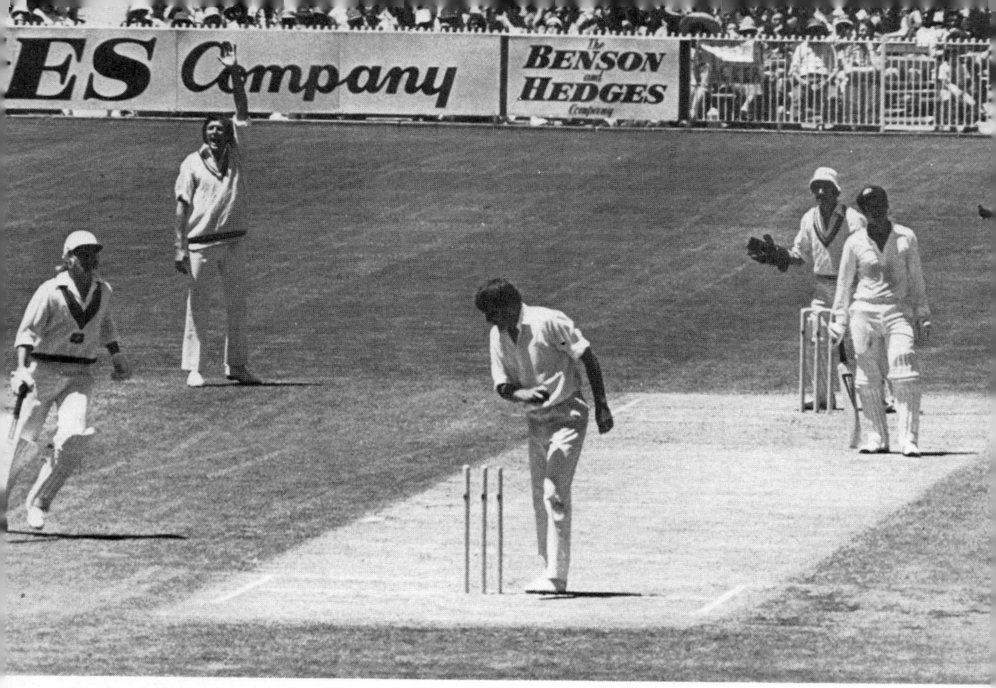

17. Australia's opening batsmen established an unwelcome record during the series when in each of the six Tests one of them was run out. Rick Darling is the victim here at Melbourne — a fate he suffered twice in four Tests

18. Hundreds of V for victory — or victim — signs signal the end of Mike Brearley's first innings at Melbourne. Rodney Hogg, inevitably, is the bowler and crowd-leader

19. Rick Darling played an aggressive, crowd-pleasing innings at Sydney and was unfortunate to get out for 91. His hooking was very strong, if sometimes unorthodox in execution, and brought him many runs

20. Allan Border followed his debut at Melbourne with impressive not-out scores at Sydney of 60 and 45. He was unfortunate to find himself relegated to 12th man by the end of the series

21. Several sharp catches were missed in the field during England's second-innings fightback at Sydney. Here Graham Gooch watches Graeme Wood fail to hold one off Jim Higgs

22. Derek Randall played the innings of a lifetime at Sydney, 150 runs in just under ten hours, and it won the match and retained the Ashes for his side. Only on a few occasions did he allow himself the luxury of natural attacking shots such as this

23. *Kim Hughes is caught by John Emburey off Geoff Miller at Sydney to make Australia's second-innings total four down for 64, with now little chance of reaching the series-levelling 205*

24. *Mike Brearley seems to indicate that the ball hit his arm and not the bat, but it made no difference to the umpire's decision, caught at the wicket off Rodney Hogg at Adelaide. This wicket took Hogg beyond Jeff Thomson's series record of 33 wickets*

25. Phil Carlson came into the Australian side at Adelaide after a spell as twelfth man and took this brilliant catch off Derek Randall to make England four down for 18 in their first innings

26. John Emburey administers a chest thump to Rick Darling after he had been felled by a ball from Bob Willis at Adelaide. His breathing had seemed to stop, and Emburey, trained in resuscitation by the Middlesex club, was one of the first players to come to his rescue

27. Kevin Wright took over as Australia's wicketkeeper at Adelaide and impressed with his wicketkeeping skill and determined batting. Here he appeals successfully against David Gower, who was lbw in both innings

28. Bob Taylor's outstanding wicketkeeping was greatly admired throughout the series, but his match-turning innings of 97 at Adelaide gave tremendous pleasure. Few would have begrudged him the three runs he needed for a first-ever Test century

29. Mike Hendrick has Graeme Wood caught in the slips in Australia's first innings at Sydney. Hendrick's bowling throughout the series was quite outstanding, and he became England's leading new-ball bowler

30. Geoff Boycott is out for 19 in the first innings at Sydney. His doubts, shown here, about the validity of Andrew Hilditch's first Test catch were possibly borne of frustration at yet another low score for him in the series

31. Graham Gooch is smartly stumped by Kevin Wright at Sydney for 74. This was by far Gooch's best innings of the series, and it included a crowd-pleasing straight drive onto the apron in front of the Bradman stand

32. Ian Botham didn't have a happy time against leg-spinner Jim Higgs at Sydney. Here he edges a ball from Higgs over slip fieldsman Kim Hughes's head. Hughes missed some vital catches in the slips and was eventually moved to outfield positions

surviving a close call for run-out when Randall came on the scene again with an underarm toss followed by a Michael Crawford leap over the stumps that threatened all kinds of damage.

Shortly, Border was unwinding a massive pull at a ball slightly short from Miller. It was only a yard or two short of a six, and it brought the 200 up, in the 60th over.

At a quarter to six, with the new ball in the offing, Brearley tried spin from the Southern end for the first time in the gentle, easeful shape of Emburey, whose challenge to sweep was soon accepted by Border. With two men out for the shot, he eluded Boycott for one boundary, which took him into double figures, and seemed to have done it again, except that this one slowed down and stopped. Boycott stopped chasing, which persuaded the batsmen to stop running, and when it was all sorted out only two runs had accrued.

The new ball was taken immediately after drinks, at 212 for 4, with Wood 84, Border 13, and Hendrick this time was the favoured one, running in from the pavilion end. Willis, copping the full blast from his many friends in Bays 13, 14, 15, 16 and 17, powered in from the far end.

The two left-handers took it quietly. This was a crucial stage of the day and of the match, and needed to be weathered. Australia had come alive at last, the series was showing a new competitive gloss, and consolidation was the prime need. Those who had come to the Melbourne Cricket Ground for fun didn't like it overmuch, but Wood, fighting a natural fatigue, and Border, getting the feel of Test cricket, played with fine judgment, and on a pitch that now seemed as quiet as this city on a Sunday, averted the collapse that had occurred in all four Australian innings so far in the series.

Wood crept into the nineties, and Border broke a long sequence of defensive parries with an immaculate cut for four off Willis between slips and gully to reach 21. When Willis dug the ball in nearer the halfway mark it rose with so little pace that it could be played off the front foot.

With twelve minutes remaining, Brearley called up Botham, whose first ball, from around the widest, passed a ball's width from Wood's stumps as the batsman let it go. A two through midwicket took him to 93, and, playing inside the last ball of the over, he edged fast through slip to take him to 97. England's aim must now have been to keep him from the strike, to play upon his nerves. Willis's last ball to Border was a slow half-volley which he turned for a single, thus depriving Wood of the strike for the final over—

something the crowd resented—but a leg-bye came from Botham's third ball, and Wood had his chance.

It was actually a minute or two after six o'clock when Wood on-drove Botham hard and ran three as Boycott retrieved, and the crowd acclaimed the century as it had acclaimed nothing else on this day of incident. Six ecstatic fans ran on, delighted that their hero, even though he be a Western Australian, had reached his Shangri La after six hours of dedication. It was symbolic.

It would seem that no-one, apart from Kim Hughes in Brisbane (369 minutes), has ever taken longer to reach a century for Australia in Test cricket (certainly not against England, Lindsay Hassett's 1946 and 1953 marathons and Bill Lawry's 1968 Oval record having been surpassed now by both Western Australians) and the weary figure that presented itself for interview after the day's play was ample testimony to the numbing physical and mental effort involved. Wood had only ever played at Melbourne before for the WA Colts, 'in front of 25 people'. His biggest dream had always been to make a century against England. His six-hour vigil was all the more remarkable in that he is a strokeplayer by nature, always willing to spank anything off line. While Yallop was making runs steadily, Wood had geared down and held his end. When his concentration wavered later in the day he indulged in a few airy shots. But he had survived the awkward moments and steered Australia to their soundest position in the series on a day which yielded the highest quantity of runs: 243, for the loss of four wickets. The attendance of 35,174 also took the series to a more uplifting realm. Had the direct throws hit the stumps when various Australian batsmen were out of their ground, and had all catches been held, the innings could have been all over by now, and Australia's mourning extended. That would have reflected in the Saturday attendance to come. Instead, a crowd of over 50,000 was expected.

Second day

Yallop's—and all Australia's—hopes of making well in excess of 300 were shattered in the first hour of Saturday's play. On another brilliantly sunny morning, before another big, noisy crowd, Wood batted a further 25 minutes without adding to his overnight 100. In this time he lost Border, who had steered Hendrick through slip for four in the opening over only to be caught at slip three balls later. Brearley picked it up neatly, low to his right, holding the ball aloft in the fingertips of his left hand.

At 250, Wood drove at Miller but placed the ball straight to Emburey at short midwicket. It was a second or two before it dawned on the majority that he was out, so coolly did the fieldsman accept the chance. Worse followed for Australia. Hogg, by now the subject of feature articles in almost every newspaper and magazine, was given a hero's welcome, and tackled his task confidently, until a handsome cover-drive sent his fifth ball straight to Randall. Miller thus took two wickets in an over, and Hogg recorded the second duck of the innings. Two more followed. Dymock played a straight bat at several deliveries, then dragged a ball from Hendrick onto his stumps, and after a no-ball, Hendrick struck again by bowling a scoreless Hurst. Two hundred and fifty-two for 9, and Maclean and Higgs stretching their tactical battle for the strike beyond the drinks break. In the hour's play, 11 overs had been bowled, and five Australian wickets had toppled for 14 runs, three to Hendrick and two for two runs to Miller, who gave way to Botham after his five overs.

Botham finished it, bowling Maclean and finishing with three wickets, as did both Hendrick and Miller, and Australia were left to rue a comparatively miserable total of 258. At 247 for 4 the keys to the kingdom were to hand. Now they had been dropped down the drain.

Yet if they were down the drain, they were not yet lost from view, for in the 35 minutes of play before lunch, England made a calamitous start to their innings. The mature opening pair of Boycott and Brearley marched to the middle amid a chorus of booing, and Hogg, helped on his way by the wail of his name from the bays behind him, hurled himself into the attack, this time not even treating himself to a loosener. His first ball to Boycott was very fast, and the field, consisting of a mid-on, forward short leg, backward square, wide leg slip, three slips, silly point eight feet from the bat, and a cover, crouched expectantly, eight of them in the familiar green caps.

Brearley at the other end took Hurst's first ball, an intended yorker, and drove it for a single, but to the third ball of Hogg's second over Boycott turned squarely into a defensive parry to a ball well up to him and had his wicket shattered. The crowd must have been over 30,000, but it made the noise of 100,000. England one down for two, and the biggest nuisance back in the pavilion. Better followed for Australia. Brearley's awful run continued. After Randall had done his traditional jig and placed his first ball for a single, the captain met his doom. Hogg, in the same over, brought one back at him and hit the pads as Brearley shuffled across. Umpire O'Connell was in no doubt that it was lbw. Two down for three, Hogg 2 for 1.

Gooch saw it through with Randall to lunch, when eight runs were on the towering scoreboard, but the buzz during the interval was non-stop after the fall of eight wickets for 23 runs in the morning session.

Lunch came at the right time for Hogg, who came back strong after his breather. Straight away he dug one in at Randall, who fended off to the left of Higgs at silly mid-on. If the catch had been held England would have been 8 for three wickets. Randall, standing bat raised like a backstreet mugger as the bowler brought his arm over, cut Hurst firmly enough to beat the sprinting Darling to the fence, but Gooch was repeatedly in trouble against the same bowler. He bucked himself up with a thumping off-drive off Hogg to reach 11, and both batsmen settled for the push off the pads or the back-foot placement on the off side. For Randall this was the return to his golden hunting ground; for Gooch it was one further chance to establish himself in the side, to erase some unpleasant memories.

Hogg tried a few around the wicket, but after seven fiery overs from him Dymock was called up at the Southern end and passed clean through Randall in his first over. The crowd grew ever noisier at the far end, in contrast to the collar-and-tie sophistication of the members' enclosure. The sight of so many female spectators had me speculating as to how they viewed the current heroes. Back in 1936, William Pollock wrote: 'The Australian women fell for Charlie Barnett's clear-cut features and Joe Hardstaff's fair, curly locks.... Don Bradman, "Chuck" Fleetwood-Smith, and little Ross Gregory, of Australia, were far more to them than Clark Gable, Gary Cooper, or Robert Taylor.' The only Robert Taylor around now was the England wicketkeeper, whose popularity, firm that it is, is of a much smaller calibre.

Gooch's bat was not always true to the perpendicular, but he existed and grew more settled, a Gary Cosier in bulk and phlegmatic movement. A recovery was being effected as drinks were taken, though in the over before, Randall edged Dymock very close to Border at second slip.

The breakthrough came after the pause. Hurst, bowling his ninth over, pitched one well up to Randall, who moved across his stumps, as he is prone to do, and, completely off balance, missed it. Umpire French gave him out, though he was not keen to go, and the crowd divided its emotions between the bowler, who was all the more the hero because he was Victorian, and the departing batsman, who was booed for his pains. England 40 for 3, Gooch 22, and Gower at the crease.

Before Gower had scored he had to endure a disturbance of the worst kind, for it occurred as Hurst was running in to bowl. A roar went up as a streaker descended into the arena and began to trot round the boundary. A solitary policeman gave chase and eventually caught his man as he slipped over by the sightscreen. A few more constables appeared and the miscreant was led off after a scrummage, miraculously clad in briefs, presumably now part of standard police issue during events of this kind.

Gower at last opened his score with a three, and brought up the half-century with an edgy four off Hurst, the innings just over two hours old. Now, though, Australia struck again. Gooch played at Dymock some distance from his body and the thick edge flew to Border in the slips. The fieldsman moved sharply to his right and knocked the ball up, gathering it as he fell, and England were 52 for 4, still over 200 runs behind with only Gower left of the specialist batsmen. Gooch's 25 had taken almost two hours, and with Dymock getting lift at the pavilion end life was anything but easy for the Englishmen. Yallop chose this moment to give Hurst a well-earned rest and introduce Higgs's leg-spin.

Gower, who seems not always to relish flighted bowling, enjoyed the first over, sweeping daringly forward of square for four and cutting for three. At the other end, he cut Dymock wristily on the run for what would have been four had not Darling chased and hurled himself into a slide that stopped the speeding ball, which he then threw to the top of the bails. Another swept four off Higgs and then another through the covers when he switched to around the wicket and Gower had four boundaries in less than an hour, penalty-rate production.

At tea England were 75 for 4, Gower 28, Botham 2, the crowd wide awake, and soon after resumption Dymock, bowling with a lot of life towards the pavilion end, where the ball had sometimes jumped, sometimes kept low, shot one through at Gower that hit his pad halfway up and he was leg-before, a vital wicket.

So Miller came in at 81 for 5, and immediately inside-edged Dymock close to his stumps. The fans in the outer rose like a huge sea anemone brushed by the current. After he had made a single he was in trouble again, going for a big drive against Higgs and edging to Hughes's left hand. But the chance was spilt. As the fifth hour neared completion Botham unleashed some angry strokes, driving Dymock with immense power to the cover boundary and lofting him high for two. Then Hogg was called back into the attack for the 41st over. It brought with it some excitement.

He came rushing in like a speed-skater, the full-throated howl of 'Rod-nee, Rod-nee' seeming to add an extra force to his approach. He banged one in short and Botham, every bit as much a competitor, swung into the perfect hook for four. To the last ball he tried a pull, but hit it a shade too early and managed only a single as the ball hit the diving Yallop on the jaw. At the other end, away from the hurricane, he moved casually into a cover-drive against Higgs. This time, though, the solid hit was not kept down, and Darling threw himself forward and took a brave two-handed catch.

Taylor came in as drinks were taken, but was soon dispatched by Hogg, bowled, and then Emburey propped up his end for a time, Hogg keeping the ball well up and the batsman next to statuelike as he kept it out. Finally, a yorker got through and Emburey's middle stump was plucked out. Eight down for 101.

Then followed the most tedious period of play in the match and the series. Miller was intent only on survival, as was Willis, who at least basked in the knowledge that everything would be pitched well up to him . . . until Hogg let a short one go and hit him in the left armpit. The prospect of Australia batting again this evening gradually passed, as did the expectation that England would be all out. A mere seven runs were scored in the final hour, and Miller's not-out three had occupied 110 minutes, upstaging John Murray's three runs in 100 minutes in the 1962–63 Sydney Test, when the wicketkeeper was hampered by a damaged shoulder.

What did the people think of this extraordinary day when fourteen wickets fell for 122 runs? Well, only five full days' play in the history of Test cricket had ever yielded a lower return of runs, yet this last Saturday of 1978 had embodied some enthralling cricket, some tentative batting maybe, but some fine fielding, wholehearted bowling, and that quality which can never be falsified—tension. It showed in the unwavering attention of the crowd, which built up to 40,114, and in the sharp intakes of breath, the deafening cheers, the intense concentration on the Ashes battle, for which there is no substitute. Several hours spent the following day watching the World Series International Cup match from Brisbane was like tuning in to a passing amusement before the main feature. The new game, referred to by its promoters as 'modern cricket', could never, by its very fabrication, know the profundity. Anyone doubting this need only have been at the Melbourne Cricket Ground on this gripping day to have recognised that this was the superior formula. The *Sydney Morning Herald*, in an editorial, had its own way of putting it: 'In short, you play for Australia–but you work for Packer.'

As the old year filed itself into the archives and the new one arrived, with its cargo of mystery, Australia knew they were back in the series with a lead of 151, two England first-innings wickets to take, and something in the wicket for the bowlers. It would have been added comfort to have Bruce Yardley in the side for the fourth innings, but they had the key bowler of either side in Rodney Hogg, who now had 21 wickets, as well as Jim Higgs, whose last thirteen overs on the second day were worth a pitiful six runs. For England, with the weather still beautiful, a long holding operation loomed ahead.

Third day

With the New Year came the announcement of Greg Chappell's MBE, a deserved award to a classical batsman and hard-pressed captain who had somehow maintained a public dignity through all the animosity and confusion. It coincided with an outburst—albeit overstressed by the local press—by the current England captain that might better have been left until after the match or the series. Mike Brearley spoke out, on the rest day, against the Melbourne pitch, where the bounce was uneven at the pavilion end, and Australian pitches generally, which had disappointed during the tour.

On the way to the ground, and while browsing through the cricket museum, I heard several people remark on the bad timing of the captain's criticism. It had the appearance that after fifteen Tests, faced with defeat at last, he was whingeing—something high, very high, on the list of things not to do in Australia.

However, the victory was not won yet, and though there was a good deal of lip-licking in anticipation, this day, Monday, January 1, 1979, was to be a most important day. A quarter of an hour into it, Hogg took his fifth wicket of the innings, for the fourth time in five innings (the other was reduced to only three wickets as England won at Brisbane). He bowled Miller off his pads, and England were 120 for 9, the young Derbyshire all-rounder having batted two hours and five minutes for his seven runs.

Willis and Hendrick added a useful 23 in half an hour, putting their broad shoulders to good use against Higgs and Dymock after Hogg had been rested. Willis gave a sharp chance to Border at second slip when he was 17, but it was then soon over, and at 143 England carried a deficit of 115 runs, a heartening situation for Australia as they started their second innings about an hour before lunch.

Darling and Wood made 31 in that time, and seemed in little trouble, though Willis kept one low to Darling, and there was the usual uncertainty between wickets. Botham shared the new ball, and Brearley tried Hendrick and Miller as the second wave of attack. But the gaps were found in the field quite consistently, and Australia lunched happily without loss, Darling 14, Wood 15.

It looked more like old times when they came out, for Darling had forsaken his helmet—probably too hot and the ball unlikely to fly—for a green cap, like his partner's. The first boundary soon came, but not from the bat: Wood tried to sweep Miller and Taylor was unsighted. The fifty came up in the 20th over as Wood cut Miller melodiously for two, and the lively pair continued to dash close singles and frenetic twos, the sweetest stroke so far being Darling's late cut for three off Botham, operating round the wicket.

The first wicket fell at 55, when Darling quickly saw a shorter ball from Miller, stepped back, hit it hard into the covers, and saw Randall lunge forward to take the catch. It was similar to the one Darling himself took to dismiss Botham on the second afternoon. This brought in Hughes, who was on a 'pair'. He ran a quick run from a push through square leg, and then set about taming the attack as had no-one in the match so far. He straight-drove Botham under the sightscreen at the Southern end, Boycott running urgently behind the screen to retrieve the ball as the umpire signalled the four, and then stabbed down at the pitch of a full-length ball and glanced it to the long-leg boundary. Hitting Miller for threes to midwicket and cover with all the willingness and conviction imaginable, Hughes seemed to be a man with a score to settle. It was just what Australia, and the match, needed.

A helicopter hovered and descended beyond the far end, and someone suggested it was the coming of Kerry Packer, 'to see what all the noise was about'. The noise subsided as Miller, with eight runs off his last over, made way for Emburey, who flighted straight onto a length and obtained possibly a little more bounce. At drinks Australia were 77 for 1, 192 ahead.

Wood's downfall came through bad judgment. Botham's slow ball is very slow indeed. It still has to be played, but batsmen usually seem to have little trouble in negotiating it, for it is so devoid of pace as to allow an adjustment even if the batsman is initially beaten. Wood, after over eight-and-a-half hours at the crease in this match, was entitled to an aberration, but it was of the schoolboy kind. He tried to sweep off the stumps, and was bowled. Two down for 81.

Yallop came in and began reassuringly, though a ball from Emburey which he let through ran on and missed the off stump by a sufficiently narrow distance to cause the ice-cool Emburey to hold his head and twist in agony. He was still awaiting his first Australian wicket.

While Yallop wavered again, edging Willis for four just past Hendrick's right hand, Hughes got lower and lower down over his bat in the forward defensive, breaking out just once in a while with a bold move down the pitch to Emburey. The game got tighter as tea approached, and the slow handclap made a predictable return. But the cricketers—all the Englishmen except Boycott in white sunhats—were locked in deadly conflict, the sun burning down, the breeze ruffling their shirts. Well might a banner hung from the balcony of Bay 12 proclaim: Fair Dinkum Cricket.

The hundred came up in the 39th over when Yallop took a couple off Miller, now bowling in harness with Emburey, but with two minutes to go to tea England had a somewhat unexpected success. Miller pitched one just short of a length and Yallop went back to cut. He got the thinnest of edges into Taylor's gloves as the 'keeper left the ground to take the rising ball, and it was 101 for 3 as tea was taken, with Hughes a lively 22 not out even if it had taken 77 minutes.

Soon after resumption the West Australian was delighting the crowd with the first six of the match, a compact assault on Miller from a yard or two down the pitch, the ball dropping among the fans in Bay 13. Given the opportunity, Hughes threw himself into drives and cuts, and seemed on the verge of playing one of the outstanding innings of the summer, dealing capably enough with anything that tended to keep low at the pavilion end and killing the spin with an acutely-angled bat. When he thrashed out at Emburey the ball cannoned into the arm of Botham at short leg, and for a time the injury looked serious, but the fieldsman, tough as teak, soon recovered, and was about to feature in the action again. Before that, Toohey had time to strike a four, a gorgeous drive through the covers that shot past Boycott's outstretched foot.

Emburey was bowling beautifully, swivelling languidly at the crease, wrist cocked, the ball curling to a length. The first ball of his twelfth over drew Toohey out of his crease for an unclassical crossbat swing, and the ball dropped in front of Botham at midwicket. Before it hit the ground, though, the fielder lunged forward and collected a special catch. Australia 136 for 4.

Border then came in and survived uncomfortably for eleven minutes, during which not a run was scored, before he fell victim to a lightning-fast piece of cricket. He swept Emburey, and was partly toppling forward, partly projecting a run, when Hendrick, forty-five degrees at leg slip and only five yards from the bat, took the ball and flung it at the stumps in one movement. Border was out—and startled.

The sky had clouded over by now, and the temperature dropped. Any earlier gaiety had disappeared. There was no flamboyance, even about Hughes, and no runs for over after over. England, 251 runs behind with four wickets to take, fancied themselves back in the match.

At drinks the score still hadn't moved from 136, Emburey and Hendrick having each bowled three successive maidens, and 63 balls were to go by before Hughes added to that figure with a single behind point off Hendrick. Then, doubtless encouraged, Maclean opened his account with an attractive delayed drive to the third-man boundary. Hughes then sailed into a cover-drive off Emburey for three and things were moving again. Another drive was hit a foot or two off the ground, to Randall's right and Willis's left, and reached the fence, and a top-edged sweep for two through the vacant slips region brought up the 150 in the 56th over. After bowling for so long without cost, Emburey now conceded eleven runs in an over.

A change of bowling at the Southern end brought another wicket. Botham, greeted by deep volumes of booing, took over from Hendrick, and bounded in at Hughes with all the eagerness of a ferret, a large one. Hughes met the challenge with a free-and-easy drive, but he struck a fraction too soon and Gower gobbled up the catch. Hughes slapped the ground with his bat in annoyance.

Hogg came in at 152 for 6, the pride of Northcote even if he had been forced to seek recognition in Adelaide three years ago. He wore no helmet, and Botham gave him a bouncer first ball, something guaranteed to promote an early finish to the day, as the light was now poor enough for the Press-box lights to be switched on.

It was quite a duel, the one between Hogg and Botham. Hogg avoided his 'pair' only by the narrowest margin, but his obstinacy and straight bat won admiration, until Botham sent down one of his supercharged yorkers and hit the off stump. That made it 157 for 7, an overall lead of 272, which, according to the pattern of the match, ought to have been safe for Australia. But 300 would seem so much more of a mountain. Starting with their first-innings lead of 115, Australia would have wanted another 220 or so, and in reasonably quick time, for England could well be helped in any delaying action by the weather, which showed signs of turning if not to the horrors of the current European freeze-up then at least to something in contrast to the glorious days we had recently known. England had contained well this day, which finished with the new ball just due but not taken. The bowlers had stuck to their task, and there had been few blemishes in the field, the three out-catches that were taken all being difficult forward-diving jobs and Hendrick's flick to run out Border nothing less than brilliant.

Dymock and Maclean saw through the last twenty minutes, and Australia rested at 163 for 7 after another engrossing day, watched by 30,038 people, taking the attendance above the 100,000 for three days. A watch would now be kept on the weather.

Fourth day

England could not have done a much better job in disposing of Australia's last three wickets. In 25 minutes Hendrick and Emburey overthrew Maclean, Dymock and Higgs for only four runs, to set themselves a target of 283 in 11½ hours. It was still a lot, with the pitch creeping as it was, but it could have been so much worse.

Maclean fell to the fatal charms of the sweep, topping the ball high and easy to Hendrick at backward short leg. The fieldsman then struck as a bowler by having Dymock, the left-hander, caught low down behind square leg by Brearley off an ambitious forcing shot off his toes. Emburey completed the job by luring Higgs forward and having him stumped, his second wicket of the morning.

Australia's second effort—167—was disappointing, but it was a credit to England's bowling, fielding and generalship, and it left the touring team in with some sort of chance, even if the requirement was the highest of the match. Time was no real consideration, but the dubious nature of the pitch was, and so was Australia's determination to narrow the gap.

Within minutes the complexion had altered. Boycott faced Hogg, the major personal contest of the series renewed, and began with a maiden, the last ball of which almost decapitated the Yorkshireman. It pitched short, he ducked, saw it stay chest-high, and raised his head just in time. The danger was going to be in this shorter ball.

At the other end, Dymock bowled to Brearley, who hit a no-ball sweetly to point for no runs, and then played at one moving across him and got a fine touch to Maclean. The captain's duck made his macabre run of Test scores read: 6, 13, 17, 0, 1, 0. With the dropped catches considered, a crisis was brewing again.

And that was not all. Randall, possibly England's central hope aside from Boycott's likely long-term encampment, made only two before Hogg trapped him in front, leaving him the same forelorn, spreadeagled figure as in the first innings. It was a sickening setback for England, now two wickets for six, and Australia automatically had a clearer sight of the light at the end of the tunnel.

In the remaining 67 minutes before lunch Boycott and Gooch fought hard. They got onto the front foot at every opportunity, guarding against the low ball, and took advantage of the wide spaces resulting from Yallop's attacking field. Gooch, in particular, looking very much the Roman gladiator in his helmet and stiff pads, brought off some stirring shots, placing Dymock to third man and driving square, both times for four. When Hurst took over from Hogg he cut for three, and when Higgs was tried at the other end he crashed a four off the back foot with the strength of an elephant. Boycott applied himself as if his life depended on it, but treated himself to a glanced four off Hogg—his first Test boundary since Brisbane—before the fast bowler was spelled. By lunch the recovery had taken the score to 50 for 2, Boycott 15, Gooch 26, and people were not quite as certain where to put their bets.

Dymock bowled round the wicket after the interval, and Gooch got one magnificent drive away to the fence, reaching wide and throwing the bat with just enough precision. The third-wicket stand moved to 65, the barge now steady and moving centrally down the canal. Then somebody closed the lock-gate again. It was another dismissal unblessed by the acquiescence of the batsman. The inevitable Hogg hurled one down at Gooch and struck his pad as he moved towards the off side. Umpire French gave the fatal signal, and a promising, attractive innings had ended—40 in 97 minutes, a reprieve, perhaps, for the next Test (which was scheduled hard on the heels of this one) for a batsman who had known what it means to struggle throughout most of the tour.

Higgs bowled from the Southern end into the suspect end, and beat Boycott from time to time with sharp spin and high bounce. Boycott, the anchorman, crouched over his bat and leaned into his stroke like a professor examining a moth never previously espied. This was one of the biggest assignments in a career crowded with responsibilities, and never would his concentration have been more intense.

At drinks Boycott had made only 20 of the 86 for 3, with Gower 10, looking relaxed. A few overs later the left-hander liberated a bold slash-drive off Higgs that slipped easily over the outfield behind point for four, and just after three o'clock Border came on at the pavilion end to make an all-spin attack. The sky was sapphire blue, with no sign of the unidentified flying objects picked up on radar screens the previous day off the east coast of New Zealand, as this hard-fought Test match moved ever so gradually to its climax. The hundred was generously applauded as Boycott worked Border away to leg for three, and there were catcalls when Gower drove over a ball from the same bowler and Maclean helplessly allowed four byes. With tea almost upon us, Yallop gave more work to Hurst, who had bowled only four of the 39 overs to date. Boycott played him attentively, Gower sedately and then contemptuously as his heavy bat gathered three through mid-off. This brought

Boycott to strike, and all hell broke loose in the stands as Hurst hit his pads as he played forward, tumbling out of his crease, and umpire O'Connell gave him out leg-before. It was a huge setback for England, who went to tea at 123 for 4, Gower 23, Botham yet to score.

Boycott's 38 had taken 198 minutes, with one boundary, and it fell well short of the expectation of him, so toweringly important was his role.

Australia's marksman-in-chief, Rodney Hogg, took up the action for the last session, and gave himself some lung exercise with several appeals for leg-before. Hurst did the same at the other end, and apart from the odd aggressive gesture such as Gower's drive backward of point, which eluded the fieldsman and ran for four, the batsmen kept their heads down in the knowledge that the pitch could not be trusted. Head groundsman Jack Lyons, who succeeded the legendary Bill Watt, whether with excuse or otherwise, had simply failed to produce a wicket of Test match quality. The awareness that the ball will not lift is not enough to save a batsman, any more than forewarning of a tyre blowout guarantees survival. The technical requirement is immense and unrelenting.

Gower had luck when 32. Hogg, bowling round the wicket, caught the edge of his bat, and a catch flew fast to Maclean's left. The bulky wicketkeeper could not get down in time, and the chance went begging. How crucial this was would have to be assessed later. Hurst meanwhile was getting a lot of movement off the seam, and also chose to come in at the left-hander from around the wicket. Gower found it necessary to alter his guard.

A glance by Botham took England to 142 for 4, just past the halfway mark, and a square-cut glowing with health took Gower to 42 and the total to 151 in the 48th over. A bad bounce through Wood at extra cover gave him two more runs, and the question arose, as it often does with an hour and a quarter to go, how many might England be this evening? Two hundred without further loss would set up a thrilling prospect for the final day.

Dymock broke through Gower's defence just before drinks were taken, and the urgent shout must have been very close to being answered in the affirmative, but England were still alive at 159 for 4, Botham 9, Gower three short of his half-century.

At a quarter past five Australia moved nearer victory when Higgs deceived Botham with a googly and then drew him forward, clipped the edge, and saw a delighted Maclean secure the catch—a conventional leg-spinner's dismissal. At 163 for 5, Miller joining Gower, there was a lot left to do by England. A couple of minutes later they were surely done for. Dymock smacked Gower's pad, by way of rehearsal, and did so again, this time getting the verdict, the fourth lbw of the innings. The crowd, totalling 23,432 this day, erupted as if boiling water had been poured over the terraces. For Gower, one short of his fifty, there was only the long walk back to the shadows; for the Australians there was a renewal of endeavour, a growing realisation that victory over England, something they had been told was impossible this series, was fairly imminent.

Dymock bowled to a length and beat the bat often, and Higgs, full of confidence, tossed the ball up and imparted loads of spin. The field crowded in. Taylor was watchful, Miller likewise. Then Miller played hesitantly at what seemed to be a Higgs top-spinner, and the ball lobbed from the pad to Hughes at short leg. The shout went up, and the Derbyshire all-rounder was out: 167 for 7, Australia anxious to finish it tonight, just in case the weather happened to change for the worst.

Taylor appeared to give a catch to slip, expertly taken left-handed by Darling off Higgs, but umpire O'Connell disallowed it, to the utter amazement of all the fieldsmen, and next over, with a quarter of an hour remaining, Hogg was called up. He hit Emburey's pads, but the batsman escaped his 'pair' with a two through square leg, and it became certain that we should all be back tomorrow—when the gates were to be opened free of charge.

The Australians got carried away with some of their appealing in the dying minutes, but one which brought results was against Bob Taylor, who played forward to Hogg and seemed astonished when the umpire raised his finger. It turned out to be the last ball of the day, and England, now 171 for 8, were as good as beaten, short of the arrival of that rain which we had been promised for days but which had considerately stayed away.

Fifth day

The match was soon over. Six or seven thousand people turned up to share in the young Australian cricketers' hour of glory and fulfilment, and with a bugle blaring tunefully and dramatically, and the fieldsmen appealing raucously for everything in sight in their enthusiasm, Emburey glanced and Willis carved for a few token runs before the hungry Hogg moved in for yet another five-wicket haul. Willis was caught by Yallop at short leg, fending off a lifting ball, and Hendrick was bowled two balls later. Within seconds the ground was swathed in jubilant people.

The margin was 103 runs, and the twin significances were that the series was brought back from the dead and 'established' cricket could now hold its head up—so much so that some people had fears that the Australian Cricket Board might harden its attitude further, if that were possible, in the matter of seeking an accommodation with World Series Cricket. Charles Palmer, David Clark and Jack Bailey were in town for informal talks with WSC officials, and while the main topic was supposed to be the Prudential World Cup scheduled five months hence, long-term problems must surely have come under discussion. Yet again, the candles of hope were lit by shaky fingers.

Australia were now only two-one down, and their captain had a cocky look in his eye as he faced the same old Press brigade after the match, this time with a new set of questions. Yes, the patience of his players had been rewarded. Yes, there were still a few things to be ironed out. 'I knew we had it in us. It was just a case of putting it all together.' It was not a match-winning toss, he said, but no-one likes to bat last on this wicket. He didn't think it played all that badly. The odd ball kept low, but it was a reasonable batting wicket. When England were 163 for 4 he got 'a little bit anxious', but he had confidence in his bowlers.

Yallop had stressed the need to get onto the front foot when batting in the first innings, and he was very pleased at his players' improved application. After all the flak hurled in his direction he was gratified at getting complete public support here in Melbourne.

Asked to describe his feelings, he said he was 'totally ecstatic'. This became even more understandable when it was realised that this was Australia's first victory against England in an Ashes Test match since the Edgbaston success of 1975. Ten Ashes Tests had intervened.

Graeme Wood was voted Man of the Match, a perceptive choice by the five judges, for though the phenomenal Rodney Hogg again bowled valiantly, collecting ten wickets yet again, it was Wood's disciplined century that set up final success. It was the pair of opening stands, 65 and 55, by Wood and Rick Darling that gave Australia the long-awaited sizable starts—in such stark contrast with England, who were two down for three and two down for six. That is where it counts: at the start.

Brearley's disastrous form, with bat as well as in the slips, had become a major worry for England, and Willis's lack of success was something feared all along. As Hogg gathered in his sensational harvest of 27 wickets in three Tests, it could easily have been forgotten that Willis was also by a mile his country's prize attacking weapon. Botham continued to be kept in check, with bat and ball, and Boycott was never going to take command. Randall simmered, always likely to burst out in a match-winning innings, and it seemed for a time that Gooch was going to show Australia what he was really worth. Hendrick bowled well, as he always does, but his best figures in eighteen Tests remained a mere 4 for 28, four-and-a-half years earlier. If chosen, Old must have made an impression on this match. And David Gower, who eight months ago had yet to play in a Test match, top-scored in each innings with 29 and 49, and demonstrated a maturity beyond his years. England owed much to him in Melbourne, as they did to the youthful Cowdrey four-and-twenty years before.

The scene in the Australian dressing-room was one of joyful fatigue and open friendliness. Bob Parish gave me a glass of champagne, and Ray Steele topped it up. Graeme Wood looked both reflective and content. Drinking and chatting together, Alan Hurst and Graham Gooch were like longlost brothers. Selector Neil Harvey looked very happy. David Gower was worried only about a stain on his swimming trunks. Rick Darling heard of my anxiety at having no boots for tomorrow's 'Press Test' and gave me his without hesitation.

Australia Day had come over three weeks early.

THIRD TEST MATCH

Melbourne, December 29, 30, January 1, 2, 3

AUSTRALIA

			Mins	Fours			Mins	Fours
G.M. Wood	c Emburey b Miller	**100**	390	6	(2)b Botham	**34**	136	0
W. M. Darling	run out	**33**	93	2	(1)c Randall b Miller	**21**	100	0
K.J. Hughes	c Taylor b Botham	**0**	3	0	c Gower b Botham	**48**	153	4*
*G.N. Yallop	c Hendrick b Botham	**41**	82	4	c Taylor b Miller	**16**	41	1
P.M. Toohey	c Randall b Miller	**32**	80	1	c Botham b Emburey	**20**	32	1
A.R. Border	c Brearley b Hendrick	**29**	106	4	run out	**0**	11	0
†J.A. Maclean	b Botham	**8**	70	0	c Hendrick b Emburey	**10**	90	1
R.M. Hogg	c Randall b Miller	**0**	3	0	b Botham	**1**	42	0
G. Dymock	b Hendrick	**0**	16	0	c Brearley b Hendrick	**6**	41	0
A.G. Hurst	b Hendrick	**0**	2	0	(11)not out	**0**	5	0
J.D. Higgs	not out	**1**	25	0	(10)st Taylor b Emburey	**0**	11	0
Extras (8 lb, 6 nb)		**14**			(4 b, 6 lb, 1 nb)	**11**		
		258				**167**	*plus 1 six	

Fall: 65, 65, 126, 189, 247, 250, 250, 251, 252. 55, 81, 101, 136, 136, 152, 157, 167, 167.

Bowling: Willis 13-2-47-0, Botham 20.1-4-68-3, Hendrick 23-3-50-3, Emburey 14-1-44-0, Miller 19-6-35-3.

Second innings: Willis 7-0-21-0, Botham 15-4-41-3, Hendrick 14-4-25-1, Miller 14-5-39-2, Emburey 21.2-12-30-3.

ENGLAND

			Mins	Fours			Mins	Fours
G. Boycott	b Hogg	**1**	13	0	lbw b Hurst	**38**	198	1
***J. M. Brearley**	lbw b Hogg	**1**	17	0	c Maclean b Dymock	**0**	7	0
D.W. Randall	lbw b Hurst	**13**	88	1	lbw b Hogg	**2**	7	0
G.A. Gooch	c Border b Dymock	**25**	110	1	lbw b Hogg	**40**	97	5
D.I. Gower	lbw b Dymock	**29**	61	4	lbw b Dymock	**49**	169	3
I.T. Botham	c Darling b Higgs	**22**	84	3	c Maclean b Higgs	**10**	78	0
G. Miller	b Hogg	**7**	125	0	c Hughes b Higgs	**1**	19	0
†R. W. Taylor	b Hogg	**1**	5	0	c Maclean b Hogg	**5**	36	0
J.E. Emburey	b Hogg	**0**	13	0	not out	**7**	46	0
R.G.D. Willis	c Darling b Dymock	**19**	88	0	c Yallop b Hogg	**3**	21	0
M. Hendrick	not out	**6**	32	1	b Hogg	**0**	2	0
Extras (6 b, 4 lb, 9 nb)		**19**			(10 b, 7 lb, 1 w, 6 nb)	**24**		
		143				**179**		

Fall: 2, 3, 40, 52, 81, 100, 101, 101, 120. 1, 6, 71, 122, 163, 163, 167, 171, 179.

Bowling: Hogg 17-7-30-5, Hurst 12-2-24-1, Dymock 15.6-4-38-3, Higgs 19-9-32-1.

Second innings: Hogg 17-5-36-5, Dymock 18-4-37-2, Hurst 11-1-39-1, Higgs 16-2-29-2, Border 5-0-14-0.

Toss won by Australia. **Umpires:** R.A. French & M.G.O' Connell.

*Captain †Wicketkeeper

AUSTRALIA WON BY 103 RUNS

7. BREATHLESS PAUSE

Quite a lot of activity was crammed into the two days separating the third and fourth Test matches. Before we left Melbourne, Australia announced the same twelve for the next Test, and on January 5, the day before the start, Mike Brearley told newsmen in his hotel room in Sydney that not only were England trusting in the same eleven, with John Lever again twelfth man, but the batting order would remain the same, i.e. he would open and Gooch would go in at number four. The Essex man, said his captain, 'was keen on the idea'.

The delicate matter of Brearley's own run shortage was approached with a great deal of courtesy, almost sympathy, by the gathered journalists, and he explained simply that it was felt that he and Boycott were the best opening pair available. Several possible means of strengthening the batting had been considered, but the Melbourne combination was being stuck to. It had been the shortest Test selection meeting of the tour so far.

Meanwhile, Australia's wicketkeeper and vice-captain John Maclean had sustained a wicked blow just above his left eye when a ball from Alan Hurst kicked up while he was batting at the Sydney No. 2 ground nets. Twenty-four hours before the Test was due to start, 'Macca', after a night under sedation, looked like the loser in a fight to the finish—Carmen Basilio, perhaps. The Queensland-NSW Shield match was just beginning, which ruled out their wicketkeepers, and Steve Rixon had a damaged hand. Kevin Wright, the brilliant young Westralian, was thought to be too far away (in Perth) under the circumstances. That left the Victorian 'keeper, Ian Maddocks, son of former Test 'keeper and Board delegate Len, and Trevor Robertson of South Australia, who happened to be Test selector Phil Ridings's son-in-law. The Tasmanian wicketkeeper presumably did not come seriously into consideration. Maddocks was the lucky man to be called up on standby duty. But Maclean continued to hope for a speedy recovery.

The Sydney pitch, on the day before the match, was heavily grassed, but quite firm. Neither captain would commit on preference of innings this far ahead, but the surface was interesting, to say the least. The sight of the pylons still jarred, and the mess where the new stand was being erected still forced the eyes to redirect to a more pleasant view. Sadly, there is not a lot left to contemplate at this ground now. Only the 'showboat' pavilion, which Heaven preserve, and the Sheridan Stand, where I sat for ten mind-bending minutes, totally alone in the dazzling sunlight, hoping for visions to appear. Nothing happened. Lindwall, Hutton, Harvey, Worrell, Miller, May—they were all gone. All I could see were about fifty World Series Cricket emblems affixed to the boundary fence. I supposed they would be removed by the start of play.

After a pleasant TAA flight, the industrial troubles now mere memories, I broke away from my bachelor existence—now shared happily if somewhat basically with my son at Maroubra—to partake of the 'Press Test' between teams of Australian and English journalists, a sequel to the game at Harrogate during the 1977 Ashes series, when Kerry Packer was allowed to play, amazing to relate. This time the event was played with serious undertones.

When the machinations of team selection were over and done with I found myself with the English side, thus doing a kind of 'Midwinter'*. The match was played on Benson & Hedges' ground at Kensington, and sponsored by that cricket-minded company, who saw to it that the players went to their task with full stomachs and were never allowed to go thirsty in the field. As usual in these matches, the first half-hour was the most serious, and the English XI lost three wickets in no time to the fiery new-ball attack headed by Peter Meares of the ABC, who went on to take 7 for 18 and win the Man of the Match award. Ken Barrington, England's allotted star player, made a nostalgic 84, growling at one point that I was worse than Boycott at stealing singles from the last ball of an over, and Australia's big name, Bob Simpson, stroked 78 as the home side waltzed to an eight-wicket victory. Their 190 runs came with the greatest of ease.

Peter McFarline enjoyed himself with a laborious but invaluable unbeaten half-century, but Chris Martin-Jenkins of the BBC had a mixed match, dropping Simpson after having been dropped by Simpson, and bowling the former Test star after being thrashed by him almost the length of Todman Avenue. Peter Laker, our captain, made a few for the English XI and somehow won a pair of nutcrackers of obscene design for being 'personality of the match'. The trophy, to be known as The Ash, was presented to McFarline, and presumably will be fought for in 1981, by which time several of the 1978–79 combatants will have been forced to hang up their boots.

As for the author, he pulled his nose out of the path of a bouncer from the red-headed tearaway son of Dick Tucker with only a centimetre to spare. Chapter 6 was almost the final chapter in this book.

* Bill Midwinter is the only man to play for Australia against England and *vice versa*.

8. THE FOURTH TEST MATCH

SYDNEY, JANUARY 6, 7, 8, 10, 11

First day

Rodney Hogg looked like a West Point cadet as he strode to his mark with a belligerent air and a glistening new ball in his right hand. England had won the toss and were to bat on a green-tinged wicket on a day when the temperature was already hovering around the century. Bowlers would be operating in shortish spells and batsmen would be contending with sweaty eyebrows and other parts. Even in the shade of the Press-box my light-blue shirt turned to dark after the climb up the flights of steps. It was some comfort to hear gnarled oldtimers complain of the heat.

Maclean convinced doctors and selectors that he was all right to play, so Maddocks's journey was in vain. Yardley was again twelfth man.

Hogg ran in from the Paddington (pavilion) end and flung down two wides before Boycott was called upon to consider line and length. There was lift in the pitch, and twice in the opening over Boycott had to duck. Dymock took the Randwick (Hill) end, and twice hit Brearley's pads. The first run from the bat came off his seventh ball.

Hogg was bent on using what first-day bounce there was in this pitch, and soon Maclean was jumping to take a screaming lifter above his battered head. Brearley took one in the chest and could scarcely refrain from rubbing the outraged part, but Boycott kept out of trouble, and opened his score with a two behind square leg off Dymock.

The heat now got at Hogg, who left the field, and Hurst took over, Boycott pushing him for two through cover. Next over, Brearley edged a full-toss from Hurst on the bump to Border at second slip, who put it down, for what it was worth, and the bowler fired down a couple of bouncers at Boycott in a display of strength that was never likely to draw hostile retaliation. When he pitched a quick one on a length, however, he got results. The ball clipped the outside of Boycott's strictly defensive bat and flew between first and second slip. Border threw himself to his left and clasped the catch with both hands, and England's first loss had come at 18, Boycott 8. It was to be part of a double setback.

Randall brought his own special carnival to the field, playing all sorts of strokes, jumping on the spot, swinging his arms. He played Hurst's first ball back, and then swung into a virile pull stroke against the next, which was short. Wood as short leg had a fraction of a second to sight the ball as it blurred towards him, but he got his hands to it as the force knocked him over, and the catch was secured as he rolled ecstatically over. The Australians forgot the heat in their exultation.

So England had failed yet again to get a solid start, though Boycott and Brearley had gone sensibly about their job. Randall played instinctively, and was not to be condemned. The hook and pull are specialty shots of his. This one went straight at the man. That was its only fault.

The running when Brearley and Gooch were together was cautious, understandably, but when Hogg came back for Hurst 28) Brearley drove him confidently for two and Gooch drove square for three with power and style. When Brearley drove Dymock for three towards the Sheridan Stand it seemed that a kind of tranquillity was returning, but no sooner had note been made of Brearley's reversion to the old bat-raised stance than Hogg, who was beginning to look ragged, whipped a leg-cutter through to knock Brearley's off stump out of the ground. England 35 for 3, last man 17.

Gower was struck on the pad first ball, Hogg bowling round the wicket, but when Dymock (8–1–12–0) made way for Higgs at 12.40 pm Gooch took a nice three to midwicket. Gower's first run came from a pull at a long-hop, Border's accurate return winning much more applause than the stroke, and if there was any obvious cause for English concern it was the way Gooch used his pads at every opportunity against Higgs's leg-spin. The googly, sparingly used that it is, could be a very great danger.

Hurst came back for his third spell, and Gower played him firmly through mid-off for two. Then, at six minutes to one, after 114 minutes' play, Gooch registered the day's first boundary, a sweep off a Higgs long-hop. Gower ran a very quick two in the last over before lunch to bring up the half-century in the 21st over, and England appeared to be safely into the refreshments when Hurst's final ball, bowled from around the wicket, came in nastily at Gower and brushed his glove. Maclean took it, the appeal echoed, and umpire Bailhache, after a long pause, gave Gower out. He was crestfallen, not in disagreement but in the harsh knowledge that it was all over so soon after it had begun. England were 51 for 4, and the Australian advance of Melbourne was being reinforced by the hour.

The four wickets had been earned, without question, but it seemed an appropriate time to ponder on Boycott's fortunes. The dominance of old was gone, as well as the aura of invincibility, and if it was not age that was dimming his eye and reflexes then perhaps it was time to recall the turmoil into which his life was dipped in 1978, after the thrills and glories of 1977. The troubles had left their mark, and while he had proclaimed that he wanted only to get to Australia to immerse himself in the Test series, the mark was now visible with every match.

So many of the growing crowd had come to see Hogg, but the pre-lunch hero was Alan Hurst, who bowled with more fire and determination than I had seen from him before. The prize of Boycott's wicket and the rather fortunate capture of Randall's spurred him on, and after lunch, when Hogg had bowled three more overs, finding the inside then outside edge of Botham's bat before drooping away in some distress, Hurst came back at the Paddington end. But for the moment, the action was at the opposite end.

Gooch unwound a big pull against Higgs, in line with the small stand at the southern end of the 'bob' stand. Would Toohey get across in time to cut off the four? He made good ground, judged the swooping ball perfectly, and slid beneath it baseball fashion to take an astounding catch that raised howls of acclamation from every enclosure. It was a good time to have drinks.

John Maclean was obviously unwell, and Bruce Yardley towelled him off as the liquid did its job down parched throats. The 'keeper was to feature on the scoresheet one more time before his condition overcame him.

Miller made just four. It was a boundary off Hurst, a kind of off-glance through slips, but a straight ball then accounted for him, finding the edge and careering comfortably into Maclean's gloves. England now 70 for 6, and the tail exposed.

At this point, 2.50 pm, Maclean had to go off, his shirt sticking to his back, his legs not completely steady. The tension and the drugs had numbed his hands and stiffened his shoulders. Yallop put on pads and gloves and earned a loud cheer when he took Hurst's next ball cleanly, and when he stood between deliveries, relaxed, with arms akimbo, he somehow resembled the famous posed picture of Bert Oldfield. He certainly moved more with the grace of the great oldtimer than the unlucky current wicketkeeper whom he was forced to replace.

It all rested on Botham's broad shoulders, and he moved into gear with a thunderous boundary hit off the back foot off Higgs in the direction of the construction site. Dymock replaced Hurst, and Botham attacked, taking two twos off him, and when Higgs let go a full-toss Taylor gratefully whacked it to the fence at the foot of the hill.

Higgs was getting a good deal of turn out of this first-day pitch, and Botham was often in trouble, but he tried hitting his way to parity, and survived. Taylor was the one to go. He played from the crease at a leg-spinner and Border snapped up the catch at second slip. The stand of 24 for the seventh wicket was the best of the innings so far.

Emburey brought matters of a diplomatic nature with him to the wicket. He politely objected to substitute fieldsman Yardley being stationed in his specialist position of gully, and the switch was duly made at the behest of the umpires. A second objection was made an over or two later.

Emburey did not last long. He was missed by Higgs at short leg off Dymock, a direct catch off a forward prod, and the same kind of parry at Higgs's bowling saw him caught by a diving Wood at forward short leg.

The hundred came at last, Botham cutting edgily for four in the 41st over, and in Dymock's next over Botham really got into it, hitting him hard through cover then through mid-off, both times for four, and then pulling for two. Willis had no clues at all against Higgs, but survived, and at tea England were 119 for 8, Botham a vital 40.

Ten minutes after the interval he had his fifty, taking a stream of runs off Hogg – a hooked four and a healthy off-drive with similar result – reaching his half-century in 135 minutes. The field spread out, offering a single to get at Willis, and Hogg dropped one short. Botham hooked, top-edged, and got four more. Then a slower ball was dug out, all this appreciated by a crowd that recognised a man-to-man confrontation. Hogg triumphed in the end. He bounced another, Botham hooked but thin-edged to Yallop, who took the catch well, the stand of 43 having lasted 44 minutes, Willis making seven in that time.

I had that feeling that Botham's innings was going to have a heavy bearing on the match. Without it, England would have fallen well short of a hundred. With it, assuming the animation remained in the pitch, fifty was going to be a good score. It was a good wicket, but it offered something to the bowlers, and with the perceptible shortage of class in the batting of both sides another fairly low-scoring game could have been in the offing.

Hendrick and Willis put eleven runs onto the total before Hurst bowled Hendrick, and England were all out for 152. Hurst, slapped on the back by all his team-mates, took the bowling honours with 5 for 28, his best in Tests, and left the field beaming, his moustachioed face as radiant as any victorious Western hero's. For weeks I'd been trying to think whom he reminded me of, and now I knew: it was Slim Whitman. He had just won a High Noon of his own.

So at 4.40 pm England's first effort came to an end, and their 152 was just two runs short of their first innings in the memorable Sydney Test of 1954 – Tyson's match. If we were in for another nerve-tingler like that it would be no bad thing.

The ground soon came alive again. Willis, from the Paddington end, bowled a no-ball to start, but his fourth ball, which would have passed well away from the off stump, found Wood indecisive, and the ball clipped the inside edge of the bat and broke the wicket. One for one.

Hughes took a single, and then Darling was in trouble, hooking and being caught behind – but it was a no-ball, and the great-nephew of Joe Darling (whose brother Laurie still lived in an old folks' home) lived to fight again.

Some fighting strokes followed. Hughes drove Botham to the construction site (how I hope they *do* call the new edifice the Victor Trumper Stand), and when Willis dropped short Hughes dispatched him high over mid-on for four. Darling, his white crash-helmet off as his scalp breathed, watched this and then emulated it after a fashion by pulling square with a resonance that would have pleased a piano-tuner.

The opening attack soon seemed to lose its edge. Hughes and Darling played their strokes, ran their runs fast, observed most of the tenets of batsmanship. Darling in particular let himself go, firstly mis-hooking another Willis no-ball over Miller's head for two, then getting all the components together for a lovely four in the same direction. When Willis bowled off a short run Darling hooked him again, this time beating Boycott at long leg and Miller at backward square. Willis slumped his way from the field after that.

Botham now took some stick. Darling, the hook stroke working like a dream, got four more, and after a painful blow above the left knee, cut juicily for yet another. After four overs costing 20, Botham made way for Miller, and Hendrick held the Paddington end, the fifty coming from his bowling in only the 11th over. In the final over of the day Darling was still looking for runs, and his sixth boundary came from a pull off Miller, the ball not exactly getting up, but meeting the middle of the bat nonetheless. It took Australia to 56 for the loss of Wood, with Darling 35, Hughes 15, and the innings only 67 minutes old. It was much too early to say, but the faintest whiff of victory would have been drifting into Australian nostrils this Saturday evening.

Second day

It was just as hot and humid on the Sunday, and in large numbers again the men and women and boys and esky containers filed through the gates, eager to see Australia assert themselves further. Hendrick beat Darling in the first over, but he and Hughes applied themselves, got a good sight of the ball, and made the strong resumption so necessary to Australia's cause.

The first boundary came from Hughes, a beautifully-balanced off-drive off Botham. He then steered Hendrick past Gooch at third slip for another, and after 35 minutes Willis removed his white plantation-overseer's hat and came on at the pavilion end. Darling took an easy two, and then two more that he ran so fast he must have broken the world 40-yards sprint record. It was followed by the cheekiest of dabs to third man for a single. Already the crowd were sensing that this was going to be their day.

Emburey took over from Botham at 82 for 1, with Darling on 43 and Hughes 32, and just before drinks, Willis began to bowl very well, troubling Hughes with movement both ways, hitting the pads, finding the inside edge. But there was no breakthrough. Botham transferred to the pavilion end, and with Emburey bowling very accurately at the other, England were at least containing the batsmen. Then, for a brief period, Australia broke loose. Darling had not added to his rush of fours the previous evening, but a pull for three off Botham took him to 51 (108 balls), his first Test half-century against England. The round-faced, fair-haired 21-year-old, who might have walked into the ground from any of Australia's glorious beaches, slipped his white helmet off and raised his bat in acknowledgement of the rousing cheers.

Hughes slashed at Botham and sent the ball flashing over Gooch's head at third slip down to the Hill boundary, and then Darling unwrapped some daring shots, putting Emburey to the midwicket boundary twice in an over, raising the hundred, and the century stand, in a time of two-and-a-half hours. For England it was rapidly becoming an Australian Test match of the old order, with the heat, the humidity, the partisan crowd, the curiosity as to where the next wicket was going to come from, and an eye on the clock for the next interval. The bowlers were being used in short spells, and looked short of breath when they came off, though when Emburey's tidy spell (7-4-13-0) ended and he called for a sweater he was loudly applauded by a bemused audience.

Miller took over from him, and was hit muscularly by Hughes to the 'bob' stand fence. Off-spin was going to present no terrors – yet at least. What was needed was leg-spin or better still left-arm spin. Edmonds would have been worth a gamble in this match, even if he had played little and bowled poorly. He is a good enough bowler to be able to stage a comeback during a Test match. Watching Hendrick too, honestly and well as he bowled, brought back the thought that Old would almost certainly have got more out of this pitch. But England were committed, and were paying the price of weak batting.

Hughes lashed a four to midwicket off Miller just before lunch, taken at 126 for 1, 26 runs behind, with Darling 69 and Hughes 48. Here England pulled one back.

Self-destruction would define Hughes's downfall to the first ball after the interval. Willis bowled just short of a length and the batsman committed himself to a brazen off-drive, coming forward with the stroke. The ball sank into Emburey's hands at extra cover, and Hughes walked off a very angry young man.

Yallop was watchful. Here was the chance to steer the ship to the Land of Equality, where fruit was bountiful and the gratitude of the nation was guaranteed. Willis tested him for a while, then left the field and returned to the team's hotel, overcome by heat and a gastric upset. Before long, Hendrick, having bowled another few overs, also left the field, and Edmonds did thirteenth-man duties. 'They're dropping like flies,' exclaimed a toothy oldtimer. But there was always Chris Old, batting at the Number 2 ground, to come on next if needed, and Roger Tolchard looked pretty fit when he brought out the drinks.

Just before the refreshments Australia had gone ahead when Darling pulled a slower ball from Botham for four, and after drinks, because of the heat and the dependable bounce, Darling exchanged helmet for cap. Looking at him bareheaded again, I realised at last whom *he* reminded me of facially: Steve McQueen. Botham saw only an unprotected head, and he let Darling have a bouncer. He did the same to Yallop several times, but the captain was untroubled. He hit Emburey high to the fence at long-on, and Darling came back into the picture with a pull for two off a Botham no-ball. Just after three o'clock Gooch had a try, whirling his first two balls down the leg side to Yallop and bringing the best out of Taylor. Yallop swept him off his leg stump for four, and the focus turned to Darling, who was nine runs short of a century.

He missed it. Miller floated one up to him and he moved forward, glancing firmly. Botham at leg slip took the catch two-handed by his left calf.

There were very few people present who would have begrudged Rick Darling his first Test hundred. He had batted for four-and-a-half hours and exhibited some spirited strokes in an innings of great significance. Not only had he set up a sound position after the work of the bowlers the previous day, but he had established for himself a new set of credentials. Great-uncle Joe would have been very proud of him.

Toohey came in to deafening cheers on this home ground of his. But be failed again, and the Peter Toohey Stand banner was taken down from the Hill awning. He got off the mark only through a fumble by Gower at fine leg. Then, in his 16th over, the valiant Botham, who had taken some salt tablets minutes earlier, pitched one just short of a length and Toohey tried to cut when the line was too near his body. The cramped stroke sent the ball to Gooch at third slip and the catch was well taken just above knee height. Australia were now 179 for 4, and Hendrick was back on the field, showing his sharpness at backward short leg and drawing deep breaths in preparation for the new ball, due after tea.

Border opened his score with a clunk, pulling Miller to the mid-wicket fence, but that was his limit before tea. Yallop hit Emburey through point for four, an untrained youngster running on to retrieve the ball when it still had twenty yards to run, and then banged Miller to long-on and cut him fine for three. The sun disappeared behind wide cloud-banks, the new ball would now be used when the atmosphere was heavier, and suddenly Australia were in command but no longer crushing their opponents. The score was 199 for 4 at tea, Yallop 40, Border 4, and the only incident of note during the twenty-minute pause was the repeated exposure of his backside by a poor wretch who left the security of the Hill for a few minutes to exhibit himself in the outfield.

Botham took the new ball at 200 for 4, and Hendrick, probably dreaming of Derbyshire's cool climate and sporting wickets, operated from the Noble Stand end. Between them they fished out England's next wicket. Hendrick forced Yallop to play indeterminately at a lively ball that flew from the edge wide of second slip. Botham fell to his left and collected a wonderful two-handed catch near the turf to make Australia 210 for 5. After a morning session in which 70 runs had been scored and an afternoon session bringing 73, England were still holding on gallantly to a share of the match, minority share though it was.

Maclean came in, damaged brow ensconced in a white helmet, and a tough period of play followed. Border could not quite manage to get his strokes away, and Maclean seemed content just to prod. An edge went for four, and when Border clipped Botham hard past point Lever emerged from a flock of seagulls to cut off the four. The crowd of 20,485, a few hundred down on the previous day, and incidentally 53,000 down overall on the first two days of the 1974–75 Ashes match, seemed to understand Australia's need. With the prospect of batting last against two off-spinners, Australia would want nothing less than a lead of 200.

At ten-past-five Emburey came on, the pace of the game having been slowed right down. The crowd were restless now. They wanted some visible effort from Australia towards attaining their aim. Brearley, for the first time in hours, was moved to crowd the bat. Maclean played doggo.

Eventually another breakthrough came. Emburey gained his reward with the first ball of his 21st over, Maclean playing not far enough forward to kill the spin and being trapped leg-before: 235 for 6.

Hogg entered, to affectionate applause, and after a couple of sighters he timed Emburey sweetly to the base of the Hill, a kind of thank-you to his patrons. An absolutely enormous man climbed over the Hill fence about this time and gave Boycott, fielding at third man, the fright of his life when he turned round and saw him. He gave the visitor the regulation handshake, accepted a green cap which he placed over his England cap, bade him farewell, and kicked away a few stray beer-cans littering the field.

The ball was keeping low now, Taylor taking it around ankle-height and sometimes on the bounce from Hendrick.

Australia fell a further peak away from expectation when Hogg was out – this time to a misunderstanding in the field and not directly to the persistence of the bowling. Border played to mid-wicket, saw Hogg stop, stopped himself, and then they both ran on. Gower's fast underarm throw missed the bowler's stumps, but Miller gathered it and promptly hurled to Taylor at the other end with Hogg hopelessly adrift. That made it 245 for 7, and England could now be permitted quite congratulations. At lunchtime there was only one side in it, and an Australian advantage this evening of 180 was the expectation. As it was, Miller came up for the final over of the day – a maiden – with the score 248 for 7, a lead of 96. In trying conditions, with Willis absent from two o'clock onwards, England had earned a few medals for endurance and tactical acumen. Never were Australia running amok, and though it was their day, England's traditional skill at keeping things tight shone through. With three days left it ought to be Australia's match, but the prospects of a runaway win had been considerably reduced.

The fast bowlers, Hendrick and Botham, had won heaps of admiration for the way in which they stuck to their task, and Brearley's generalship and deployment of his reduced resources had one columnist suggesting he had earned his place even if he continued to make few runs.

In all the recognition of England's courageous holding operation, and in all the condemnation of Australia's failure to run away with the match, it was not to be overlooked that the home side had control. Not for the first time, we were looking forward to a day of profound significance. An early dismissal for Australia and an England total of 350 would set up an exciting prospect. But few felt England had it in them to make that sort of score. Bowlers are always prepared to tell you that their efforts are so often undone by the batsmen.

Third day

I know of no better way to start the working day than by taking a ferry across Sydney Harbour. Friends at Mosman had offered all the comforts of home, and after breakfast, with the cicadas already buzzing, and with no time for an hour or two at the Zoo, welcome as it would have been, I found the deep green water a relief from the gathering heat.

The England players – except Willis, who looked seedy and again did not take the field – trotted out as if they had forgotten yesterday and expected today to be cool and mild.

Border quickly brought the 250 up with an off-driven two off Hendrick, and his first boundary of the morning came to third man off Botham. When he edged Hendrick he was relieved to see the ball fall short of Gooch's outstretched hand, and in accordance with the strategy aimed at combating the heat, the bowlers were soon being switched, Emburey for Botham, Botham for Hendrick. When Botham dropped one slightly short, Border heaved into a pull that looked incredibly like Neil Harvey's most spectacular shot, and a three glanced off Emburey took him to his first Test fifty, in 190 minutes, with three boundaries. He raised his bat and then slapped his pad with it in delight.

There was an incident when Botham grew tired of the sight of Dymock and bowled him a bouncer from around the wicket, drawing a warning from umpire French that had Brearley running down for a long discussion. He had been through all this before. Botham settled the matter in the best way possible. He knocked Dymock's off stump out: 276 for 8.

Taylor was given a remote chance of stumping Border as a ball from Emburey rebounded from the batsman's pad to his left, but he couldn't retrieve in time, though the demolition of the stumps was a major spectacular

Now we were into the cat-and-mouse period, the field spread out or packed, depending on whether England wanted Border on strike or the incompetent Higgs. Higgs, however, almost trebled his previous highest Test score of four, and hung around for 40 minutes despite Brearley's precise field placement. A cover-drive for three off Miller produced tremendous applause, and when he went at last, deftly caught at second slip, low, by Botham to give Hendrick his second wicket, he could be justly proud of his 11 runs, and Australia were now, at 290 for 9, 138 runs ahead.

There was no last-wicket stand to speak of. Border hit Miller for four to reach 60, but a suicidal attempt at a single saw Hurst barely over halfway when the bowler's underarm hit the stumps.

So Australia's lead was 142, and the innings of 294 had taken eight-and-three-quarter hours. It was time to draw breath again. But not before England had negotiated the ten minutes before lunch. And suffered a grievous loss.

Hogg stuttered and broke into his run, sixteen longish paces, and sent down the first ball of England's second innings. Boycott moved across and forward, missed the incoming ball and was struck on the back leg. The appeal was not the loudest of the summer, but it was productive. Umpire Bailhache gave Boycott out, and you would have thought the match was all over by the jubilation inside the boundary and outside. It was Hogg's thirtieth wicket of the series, and the fourth time in Tests that he had taken Boycott's.

The rest of the over produced runs, a single and a two to both Randall and Brearley, and at the end of it Brearley decided it was lunch and was thirty yards away when the umpire called for a second over. It was almost fatal to Randall, too, for Dymock brought one back to smack him on the pads when he must have been in front of all three sticks. But he survived, driving the next for four with an aggressive spread of his elbows. England were 11 for 1 at lunch.

The SCG catering facilities were hopelessly inadequate, and half the interval was wasted queueing for a hot-dog and coke, a miserable experience, though Geoff Boycott will have had a much more rueful time of it.

Hogg had a spate of no-balls after lunch, but he sent one or two through Brearley's guard after Randall had placed him for four to the empty seats in front of the pavilion at third man. When Dymock dropped short, Randall played his inimitable pull square for four, and the shockwaves following Boycott's first-baller began to recede. Yallop switched his bowlers in short spells, reversing Hogg and Dymock per medium of a Hurst over, and once again we saw Brearley survive the early threats and raise guesses as to whether this innings was going to be the long-awaited big one. When Hogg sent a short one over the off stump he played it unconvincingly, but with slackened wrists, so that while the effect was tremulous the house was intact.

At drinks England had moved smoothly to 49 for 1, Brearley having equalled his highest score of the series, 17, and Randall looking good for a lot of runs, 28 already.

Higgs came on and bowled a big-spinning maiden over, and Dymock bowled a good-line, short-of-a-length maiden at the other end. The drought was broken with a risky single by Brearley, bringing up the fifty, but the introduction of Hurst led to a free-scoring spell, the bowler becoming more distraught at every push and nudge, while the breeze revealed the outline of Brearley's torso-protector.

Border came on, bowled a maiden, and came off, allowing Higgs to switch ends with Hurst and to beat Randall's attempted cut with a high-bouncing leg-spinner. Hurst was equally unlucky, Brearley cutting head-high through where a third slip would have been and finding the fence.

As the afternoon wore on both batsmen were a mass of concentration. Higgs bowled an immaculate length, demanding careful forward play, which Brearley and Randall chose to mount from the crease. Brearley was once in great difficulty with the googly, but stayed calm, relishing the experience of being in the thirties, a run-zone long forgotten to him in Test cricket. At tea England were secure on 74 for 1, no wicket lost in the session, Brearley 33, Randall 37 and Higgs having allowed only two runs off his six overs.

That stranglehold was freed, for one ball at any rate, in the next over when Brearley pulled a shortish wrong'un for four, but the battle continued with all the pre-tea intensity, with pleasing strokes less frequent than the careworn defensive variety. Brearley was enjoying the intellectual challenge posed by Jim Higgs, but when he inside-edged Hogg for a single he deemed it politic to apologise when he got down to the bowler's end. 'Hoggy' seemed to grunt.

A Brearley cover-drive brought three off Higgs, reduced by a short run, and Randall helped make up for the lapse with a perfect on-drive for four. The leg-spinner seemed to be turning more and more each over, with Maclean taking the ball well above his right shoulder.

Higgs switched to the Paddington end, loping in with a lovely rhythm and a model side-on delivery, sending the odd 24-yarder down, compelling constant scrutiny by all in his sights, batsman, 'keeper, slips men. The score stayed poised on 99 for a long time, as shots went to fieldsmen and acute spinners were let go, but at last, at exactly five o'clock, the hundred came, in total and partnership, the batsmen 47 each, a tidy moment for drinks.

Brearley won the 'race' to fifty, hitting a full-toss from Border for a couple after having batted for 207 minutes and faced 182 balls, as satisfying a half-century as he can ever have made. Higgs then decided to bowl around the wicket, and Randall actually *drove* his first ball through square leg for two to make his own fifty. Shortly it was 111, and again the evil treble struck. If no further wicket fell this evening, the match would have been poised intriguingly, but Australian faces lit up when, out of the blue, Border took his first Test wicket, getting one through Brearley as he pushed forward.

Gooch came in with forty minutes to go, and listened to a few words from his captain at the gate before knuckling to his task. It was almost a quarter of an hour before he stole his first run. The ground was quiet now, and the mess was beginning to show as many of the crowd of 13,659 departed to reveal a stack of litter. During the Randall-Brearley stand a cluster of young Englishfolk by the 'bob' stand were going through their dischordant repertoire, appropriating the World Series chorus with the adaptation 'Come on, Pommies, come on', and failing disastrously to reach the high notes in *You'll Never Walk Alone* and other soccer songs. The bigger, browner Australians all around them grew tired of this, and began the slow handclap, which the semi-delirious group, swaying in the burning sun, cleverly used for their own purposes, changing their beat. There seemed no problem out there that a piece more ice on the head would not fix.

Higgs might have been tiring as he let go a full-toss to Gooch which was gladly pulled for three, but Randall was quite startled by his, which was practically head-high. He smashed it for a single.

Hogg came on for a final plunge with ten minutes to go, a move which Gooch would have greeted with pleasure – Randall too, after the strain and restraint of so many overs of spin. Higgs had bowled 18 overs for 31 runs.

A pull for three by Randall off a short one from Hogg and four to leg off a friendly full-toss from Border were the last shots in anger in a day of few such shots, and England went to the rest day 133 for 2, just nine runs behind, with Randall 65 (in 254 minutes) and Gooch 6. Yesterday's fightback in the wake of the dismal first day had been followed up stoutly, with the only hiccough coming in Boycott's shock dismissal. It was truly a fight for the Ashes, with many answers still forthcoming.

Fourth day

Mike Brearley said on the rest day that he wanted to set Australia at least 200, and felt that 230 would take some getting. He also referred to the ordeal undergone by Geoff Boycott when fielding on the boundary. Eggs, fruit, ham, gherkins were thrown at him and there was a stream of abuse to go with it. His plight worsened with that duck – his first in Tests for just on ten years – and a misunderstanding as he returned to the dressing-room after it. Jack Birney, a publicity-conscious politician, offered condolences but received for his trouble a comment to which he took exception. A request for a written apology was said to be on its way – on Parliamentary notepaper.

The heat was still excessive as England started the quest for security. Everyone was wilting in the heat. Yet it was odd to overhear Alex Bannister say to the telephone operator as he finished putting his story through to London: 'What's the weather like?' After being told of the snow and ice and chaos, he retorted: 'It's not too good here either!' Different problems though.

A look through the museum helped focus attention before play began. It is modest in size but houses such items as Arthur Mailey's boots, Victor Trumper's bat, Reg Duff's cigar case, Hedley Verity's cap, and Bert Oldfield's caps and gloves. There is also a silver hat, about three inches high, given to C. T. B. Turner after his hat-trick against Victoria in 1886, and some of 'Fergie's' score-charts. Charlie Macartney's and Alan Davidson's boots repose there, as well as the bat with which Syd Gregory scored 201 against England in 1894. Most unusual is the 'box' dented by Jack Gregory.

From one end, the Hill end, there was no danger of dented boxes for an hour and a half as Jim Higgs sent down eight overs of leg-spin. He came close to a wicket twice, when Gooch played forward and Wood at silly mid-off narrowly failed to hold the catch as he hit the ground, and when the same man edged fast between Hughes at first slip and Border at second. The Victorian's luck was to improve when he changed ends.

Hogg's opening spell of three overs yielded only two runs, and he got one up nastily at Gooch in his second. Hurst, who replaced him, flung a full-toss at Randall, waist-high, but a cover-drive for three took him to 70, and England at last drew level on aggregate when Gooch took a single off Hurst even though Toohey retrieved from a diving save. After a three through slips by Randall, the first of two drinks breaks was taken, after which Gooch had his escape.

An ABC cameraman fell from his parapet behind and above the

sightscreen at the Noble Stand end at this point, causing himself some nasty damage and Randall to pull away from the wicket as Hurst came in. Once again calm was restored with a boundary, an easy pull in front of square. Dymock replaced Hurst, and the fifty stand came in 108 minutes. Still Yallop refrained from taking the new ball, putting his trust in Higgs and Border.

Higgs struck at last when Gooch tried to punch him to cover but succeeded only in lobbing the ball to Wood's left at silly point. The fieldsman threw himself spectacularly and held it one-handed. Three down for 169, 27 ahead, and Gower in, his state of health giving some concern. Like the weather, he had an abnormal temperature.

Leicestershire's slender genius saved England from returning a completely palsied run-ration in the morning session. He immediately cover-drove Higgs for three and then placed a full-toss for four. Soon he was sweeping fine for another boundary and on-driving the toiling Higgs for three more runs. Randall was not going to get his century before lunch, if he was getting it at all, and the crowd, well down on the previous days' attendances, grew more and more frustrated and restless.

At lunch England had made 191 for 3, Randall 87, Gower 18, with the two hours' play having produced 58 runs, Randall 22 of them. It was hot in the Press-box and hot outside it, the sweat dripping onto the typewriter, the brain steamy, the eyes stinging with salt. What it was like out there in the middle, under a crash helmet, or, worse still, to be bowling, goodness only knew.

Dymock and Higgs got things under way again, each with a maiden, and Randall moved off 87 after fifteen minutes on the sinister number. When Gower let his bat drop like a heavy pendulum on an off-break (to him) from Higgs, the ball blistered across the outfield to the fence in front of the pavilion. He pulled a long-hop from Higgs that kept low to raise the 200 in 82 overs, and at 204 for 3, after 84 overs, the new ball was taken at last. Randall liked the look of it, driving Dymock square for four and taking two backward of square leg to go to 95. Then Hogg paced out his run.

If there is one thing Derek Randall seems to enjoy above all else when batting it is the short ball. 'Hoggy' gave him one and he pulled it with the relish of a drunk offered a beer. That took him to 99. Would he hover there for long? The next ball was short too, and the shot was repeated, for another four, and he had at last added a mate to his 1977 Centenary Test century. The surprise was that he of all people should have taken so long. Not only had it gone a long way towards saving England, but it had occupied longer than any other century in the history of England-Australia Tests, another Englishman, Bob Woolmer (The Oval, 1975), having held the previous record of 396 minutes. Randall's hundred came in 411 minutes, was built on grit and stamina, and contained nine boundaries, and it was questionable whether this or the 1977 Melbourne century was the greater effort. Both were monumental in their response to England's desperate need, and both showed that, for all his jinks, Randall is more than a 'Flash Harry'.

Before the over was out Hogg dug another one in and this time Randall hooked fine, beating the fieldsman to the fence – or what there was showing of it through the advertisement boards. The scoreboard, too, which has told so many, many tales over the years, is plastered with garish ads. But it now had to update the story by recording Gower's dismissal. With Hogg bowling round the wicket, there were almighty shouts for a catch behind and then an lbw, but the first ball of Hogg's 18th over was a foot wide of off stump, inviting the drive from a person like Gower, and the edge whistled through to Maclean, who now seemed to be back to his old self. Gower would not have walked, but the umpire gave him the signal, and his useful 34, off 68 balls, made way for Botham, England 237 for 4, 95 ahead. Hogg, deliberately or otherwise, was soon probing Botham with a bail-high full-toss, which was played back by a startled Roman legionnaire.

Australia's next chance came when Higgs came back and had Randall, 113, in two minds with his first ball. Playing a kind of stand-up cut, he edged low towards Hughes's left hand, but the slipsman was on his heels and got down to it too late. An inside-edge by Randall off Hurst put England 100 ahead, time for further fly repellant to be applied to Randall's sweaty brow by the umpire – something which caused Yallop to protest. This should not be done during an over, he said. The Australian captain also took it upon himself to galvanise the slips field, putting Hughes out at silly mid-on. Hogg had left the field now, anxious to stay alive, as were we all. The concentration was giving best to the sticky heat, and batsman and wicketkeeper were party to a piece of poor cricket when Randall on 117 played loosely at Hurst and inside-edged low to Maclean. The 'keeper hadn't even to recover from being wrong-footed, but he fumbled the catch and put it down. Australia's morale was again put to the test.

The longer this day went on the more the game resembled that which Americans and certain others have never been able to grasp. It seemed to slow down just short of a halt. Yet there was a lit fuse fixed to it. A rush of wickets, and Australia were in with a chance to make the series two-all. An acceleration by England, particularly if allied to a collapse (for no declaration was likely to leave Australia a challenge), could see Australia facing a kind of embarrassment tomorrow evening. The match had shifted face, slowly as a stirring sea-monster which was just as liable to revert to sleep or rise heavily and dramatically to the surface.

At tea England were 247 for 4, Randall 119, Botham 2, 56 runs having been made since lunch, two fewer than in the morning session. Higgs and Hurst resumed after the break, and Randall, soon after pulling Higgs for four, was missed off him at slip, Yallop this time being the offender. It was not a difficult catch, going to his left (natural) hand, but it made Australia's task that much more tantalising. England's saviour had now been missed three times between 113 and 124, and had also survived a concerted appeal for a catch at the wicket down the leg side during this period. Border, with his sleeves buttoned at the wrists, came on around 4.30 pm.

There was a four, all run, for the perspiring Randall when a back-cut got past a tumbling Darling, and his score now, 132, was the highest of the series so far, passing Hughes's 129 at Brisbane, and after drinks there was a further landmark when Higgs conceded his hundredth run. It had taken England 41½ Higgs overs to get him to the century, and it triggered a wicket. Botham popped the next ball up for Wood, at short cover, to run in and collect the catch low down. At 267 for 5 England now led by 125, and Australia were in with a chance again. Derek Randall – 'Arkle' – was still out in front. Would he fall at the next fence? Would his lungs stand up to the strain? Or would his brother runners shield him from being overtaken?

He pulled a short ball from Border from outside off stump through midwicket for two in a manner reminiscent of Denis Compton, and Miller was reassured enough to discard his helmet for a sunhat. A rare Higgs full-toss went from Randall's bat to the Hill boundary with a minimum of delay, and at ten-past-five Hogg came back. This was going to be a crucial thrust as well as a test of his character.

Randall called for a quick single and had his 150, and when the kids and others ran on, for once he didn't want to know, down on his haunches, breathing deeply. Drinks soon came out once more, giving Miller the chance to reclaim his helmet, and when Hogg embarked on his 22nd over, the breakthrough was imminent.

Randall seemed to be lbw when only three, a day and a half ago. Now Hogg struck his pads, and umpire French thought about the loud appeal for only a second or two before giving the batsman out and bringing the fieldsmen back to life like the resumption of frozen movie footage. Randall's epic was over after twelve minutes short of ten hours, but he did not go willingly. He glared at the umpire most of the way and spat his gum out with an angry twitch of the neck. The decision looked perfect.

The lead at this stage was 150 (Randall's total, by chance) with four wickets to fall, not one of them in any way commanding, and Australia must have felt close to a golden opportunity after a gruelling day. When Taylor was hit on the pads first ball hearts were in throats, but the new batsman and Miller went carefully about their task as the clock-hand moved up to complete the last hour. Higgs, whose length was now open to sympathetic criticism, was placed through cover by Miller to raise 300 in the 125th over, Australia having been in the field for ten hours and five minutes.

At the close of the fourth day England, 304 for 6 (Miller 16, Taylor 3), led by 162 runs, which gave Australia an edge, even if not pronounced. The fightback by England met with anything but universal approval, the feeling being that runs made were as important as hours used up, but wickets lost to adventurous strokes would have dashed to pieces the big rescue operation, and it was, after all, England who held the Ashes and had to be robbed of them.

Graham Yallop, unusually subdued that evening, agreed that the Ashes had once again thrown a series into a negative mood. He could not quite bring himself to confess that in the same position he would have demanded complete caution, but the Australian Press was united in its condemnation of England's tactics. For a batsman with Botham's aggressive instincts to make six singles only in an hour and a half there had to be very firm instructions from the pavilion, and for a man of Randall's bubbling energy to deny himself all risk for nearly ten hours there had to be a ferocious determination throughout the English camp to wipe out all memory of the pathetic first innings. Frustrating as it was for the Australians,

I could not feel anything but admiration for the way the batsmen sold themselves so dearly. More runs would obviously have been welcome, but rearguard actions are a frame of mind. There is no in-between. It has to be total commitment of the mind. As it was, by losing Randall towards the end of the day England were still some distance from safety. Yallop gave a guarantee that he would chase any reasonable requirement on the final day. No Australian would tolerate otherwise.

The Australian captain paid fulsome tributes to Higgs for his marathon performance, and to Border for his 1 for 23 off 21 overs, but asked for an adjective to apply to Randall's efforts, he said, after some thought, 'Patient'. Nothing else.

Fifth day

England lost only one wicket before drinks were taken after an hour's play. Australia's frustration continued, with the eventual target growing more remote. Two byes came in Higgs's opening over, and he had Miller in all kinds of trouble, especially with the googly. Hogg bowled from the Noble Stand end and tested Taylor with a bouncer. Soon he broke through for his 33rd wicket of the series, equalling Jeff Thomson's record for an Australian fast bowler against England. He had Miller leg-before, playing only half-forward, his 17 having taken 96 minutes.

Emburey looked a lot more confident than usual. He steered Hogg's slower ball to third man for two, and attacked Higgs with a series of sweeps. More precious runs came from an elegant square-drive for two by Taylor, and it was Emburey's job next to weather two successive short ones from Hurst. The first dropped just short of Dymock at square leg and the other flew past Wood at silly mid-on. A fine sweep for four off Higgs took Emburey to 12, and at drinks England were 327 for 7, 185 ahead. Emburey at this point deemed it prudent to put his helmet on.

Border came on for Hurst, but it was the toiling Higgs who was about to reap his long-overdue desserts. Emburey tried to on-drive him, and the ball curled out to cover, square, where Darling hurried in for the catch. Next ball, Willis played predictably forward and was taken by Toohey at second slip, and suddenly there was the prospect of a hat-trick. Hendrick, phlegmatic as ever, saved it.

The Derbyshire pair put on a dozen vital runs for the last wicket, Taylor swinging a Border full-toss for four and Hendrick hitting Higgs through cover for another. Then, at 12.22 pm, Australia's torment was over. Higgs found the edge of Hendrick's bat, Toohey took another catch, and England's two-day innings was over for 346. The official time of the innings was 703 minutes, and Australia's target was 205 in four-and-a-half hours – or to be precise, three hours 28 minutes plus 15 overs. In other words, 45 runs per hour, about 50 per cent above the rate for the first four days and a bit. It threatened to be a gripping afternoon.

Willis opened the attack, but after two overs, the first of which had Darling in trouble, the second seeing a Wood hook land first bounce into the pavilion seats, he left the field.

Brearley fielded out at mid-on, and fell on his bottom as he chased a Wood on-drive. Meanwhile, Hendrick and Botham guarded the slips in a field that combined attack with defence as nearly perfectly as human calculation would allow at this stage.

Emburey, perhaps Australia's biggest hazard, bowled the last of the five overs before lunch, and turned a couple sharply on Darling. But the leg-trap had to wait for the time being. Everyone had a thoughtful lunch.

The 15 without loss off five overs at the interval was soon enlarged as Wood and Darling went for their strokes. Wood pulled Emburey shakily for two but followed it with a cut and a sweep, both for four, and when Emburey, the potential danger-man, went over the wicket Darling pulled him for four. The same stroke against the same bowler then brought trouble to Botham, who was fielding close at square short leg. The full-blooded shot cannoned into his helmet, inflicting a split in the plasticised surface and leaving the fieldsman very dazed when he eventually got to his feet. After a glass of water and a delay of several minutes he carried on, though positioned now out at mid-off. Without the helmet he might have been killed. Without it he would almost certainly not have been fielding so close. Which again raises the question of whether this armour should be permitted to fieldsmen.

Whether or not he was shaken by the incident, Darling's time was just about up. He played defensively at Hendrick and Gooch fell to his right to scoop up the catch, Australia's first wicket tumbling at 38 after 51 minutes.

Emburey's three overs cost 19 runs, and Brearley chose to put him back on ice and give Miller a try. Wood sliced a drive into the cover regions for two and then hit Hendrick straight back into the stumps. When Hughes crossbatted Miller for two more and Wood was in some discomfort against Hendrick the task began to loom ominously large. Yet it was indiscretion, not England pressure, that brought about Australia's second setback.

Wood drove pleasantly to cover's right and set off for a run. Hughes hardly left his crease, seeing the ball go Botham's way, and turned his back after refusing a run. Wood carried on running, Botham fielded and returned by the side of the bails for Taylor to remove them, and Wood was run out by almost the length of the pitch. It was a savage blow to Australia's hopes, made the worse by its unnecessary nature.

With both openers gone for 44, Australia were really on the defensive. To go down here, guns blazing, would mean no Ashes for a couple more years at least. It was wickets in hand that mattered if a last-hour assault was to be launched.

Their position deteriorated further eight minutes later when Yallop, having made only one, misunderstood Hendrick's slower ball and was caught by the bowler. He was starting to turn his wrists, detected the reduced pace, and held the face of the bat forward. But he could not keep the ball down. He might have profited after all by playing it at an angle. Anyhow, he was out, and he glared unforgivingly at the pitch as he departed.

At three down for 45, the general feeling seemed to be that Australia were done for. None of the top three was now going to make the eighty or so that was considered vital to victory, but the requirement remained a fairly ordinary 205, and it needed only one man to run amok for half an hour for England to have to tighten up.

There were some fighting words on some of the banners draped over the pickets, one of them suggesting that 'Bob (Willis) bashes the Bruces (Aussies)', another that it was 'Ashes to England, Australia to dust'. And soon after Hughes had raised the half-century with a lofted on-drive off Miller, the latter slogan came closer to reality. Hughes stood up to play the spinning ball from Miller, and Emburey, in helmet, took a simple catch. Four down for 64, and the self-sacrificing efforts of Randall and company beginning to take on greater significance.

Emburey joined Miller in the attack, both men having seven men on the leg side to Toohey, Hendrick having returned an admirable 10-3-17-2. Toohey was soon putting up a sharp chance to square short leg, Gooch, which the fielder could not arrest, but Border raised a big cheer when he opened his score with a massive pull off Miller.

Botham split his pants getting down to a Toohey hit to mid-wicket, but two lovely strokes by Border, one to leg, one to the off boundary after two steps down the pitch, threatened nobody's attire, only the woodwork on the boundary fence. It was heartening for the spectators, but their collective heart sank just afterwards when Toohey failed again. He played over a ball from Miller, and his being bowled saved him from being stumped. Australia's biggest hope at the start of the season had now returned scores of 1, 1, 81 not out, 0, 32, 20, 1 and 5 – 141 runs at an average of 20. He would be a lucky man to hold his place now.

Maclean headed the tail, but gave it no inspiration. He played helplessly forward to his 11th ball and gave a bat-pad catch to Botham on the off side which he accepted in an attitude of prayer. That sent Australia to tea in a sick state at 76 for 6, with the not-out batsman's task 'Bordering' on the impossible. The New South Welshman was 13 and looked in no difficulty, because he judged the line and the length, did not panic, and used his wrists skilfully. He was always balanced, always ready to use his feet, and the comparisons with Neil Harvey took on more validity all the time.

Border's dazzling pull stroke came on display often after the interval, with Australia needing 129 with only four wickets left. He caned Emburey for one boundary, and in a Miller over he twice battered the boards in front of the construction sight.

But between these two overs Australia suffered two more casualties. Dymock played Emburey into his stumps and five minutes later, also scoreless, Hogg came forward and gave Botham an innocent bat-pad catch. That made it 85 for 8, and an early finish seemed certain.

There was an amusing moment when Border objected to substitute fieldsman Lever being positioned at silly mid-on, *not* his specialty position, and he was moved back to mid-on, where he was more at home. Higgs continued to hang on, irrespective of who was breathing down his neck, winning enthusiastic applause every time he played out an over, and Border went on looking for the hittable ball, swinging Emburey for another four to bring up the hundred in 178 minutes, and off-driving him with the sweetness of a low golf drive to the members' stand.

Higgs's stay at the wicket, 31 minutes, was longer than that of four of his seniors, but Emburey beat him in the end, lbw, and with one wicket standing and the time only 4.41 pm everyone held his breath for the *coup de grace*.

False alarm number one came when Gooch at slip thought he had caught Hurst off Emburey. The ball was tossed high and the fieldsmen made to race from the arena. But umpire French was unimpressed. Number two came when Brearley thought he had Hurst off bat and pad. Again the ball got a prodigious tossing into the stratosphere. This time Miller was the disappointed bowler.

When Border leapt at Emburey and hoisted him to deep mid-off the match was all over again ... but Lever spilt the catch off his fingertips, running away from the wicket, to howls of excitement and discouragement, and there was still all to play for.

Brearley was unhappy when Border called for a drink just as the final 15 overs became due, but there was only one blow to come from the bat, a huge off-drive by Border, his ninth boundary, which had no backspin on it, or it might have given him a three instead, and kept him the strike. At the other end, at four minutes past five, and the total menacingly on 'triple Nelson', Hurst was bowled swinging at Emburey and England had retained the Ashes.

There were the customary scenes of jubilation on the field as players hugged one another, but outside the fence there were areas of stunned silence. Hope had turned to frustration as the days passed, then hope had returned, pursued by apprehension, and finally desolation. Two-two had been on the cards, but now it was three-one and there seemed nothing left to fight for, by either side. The feeling would pass. But in two-and-a-half hours the possibility of a pulsating series had been dashed in the faint puffs of fifth-day dust, Australia's confusion and incompetence scratched in it in large lettering.

While Graham Yallop got away from it all with a two-mile run, and Rick Darling immersed himself in a newspaper, Graeme Wood and Geoff Dymock vented their feelings on a heavy punchbag in the Australian dressing-room. Rodney Hogg had a gentle rub-down, and gave me a tired, resigned wave. Jim Higgs looked very tired. Alan Hurst still looked like Slim Whitman, ready now perhaps to sing the sad *Song of the Old Waterwheel*.

At the other end of the old pavilion sat Michael Brearley, drinking champagne, a regular tipple for him since he took over the captaincy. Derek Randall, Man of the Match for the third time in five Tests in Australia, had sprayed everybody on the verandah with the sacred brew, and Geoff Boycott had permitted himself a good look at the massing fans through the dressing-room window, clad only in a towel. Alec Bedser, proud chairman of selectors, beamed, as did fellow selectors Charlie Elliott and Ken Barrington. The main objective had been achieved, and the men who chose the winners were entitled to some congratulations.

Brearley described the match as the best 'coming-back-from-nowhere' match in which he had played, and one incorporating an accumulation of problems unique in his experience: the intense heat, the illness of several players. 'If you get enough disasters you've got nothing left to do!'

Questioned on the matter of Botham's head blow, Brearley raised his voice: 'After all the crass statements we've had to listen to regarding helmets, this just shows you.' I asked him if Botham would have been fielding quite so close if he had been bareheaded – and earned a bouncer of my own: 'Of course,' came the sharp reply. 'Fieldsmen have been fielding there for years!' The implication had been missed, but the skipper was excused in his hour of glory.

There had been a team talk every day, and, no, he would not deny that a draw was in his sights at one point. 'We were playing for a position from which we could either draw or win.'

Not for the first time, he put the difference between the sides as England's greater depth in both batting and bowling – one bowler, Hogg, having taken about half the wickets for Australia – adding that he thought there was very little to choose between this Australian side and that of 1977.

It was a good wicket, he said, bringing out all the skills of cricket. But he regretted that England bowled too many short balls in the first Australian innings. Darling, he recalled, made about 50 of his 91 runs from cuts and pulls.

He went on: 'We shall try very hard to avoid a let-down, as happened at The Oval in '77 after we had won the series . . . and in India after we'd gone three-up. As Bob Taylor says to the other players, we must imagine every day is the first day of the series.'

It was, he said, 'very pleasing, very deep. Marvellous feeling.' And his parents, Horace and Midge, had been there to see it.

Nonetheless, World Series Cricket hardliners would be rubbing their hands with glee at the fact that the great Test revival in Melbourne had been short-lived. With two Tests still remaining, the wind was now taken out of the sails of this series. It was estimated that takings would be down by a quarter of a million dollars on the remaining two Test matches, so if Australia's comeback in Melbourne might have led to a toughening of attitude by the Board, one might now perhaps assume that England's sweeping victory would ease the way for a settlement.

FOURTH TEST MATCH

Sydney, January 6, 7, 8, 10, 11

ENGLAND

			Mins	Fours			Mins	Fours
G. Boycott	c Border b Hurst	**8**	55	0	lbw b Hogg	**0**	1	0
*J. M. Brearley	b Hogg	**17**	97	0	b Border	**53**	217	2
D. W. Randall	c Wood b Hurst	**0**	1	0	lbw b Hogg	**150**	589	13
G. A. Gooch	c Toohey b Higgs	**18**	105	1	c Wood b Higgs	**22**	130	1
D. I. Gower	c Maclean b Hurst	**7**	21	0	c Maclean b Hogg	**34**	98	3
I. T. Botham	c Yallop b Hogg	**59**	144	7	c Wood b Higgs	**6**	92	0
G. Miller	c Maclean b Hurst	**4**	5	1	lbw b Hogg	**17**	96	1
†R. W. Taylor	c Border b Higgs	**10**	34	1	not out	**21**	110	1
J. E. Emburey	c Wood b Higgs	**0**	8	0	c Darling b Higgs	**14**	49	1
R. G. D. Willis	not out	**7**	64	0	c Toohey b Higgs	**0**	1	0
M. Hendrick	b Hurst	**10**	18	0	c Toohey b Higgs	**7**	7	1
Extras (1 b, 1 lb, 2 w, 8 nb)		**12**			(5 b, 3 lb, 14 nb)	**22**		
		152				**346**		

Fall: 18, 18, 35, 51, 66, 70, 94, 98, 141. 0, 111, 169, 237, 267, 292, 307, 334, 334.
Bowling: Hogg 11-3-36-2, Dymock 13-1-34-0, Hurst 10.6-2-28-5, Higgs 18-4-42-3.
Second innings: Hogg 28-10-67-4, Dymock 17-4-35-0, Hurst 19-3-43-0,
Higgs 59.6-15-148-5, Border 23-11-31-1.

AUSTRALIA

			Mins	Fours			Mins	Fours
G. M. Wood	b Willis	**0**	3	0	(2) run out	**27**	74	2
W. M. Darling	c Botham b Miller	**91**	274	9	(1) c Gooch b Hendrick	**13**	51	1
K. J. Hughes	c Emburey b Willis	**48**	183	6	c Emburey b Miller	**15**	55	1
*G. N. Yallop	c Botham b Hendrick	**44**	140	5	c & b Hendrick	**1**	8	0
P. M. Toohey	c Gooch b Botham	**1**	5	0	b Miller	**5**	50	0
A. R. Border	not out	**60**	244	4	not out	**45**	100	9
†J. A. Maclean	lbw b Emburey	**12**	63	1	c Botham b Miller	**0**	8	0
R. M. Hogg	run out	**6**	13	1	(9) c Botham b Emburey	**0**	5	0
G. Dymock	b Botham	**5**	66	0	(8) b Emburey	**0**	8	0
J. D. Higgs	c Botham b Hendrick	**11**	40	0	lbw b Emburey	**3**	25	0
A. G. Hurst	run out	**0**	5	0	b Emburey	**0**	20	0
Extras (2b, 3lb, 11nb)		**16**			(1lb, 1nb)	**2**		
		294				**111**		

Fall: 1, 126, 178, 179, 210, 235, 245, 276, 290. 38, 44, 45, 59, 74, 76, 85, 85, 105.
Bowling: Willis 9-2-33-2, Botham 28-3-87-2, Hendrick 24-4-50-2, Miller 13-2-37-1,
Emburey 29-10-57-1, Gooch 5-1-14-0.
Second innings: Willis 2-0-8-0, Hendrick 10-3-17-2, Emburey 17.2-7-46-4, Miller 20-7-38-3.
Toss won by England. Umpires: R. C. Bailhache & R. A. French.

*Captain †Wicketkeeper

ENGLAND WON BY 93 RUNS

9. SOMETHING COMPLETELY DIFFERENT

Like an airbed with the stopper out, the Test series had undergone a sudden deflation, and it was an opportune time for attention to be diverted temporarily. The Benson & Hedges Cup match in Sydney on January 13 brought further disappointment for the sponsors, only forty minutes' play being possible before rain set in, forcing an abandonment later, Australia 17 for 1, Roger Tolchard, his fate awaiting him within a couple of days, missing two catches behind the wicket in that short time and holding one from Graeme Wood. At Newcastle a couple of days later, Tolchard took an awful blow in the face while trying to hook a short one from giant New Zealander Glyn Davis, playing for Northern NSW. One of the few England XI batsmen not to wear a helmet, 'Tolch' paid the price with a fractured cheekbone, and spent a week in hospital. Yorkshire's David Bairstow, unlucky to have missed original selection, replaced him in the side for the final month of the tour.

Geoff Boycott made 117 not out in the England XI's nine-wicket victory in Newcastle, his second century of the tour, neither of them first-class, and the team moved down to Tasmania, captain Mike Brearley remaining in Sydney. Before joining them in the island State, I took a trip to Papua New Guinea to see how that country's Prudential World Cup preparations were progressing. The opportunity, presented by Air Niugini, was too good to miss, and the findings were unexpected.

To start with, a sum equal to £15,000 was needed to send the team away, and only £300 lay in the special kitty, all approaches to local business for sponsorship having failed. PNG Cricket Association treasurer Ray Seymour and publicity officer Brian Fry understandably looked towards Fiji with envious eyes, for that nation was going to send its side to England in May with the assistance of a wealthy Arab who owned a hotel on the main island. In Port Moresby all was pessimism, with time running out, the team not yet selected, and the greatest moment in the island's 85-year cricket history apparently going begging.

The problems surrounding the survival of cricket in Papua New Guinea are unique. The towns on the northern coast are only slowly casting off the long-term German influence, and cricket is not yet played in the schools there. Club cricketers are put to great expense to play competitively, since travel between the main towns scattered throughout the mountainous jungle terrain is costly by air – and the hazards, with the mists, air pockets and multiple peaks, are such that over 170 light-aircraft crashes have been recorded in the past nine years. Very few of the players had even sampled a turf pitch, but the general feeling seemed to be that there were enough good players available to make a fight of their elimination rounds in the World Cup, where they were grouped with Argentina, Bermuda, East Africa and Singapore.

PNG's cricketing strength stems from fast bowling, and Kila Alewa, a six-foot-two Port Moresby national, is so swift that in club cricket he bowls off only five paces, for fear of maiming someone on the concrete wickets. There must be more like him, if only they can be induced to play and undergo coaching. The Association had plans to engage a national administrator-coach, probably from Australia. The game then should rise to even greater popularity. The missionaries from Britain did their stuff before the First World War, diverting men from cannibalism to cricket, and now the natives play cricket enthusiastically as well as watch it. Clive Lloyd's six out of the Sir Hubert Murray Stadium in 1975 is still talked about incredulously.

So, with players such as Sam Malum, who scored a hundred against the West Indians, Ili Tarua, a lawyer and opening batsman, Tau Ao, a fine 18-year-old batsman, and his brother Lou, a wicketkeeper, Vavine Pala, left-arm swing bowler, and Charlie Harrison, veteran bowler, all not knowing whether they would be in England in four months' time, and Sir John Guise's national record innings of 350 still unlikely to be threatened, cricket in PNG was poised either to progress or slip backwards. With luck (and all will be known by the time these words are read) the £500 Birmingham hotel deposit might yet prove not to have been paid in vain.

There was just time to drive to the beautifully laid out war cemetery within sight of the Kokoda Trail, where the white headstones stood out starkly in regimented rows against the colourful tropical vegetation, and the mosquitoes, black and weighty, showed us no mercy. General Blamey's camp had been close by, and Macarthur had been in Port Moresby for a time. Ray Lindwall had caught malaria here. Jack Iverson had developed his middle-finger spinners in a steamy jungle clearing. There was much to visualise as I stood at the highest point above town on the way back, seeing the sparkling coral reef beyond the harbour, the waterside shanty settlement, the wreck of an Australian hospital ship sunk by the Japanese, and the wing of a USAF Lightning all in one sweeping view. Soon, like so many other glimpses of another area, another age, it was receding into the memory bank, for wistful recall at the unlikeliest times ahead.

The Air Niugini return flight, when an abundance of bookings compelled me to accept with mock reluctance a first-class seat, was elevating in several senses. Champagne is a suitable antidote to many things, and I was at one with the heavens as the earphones poured Satie's *Trois Gymnopedies* (not a homily to England's slip fielders) into my consciousness.

Within hours I was at the Sydney Cricket Ground, watching the World Series one-day match between the Australians and West Indians, glad to be back with son and brother, carefree in the midst of an animated, convivial, throaty crowd, when admittedly I might soon be longing to be back on the warm hilltops of Port Moresby, with only the sound of the birds and the distant barking dogs, and the unpolluted warmth of the sub-tropic atmosphere. Was cricket losing its lifelong pull on me, I wondered? Was I a victim of the rupture of the game? Was it fatal or would it heal in time? Was I becoming another Tony Hancock, wondering what, just what, it could all be about? No fear! The World Series match elicited strong feelings. Feelings of outrage that cricketers could be allowed to take the field in all-pink outfits, and all-lemon. It made a mockery of the game. When Gordon Greenidge passed by on his exit after making nought, he looked like a cricketer who had been run down by an express train – a gory sight, red cap, pink shirt, white sweater, pink trousers, pads painted (patchily) pink, white boots. The fieldsmen all looked like service station attendants. It distracted from the ebb and flow of the cricket.

The West Indians won a match interrupted by rain. They won after scenes of confusion that would have befitted a soccer match, and Ian Chappell became very angry at everything, especially the crowds running on and thumping the players, sometimes very painfully, even though they could almost be excused on the count that they were incited in almost every way by the crowd-stirring actions of many of the participants – the box-patting, the posturing, the delayed umpiring decisions, the theme music filtered through the loudspeakers at psychological moments. Gorillas, 'Chappelli' called them. So many of the crowd did indeed behave as if they were at the zoo. The question still beckoned: What kind of spectator were the Packer matches attracting? When the attendances at the Melbourne Supertest the previous week were unexpectedly dismal it was suggested that the presence in the city of the pop group Chicago had a lot to do with it.

The inescapably amusing thing about the all-coloured strip was that coral pink, the shade forced upon the West Indians, has very strong homosexual associations in the Caribbean. The Australians could have been no happier, either, when a Melbourne newspaper editorial reminded the customers that yellow was traditionally linked with cowardice.

Sydney was proving once again to be the stronghold of World Series Cricket. The ground was packed solid, and even after the evening rain, there were many thousands at the ground upon resumption. I must have been one of the few who felt something of an intruder. For the first time in my life I did not feel at home at a cricket match, did not feel part of the occasion, even though almost every single player was a personal friend or friendly acquaintance. The stands and terraces were turned into baseball bleachers. It could even have been a bullfight, so deep-throated were the reactions of the multitude. General reporters, not cricket-writers, dwelt in the Press-box. There was some electrifying cricket, to be sure, especially when Dennis Lillee was pounding them down, but there was a bloodthirstiness and a crude fundamentalism about it all, a total lack of subtlety.

As the moths gathered in greater numbers, drawn by the fierce artificial light that flooded the air for several square miles, the match ended to a burst of celebratory fireworks that had others besides myself jumping out of their skins. It was the perfect preparation for a few days in pure and peaceful Tasmania, a journey undertaken in the hope that all the acrimony would soon be a thing of the past after the recent talks between ICC and WSC representatives in Sydney.

I thought the TAA T-Jet must have got lost. We landed at Launceston, and it could have been Cumberland or Devon or Sussex. It was also much cooler. On to Hobart, and the arms were stretched another centimetre or two as I plodded with my suitcases through near-deserted streets with night drawing in, eventually settling in at the Waratah, a cosy hotel in an area where Martin Cash, the bushranger, lay low before his capture in 1843. Before turning in, I managed a hotdog and a cup of chocolate while offering a silent toast to my second son, whose eighteenth birthday it was in faraway England. The bond was ELO's *Rockaria* on the jukebox.

The first day of the three-day match dawned in brilliant sunshine, but there was no great crowd to see the triumphant Englishmen. They had drawn over 7000 for their easy victory in the one-day match at Launceston, but there seemed to be some sort of hangover from Tasmania's splendid victory over mighty Western Australia in Hobart the previous weekend in the Gillette Cup final, when the attendance was so unmanageable that people were hanging out of the trees, the drink flowed faster than the Derwent River, and one portly man even broke his ankle trying to climb back over the fence after visiting the wicket to register his compliments.

Now Jack Simmons' heroes were up against it on a sporty wicket against Chris Old at his best. England's forgotten man took 6 for 42, including John Hampshire for a duck. Much was made of Yorkshire's new captain and the axed Boycott. If they passed the time of day to each other it was the full extent of conversation between them, and when Boycott found himself seated beside Hampshire at lunch on the third day, he quietly got up and left.

Boycott's 90 not out in five-and-a-half hours before Willis's declaration might have been turned into a century with any gesture towards urgency. But this is not Boycott's way. Gower drove with great poise and beauty in a breezy 30, triggering recollections that Frank Woolley once made 305 on this ground. His namesake, Roger Woolley, Tasmania's wicketkeeper, unhappily made only 4 and 0.

David Bairstow was given his first gallop when he was called upon to field as substitute, and his first throw from short third man clouted the umpire on the thigh, fifteen yards from the stumps. Far worse followed. On the second day, while doing hamstring-stretching exercises in the dressing-room, our accident-prone reinforcement crashed to the floor, chipping an already chronically battered nose. He was amusing during lunch, pretending, and sometimes not pretending, that he had double vision, sitting flushed and animated, towel around shoulders like a fighter after a scrap – one of those when it is not altogether clear if he won or not – scrutinising everyone in the room and passing opinion in rich Yorkshire tones.

Rain ruined Saturday's play, and after a late start on the last day Tasmania played out a draw, Willis, with his tricky sense of humour, calling upon Boycott to bowl the final over to Hampshire, who pulled a short one for four.

The hospitality of the TCA committee was something to be experienced, lunch being taken beside a full-length oil of Don Bradman, by J. C. Goodhart. The hospitality of the cricket community, too, was exceptional, and some of us were privileged to visit private homes and be taken round this elegant and historic city. When rain finally washed out the sight of Mount Wellington – which presides over all like a great dark maternal breast – and all the other mounds which constitute decorative, undulating Hobart town, the scene was more English than ever.

Another idyllic afternoon of blue sky and soft fleecy cloud, cruising over another piece of Australia, then a placid Bass Strait, with another allocation of TAA's special in-flight service. In this short break from the rigours of the tour I had incubated a growing reluctance to head for the mainland again. I was told by my hosts not to whisper a word to the world outside on the subject of Hobart's assets. But I defy that demand, knowing two things: that the town and surroundings are unpolluted, civilised, friendly and peaceful, and that the inhabitants are proud enough of their environment to forgive me for doing so. Perhaps by the end of the 1980s the island will be a semi-independent tax haven like Jersey.

Back in Melbourne for the Benson & Hedges Cup game, I was asked often what I thought about WSC's challenge to England to play a five-day match in February for a winner-take-all prize of $50,000, the money going to charity if the Australians won. The answer was all it could have and should have been: the tour programme forbade it, and those behind the offer must have known so. The only surprise was that the challenge was left so late. I felt that if the peace talks were getting somewhere, it could have made a worthwhile end-of-tour *one-day* match, perhaps even under the accursed floodlights, the takings going to old cricketers in dire financial straits – or even cricket-writers in distress. Overall the feelings were of contempt for the very idea of such a match.

But then cricket had been sullied by contempt and cynicism for twenty months now. A disinfectant swab was needed.

The B & H Gold Cup match in Melbourne resulted in a nerveless seven-wicket win for England on a pitch of variable but generally low bounce that had Rodney Hogg protesting that night that it was the worst he had ever played on. Australia seemed to be heading for a better total than 101, but Mike Hendrick, later named as Man of the Match, cut them back with four wickets, and the fielding once again was noteworthy, especially Gower's amazing diving catch at short midwicket off a bullet shot by Wood. Boycott steered the ship home – from the stern, as it were – with 39 not out, and Brearley copped an unwelcome nought at the hands of the mischievous Hogg. The crowd of 14,000 had few reasons to get worked up, and I even ventured out into the Southern Stand, where I watched Niagaras of beer go down. But they'd paid their money, and they weren't doing anything of which the roving policemen disapproved.

For England the winners' $2400, for Australia $1200 and further disgruntlement.

Once more to the tender mercies of Trans-Australia Airlines and an easeful hop beyond the Murray River, over dry brown land to Adelaide for the fifth Test match.

10. THE FIFTH TEST MATCH

ADELAIDE, JANUARY 27, 28, 29, 31, FEBRUARY 1

First day

Adelaide is yet another city of which Australia can be mightily proud. Clean (apart from its tap water, which appears to have been piped from the Ganges), squarely laid out, with wide streets and a sedate atmosphere pervading the avenues, the parks, the riverside regions. It looks marvellous from the air, set beneath the Mount Lofty Ranges – part of which, incidentally, has been painted in order to avert the eyesore which quarry work would otherwise have created. The city's hotels were almost all fully booked for the Australia Day holiday weekend and the Test match, but I managed to find a home at the Grosvenor, just a pretty walk away from the Adelaide Oval, where, on the opening day of the Test, many thousands converged from town, from farflung country areas, and from England, dozens of new tourists proclaiming themselves by their facial pallor, rhubarb-and-custard ties, and general overdressing. The teams lined up for presentation, the anthem was played, the parachutist dropped on schedule, and Yallop won the toss. To groans everywhere it was announced that Australia would bowl.

England had made no changes from the fourth Test side, but Australia dropped John Maclean and gave Western Australian wicketkeeper Kevin Wright his first cap, and Carlson came into the twelve in place of Dymock. Yardley's elevation into the eleven meant that Toohey slipped down to twelfth man and that the batting overall was slightly weakened while the scope of the bowling was expanded. Darling's right hand, cut in a recent charity match, seemed well enough knit.

When I asked a taxi-driver – among the most dependable of touchstones – why all the flags were attached to cars, he replied without hesitation that it certainly wasn't in honour of Australia's Test performances this season. Had he been at the ground on this opening day at Adelaide he would have cheered up immeasurably. Hogg began with a wide, and Hurst outstripped him with two, but England's first casualty was not long in coming. In the fourth over Hurst cut one away and found the edge of Boycott's bat and Wright held his first Test catch behind the stumps. Before this Test, Boycott had made 176 runs in eight innings in a total batting time of 1034 minutes, a rate of ten runs per hour. Against that background, the crowd could consider themselves to have been spared some tedium, albeit alongside an exhibition of immaculate batting technique.

Brearley took two behind square leg, but at 12 he fell to his doom – in the most regrettable way. Hogg, in his third over, shot one through him, and the big appeal was answered by umpire O'Connell with the finger. Brearley was recorded as caught behind, but the ball seemed to have brushed his upper arm. Young Wright, then, had written his name twice into the good book already, and Hogg had moved ahead of Thomson's series record of 33 wickets.

Gooch joined Randall, but was not to last long. Hogg greeted him with a bouncer, which he ducked, then another, from which he swayed, but in Hogg's fourth over Gooch received a very fast kicking delivery which banged into the glove as he abandoned his defensive stroke and started into an evasive retreat. Hughes ran back from slip and held the spooned catch above his head, to make England 16 for 3 after forty minutes.

Gower took strike, and Hogg gave him the obligatory bouncer first ball, from around the wicket, and struck his pads as he drove at the next. The fourth wicket, though, came at the other end. Randall edged Hurst between gully and fourth slip, and Carlson lunged to his right to bring off a dazzling one-handed catch. England now had lost Boycott (6), Brearley (2), Gooch (1), and Randall (4) for 18 runs, and Yallop's decision to put them in was vindicated.

Gower and Botham set about rescuing the side, Gower clipping Hurst past gully for the first boundary, but at 27 the fifth wicket went. Hurst had been moving the ball around a great deal off the pitch, and now he beat Gower's defensive shuffle and had him leg-before for nine. Again, England's brittle batting line-up was revealed for what it was, this time for the worst start of the series. In the best traditions, a recovery of sorts was now affected, after drinks.

Hogg, bowling as fast as at any stage of the series, inspired by his local people, peppered Botham with bouncers, but the big chap weathered them well, and erred only when he popped a slower ball over slips for four.

Yallop had to relieve Hogg (6-1-15-2) now, transferring Hurst to the River Torrens (downwind) end and giving Carlson his first bowl in Test cricket. Hurst beat Miller several times and then Carlson, from the Cathedral end, had him missed off a long-hop which he helped on its way to deepish fine leg, where Hurst muffed it. The sun was shining at him but he seemed to have positioned himself properly. The bowler could only hold his head in anguish.

Miller ran two while this was happening, opening his score, and Botham drove Carlson and then Hurst for threes. A take by Wright off Carlson drew a shattering shout from the Australians against Miller, but umpire Bailhache saw no need to budge, and soon after the fifty was raised (98 minutes) Miller edged Hurst for four and eased into a fluent pull off Carlson for four. Yardley came on just before lunch, and England went in at 71 for 5, Botham 14, Miller 25, and the lion's tail hanging limp and subdued. Hogg's figures were 2 for 15, Hurst's 3 for 26, and the ground, in which every seat was filled and most of the other space taken up, was alive with chatter.

Miller played one more nice shot, a four off his toes from Carlson, before Hogg beat him with speed and nip-back to trap him lbw for 31. The stand for the sixth wicket had picked the score up to 80 from 27, and Hogg's breakthrough meant that he had equalled Arthur Mailey's record 36 wickets in a series for Australia against England.

Ian Botham now went after the bowling, first hitting Carlson out of the attack, cutting him powerfully to the boundary by the Victor Richardson Gates and swinging the next ball through square leg for four. When Yardley came on he went for six over square leg, a blow which brought up the hundred, and then Botham ran four for a hit to long-on. The next he cut for three, but the hectic running was to bring disaster. Botham swung Yardley, and Taylor and he ran like mad. Hogg chased and cut off just by the gutter and hurled a return to the 'keeper while three runs were completed. Botham had decided there was a fourth. Taylor had stopped. And Wright's throw to the bowler's end beat him easily, although Botham was out of trouble at the other end. This made it 112 for 7, and Botham alone stood as England's hope. A dab to mid-off took him to his fifty in 128 minutes, and after drinks he swept a Yardley no-ball down to Hogg, who dropped the 'catch'. A distant hook sent the ball over Higgs's head at long leg, and a cover-drive off Hurst that hit the fence on the first bounce took him to 63, his highest score of the tour. He took to Higgs, too, when he came on, hoisting him for his second six almost into the same row of seats at square leg.

Emburey lasted nearly half an hour, but Higgs bowled him at 136, and shortly afterwards Botham's valiant effort came to an end when, facing his 100th ball, he was both caught and stumped off Higgs. He had made 74 of the 129 runs while he was at the crease, and as at Sydney, he had put some sort of face on things for England.

It remained only for Willis to extend the total with some swishing hits against the fast bowlers, making a 24 that equalled his highest Test score and had the crowd (a creditable 25,004) in convulsions. He took 18 off an over from Hurst, the first blow bringing him a remarkable six over cover point, and after a maiden from Higgs to Hendrick, Willis belted Hogg high over point for another boundary. At last, he got under one from Hogg and sent it a prodigious distance skywards for Darling to win the race and catch the ball at the stretch. It was Hogg's 37th wicket of the series, more than any other Australian had taken in a rubber against England, and behind only Laker, Bedser and Tate for the other side. It was a popular feat, recognised by the crowd and his team-mates.

So England had to make do with 169, an unthinkable kind of total on Adelaide pitches of old. But this was a 1979 pitch and these sides were 1979 sides. There was no telling any more. There was grass on the wicket, but the bounce had seemed fairly consistent, leaving the eternal query: was it good bowling and fielding or poor batting? I was inclined to believe it was a little of each.

Tea was taken between innings, and all the grief and delight was now put aside as the fifth ball of Australia's innings brought with it an accident to make even the strongest-stomached spectator feel sick with anxiety. The ball from Willis was only just short of a length, but it shot in past Rick Darling's bat and struck him below the heart, sending him straight to ground, where the urgency of the attention by fieldsmen and umpires left no-one in any doubts that Darling was seriously hurt. As he writhed, umpire Max O'Connell knelt as if to apply mouth-to-mouth resuscitation and John Emburey, suspecting breathing had stopped, administered a blow to the chest, while several players signalled frantically for medical attention. Mick Mason, the SACA's English-born physiotherapist, ran out and firstly put Darling onto his side, pulling his tongue back and the chewing gum from his mouth, and Bernard Thomas,

England's physio, also wasted no time getting to the scene. They were joined by St John Ambulancemen, and while the prone figure was lost midst helpers and distraught players, with Emburey bringing off Darling's pads, helmet and boots, the crowd remained silent, stunned, sick.

Eventually the young man was carried off, still motionless, and an announcement soon restored spirits, stating as it did that he was 'not too bad' and would be taken to hospital for observation. The game could go on. We could look to the front. It was like driving on after passing a nasty road accident.

Going in at number three in a Test match is inclined to be unnerving at the best of times. Walking to the wicket when your predecessor has been removed by stretcher is liable to prove distracting, to put it mildly. Kim Hughes – now vice-captain, ominously following Craig Sergeant, Jeff Thomson, Gary Cosier and John Maclean – got right in line, and was soon forcing Willis to the cover boundary, but Hendrick did enough with the ball to find the edge low down, and probably via boot the ball flew gullywards. Emburey projected himself forward and scooped up the catch. One down for five.

That total had only been doubled when Yallop went, getting a fine touch to Hendrick and being bowled for his first duck of the series. The pattern of the match was being established with every wicket-fall: a long stand would be the exception; Adelaide or not, life at the crease was cheap.

Border, with his Sydney success behind him, looked sound, and square-cut Botham for four when Willis was rested. He had moved to 11 while Wood stayed practically immobile, but then, driving at Botham, he got a fine touch to Taylor, and Australia were 22 for 3.

Carlson came in for his debut Test innings, but it was to last only seven minutes, and finish scoreless. It would have been no consolation that some pretty good players had begun with a duck. Botham got him, caught by the ever-reliable Taylor. The really unsettling thing about it was that Carlson appeared not to have touched the ball.

At 24 for 4, with Darling's immediate future dubious, Australia needed something courageous, and they got it in Yardley. He began to carve and pillage, much as Botham had done earlier, while Wood kept behind a rate of a run an over. When the ball was just under a length, Yardley swung at it and sent it to third man for three. When Willis came back, he looked listless, and Yardley, sensing an uncharacteristic weakness, cut him for four to raise the fifty in the 17th over, pulled him square with certainty, and an over or two later off-drove him swashbucklingly to the George Giffen Stand fence.

Wood had managed a four by steering Hendrick through gully, defeating Gower's slide at the fence. But on 16 he was missed when he edged Willis's slower ball and Botham at second slip threw himself forward to no avail.

Something similar happened when Yardley was 27. He got a thickish edge to Hendrick and again Botham floored the catch, even though it came more directly. He aimed a frightening kick at the ball in his frustration.

No more wickets fell that evening. Fourteen in a day was a fair enough ration, plus one serious injury. Yardley watched Emburey very carefully throughout four overs, all maidens, and Wood was quite indifferent towards making runs. The gulls came in, the enormous tarpaulin was draped over the square, and the crowd wended its way out, mulling over Australia's 69 for 4. It was looking like a three-day match, but a tight one at that.

Second day

Two pieces of good news: the weather, not unexpectedly, was just as beautiful on the Sunday, and Rick Darling would be fit to bat. The crowd was another large one, and the prospects for a good tussle were as strong as at any point in the series. We sat and waited.

Only three runs were added before Yardley was out, playing on to the seventh ball of the day, from Botham, and when Darling, his bruised chest protected, emerged and stepped down through the rows of seats a huge groundswell of welcome rose and spread around the arena. He took a single first ball, and the opening partnership was re-established. When he pulled Hendrick for a healthy four straight afterwards the applause was euphoric, and a bouncer from Botham saw Darling up on his toes and swinging the ball well into the seating which Botham himself had exploited with two sixes of his own. Dramatic stuff, when one remembered the winded, corpse-like figure lying by the stumps the previous afternoon. But it was all due to be cut short.

There was the trap, a square leg and a long leg, both on the fence. Botham pitched the next one up and it was allowed through to Taylor. Then the next was dug in, the irresistible Darling hook shot was unwound, and Willis, the finer of the two boundary men, had lots of time to cup his hands and bend his knees for the approaching ball. At 94 for 6 Australia were losing sight of a handy first-innings advantage.

Wright had to dig out a Botham yorker as his first ball in Test cricket, then ran a quick two, so pleased to be off the mark that he dropped his bat at the turnaround. Surviving a thunderous appeal for caught-behind off Botham, Wright raised the hundred with a three in the 32nd over, and soon the first bowling changes were made, Emburey for Hendrick at the River Torrens end and Willis for Botham. The move paid off.

Another disciplined Graeme Wood innings drew to a close at 35, after three-and-a-half hours, when he swept Emburey, lofted the shot, and gave Randall, exactly square of the wicket, time to take the catch two-handed low down: 114 for 7. Two runs later Hogg went, bowled first ball by Willis – one that came back as he moved into his stumps. The fast-bowling hero had thus made his fourth duck in six Test innings after such an impressive start in Brisbane with his top-score 36.

Higgs was having none of this duck nonsense. He had a single turned into three by a loose throw, and then defended while Wright showed what he was made of, cutting, driving, glancing, and running fast between wickets. Willis held no terrors for Wright. He once pulled him commandingly for four and a force through the covers moved with surprising speed to the fence, before his admirable debut innings ended as he played legwards to Emburey and was lbw for 29.

At 133 for 9 and with the allegedly incompetent Higgs and Hurst together, it was thought to be all over, but there ensued a frustrating – for England – and enjoyable – for Australia – last-wicket stand of three-quarters of an hour during which 31 runs were made against some not terribly imaginative pace bowling. Higgs further extended his highest Test innings to 16 before the near-infallible Gower tickled the stumps at the bowler's end to run him out, and Hurst battered 17 not out to help close the first-innings gap to a mere five runs.

Thus, at the halfway point – although the match was still less than nine hours old and fewer than 100 overs had been bowled – the balance was delicate. A substantial first-innings lead would have suited Australia, though their last innings was likely to be played on a wicket truer than on the first day and free from crumbling. It was now England's task to shut Australia out, and in the 68 minutes before tea, Boycott, 17, and Brearley, 7, embarked upon their responsibility with a determination that had some of the spectators nodding off in their comfortable seats. Hoggs finished the session by bowling off six paces and tossing down a leg-break or two, but despite Yallop's aggressive field-settings throughout the period, the Englishmen were in no trouble, and we had to dwell for the moment on the recollections of the thrills and spills of the past day and a half, and upon the fact that England had been 27 for 5 when the match was an hour old.

A quarter of an hour after the tea interval Brearley was out. Carlson, erect and clerical-looking, struck lucky at last, bringing one back a little and keeping it low to find the England captain lbw for nine. The appearance of Randall brought a sense of expectancy, but his assignment was not altogether different to that in Sydney, and nothing more than the occasional flash of brilliance was in prospect. He offered the first with a sweet cover-drive to the Giffen Stand off Hogg, but the bowler was soon coming back strong with a king-size bouncer that Wright had to take left-handed and leaping like a rocket. Hogg then confused himself and the batsman by losing his run-up but going through with a delivery off the wrong foot, rather like New Zealander Bob Cunis. It brought a few extra cheers from the embankment where a banner proclaimed The Sty, Home of the Hogg.

Meanwhile, Hurst was preparing himself to relieve his partner in pace, and when his turn came he bowled a good width, inviting the batsmen to come after him. When Randall hooked him for four a man was placed 35 yards from the bat at backward square. After drinks the hook was to prove Randall's undoing.

First, Higgs came on, potentially Australia's most penetrative bowler, curling his leg-breaks and variants from the tree-lined St Peter's Cathedral end. As always, he struck a length immediately.

Randall's demise came not for the first time from an attempted hook. He went after Hurst and topped the ball high into the line of the sun. Yardley was at midwicket, and he waited patiently and judged the catch well, making England 57 for 2.

Higgs twice fell short of a good length and was punished, Boycott and then Gooch playing similar shots off the back foot for four, but the last hour was quiet, and Boycott's concentration was much greater than that of the majority of those watching. At the close, still with no cloud anywhere visible, England had posted 82 for the loss of Brearley and Randall, in just over three hours, with Boycott happy on 38 and Gooch content on 11. The game had steadied out into the time-band wherein Australia's needs would be forged. There undoubtably would be fighting cricket ahead, and that alone would distract our minds from the overall poor quality of play.

Third day

Australia came right back into the game during the first session of this holiday Monday. With the heat even greater, the crowd was smaller but the risk of sunburn, *even in the shade*, was increased. Carlson was the surprise choice to open the bowling from the Cathedral end, a spell that was to last over an hour and a half and bring him a further wicket with the essence of economy.

Hogg took the other end, and Yallop gave him a silly point and a short gully, but they had no work to do, Gooch playing with his usual impassivity, once pulling him hard for four, and Boycott, introspective as ever, looking for that elusive Test hundred.

After four overs, his characteristic ration, Hogg, apparently without Yallop's approval, came off with 'stiffness of the inner thighs', Toohey substituting. He was to return only a short time before lunch and was therefore not entitled to bowl until the afternoon. Carlson meanwhile plugged away, and won Gooch's wicket with one that came in at the off stump and beat a wavering forward stroke. Drinks were taken at this point, 97 for 3, and Hurst came on, Boycott driving him for three to bring up 101 in 237 minutes. We then saw something that can have been witnessed very seldom in modern Test cricket: for one ball Australia had ten men on the field when Yallop, anxious to talk with Hogg, went off and no thirteenth man was to hand. He was not missed, but his return presaged the triumph Australia most wanted: Boycott got out. Hurst, having fired a few fiery bouncers past his nose, induced a back-foot cut and the snick flew just wide of Hughes, who took the chance avidly and ran round like a cup final goal-scorer.

England were now 106 for 4, and the game could not have been more evenly balanced. Gower played smoothly. It could have been any match, a charity game, a midweek county match, a backyard hit-up. He exploited the shorter side boundaries with a tuck to leg and a cover-drive off Hurst, and with Botham taking a boundary through mid-off off a Carlson outswinger, and Gower finding his way through a narrow gap in the covers when Higgs replaced Carlson, an entertaining stand seemed in the offing. But ten minutes before lunch Botham tried to force Hurst off the back foot and merely edged to third slip, where Yardley took a snap catch. That weakened England's position several points, but things got much worse in the few remaining minutes before the interval. Gower, having made an attractive 21, swung at Higgs – who was bowling around the wicket – aiming through midwicket, missed as the ball spun in, and was hit fairly high on the pad. Umpire O'Connell gave him out leg-before, and a very unhappy Gower moved slowly away with his side only 137 runs ahead overall, four wickets in hand.

Lunch was taken with England 134 for 6, Miller yet to score, Taylor 2, and the crowd's attention now riveted to events. The morning session had seemed, in prospect, to be a formality, and a dull one at that. Now the afternoon period loomed as vital for both sides, every wicket for Australia a step nearer to possible victory, every run for England worth its weight in South Australian opal.

The criticisms of the standard of batting throughout the series made tedious reading and listening, and though there was little to be gained from obsession with these shortcomings, the fact defied denial. We had seen a fair amount of grittiness, though, and now it was time for some more, from the Derbyshire pair as they gradually tugged the match back into England's grasp. Miller enhanced his confidence with consecutive pulls for four off Hurst soon after lunch, and after the new ball was taken, Taylor sent it several times to the third-man area, where fieldsmen have seldom been seen in these Tests.

Carlson, Hogg and Hurst were all tried, but in 70 minutes Miller and Taylor, sharing the duties, put fifty together by means of sensible, disciplined batting, nose over splice, mind over matter. It was in the finest traditions of Anglo-Australian warfare, and it showed, among other things and if anyone was still in doubt, that the pitch was a beauty. The stand by tea had reached 81, with Miller 31 and Taylor 46 (one run past his previous highest in Tests), and after the break the tempo continued, firm strokes, quick, alert running, enough action to keep the spectators gently on the simmer.

Boundaries were rare, but Miller clipped Higgs off the back foot to the cover fence past the fleet-footed Darling. Taylor's fifty hovered just out of reach for some time before he gained it with a four – all run – from a nice on-drive, after 144 minutes at the crease. Soon a hasty single raised the century stand, and the Woolley-Vine seventh-wicket record of 67 years ago appeared distantly in the sights just as serious thoughts of an Australian victory slowly slipped below the horizon. It was a commentary on the shortcomings of the batting that this was only the third century partnership of the series for England, the others being the 158 by Boycott and Gower at Perth and the 111 by Brearley and Randall at Sydney.

Border, diving forward at slip, got a hand to a sharp chance by Taylor, when 53, off Higgs, but Miller reached his first fifty against Australia with a soft sweep for three off Yardley, having batted just over three hours, and after another patient period a leg-bye took the stand past the England seventh-wicket record for Adelaide, set in January 1925 by Jack Hobbs and Patsy Hendren in a classic Test match won by Australia on the seventh day by 11 runs.

Hogg's incapacity kept him out of the attack and put an extra burden on the springy Hurst in particular, but the bowlers stuck to their task, once in a while leading a noisy appeal, even when the pad was struck well wide of the stumps. There was a flutter when Taylor on-drove and scuttled four, reduced to three by a short run and enlivened by Miller's helmet toppling to the ground, and the next question was whether the batsmen could beat the all-time England seventh-wicket record against Australia, held by Frank Woolley and Joe Vine since 1911-12.

First, Yallop seemed to remember all of a sudden that he had Border in his ranks, and he brought him on at the Cathedral end. The matter of the seventh-wicket record, however, was settled at the other end. Hurst had Miller playing down the leg side and the touch flew low to Wright, who got it safely into his red gauntlets. Umpire Bailhache delayed his verdict, checking with his colleague for a clean catch, and Miller left slowly, disconsolately and tiredly, though he must have felt a flow of pride in having helped make the match safe.

Taylor played quietly through the last ten minutes, with Emburey calmly beside him, and by the close England were 272 for 7, the wicketkeeper an unexpected 69 not out in 243 minutes, and the day deprived of the added distinction of a broken series partnership record by a mere nine runs.

As in Sydney, Australia had watched helplessly as the match was seized from their grasp, only this time not by any of the stars but by two of the less glamorous names in the billing, showing again what a resourceful side this England eleven was.

Fourth day

The rest day was just about the most refreshing mentally and damaging physically of the whole tour, spent in the idyllic surroundings of the Yalumba Winery at Angaston in the Barossa Valley, where mine hosts were Wyndham Hill Smith and his family and the gathering numbered a couple of hundred cricketers and cricketing people. Every label was there for tasting, and some of us went on to diving after lemons in the swimming pool and tearing shoulder muscles at tennis. Alan Shiell, the Adelaide writer who once scored 202 against MCC, drove back to the city with my shirt and trousers on his back seat, and I made it back to town later that evening wearing just Tahitian swimming trunks and thongs, a stealthy and rather sheepish return to the fold.

The raging topic now was Hogg's exit from the field on the third day, when Yallop apparently went off after him to enquire after his reasons and to persuade him to return. It seems that the fast bowler had told his captain he wanted to go off because of his leg stiffness, and when Yallop contested the matter Hogg said 'See ya' and departed. Harsh words were exchanged later in the day, and it was understood that the Board would be looking into the matter.

It was a sad episode in Hogg's otherwise gallant summer, yet if he did refuse to bowl and if he was blunt to his skipper it was, in the first instance, an expression of his sapping efforts through four-and-a-half Tests and other matches, and in the second, a symptom of the less-than-complete persuasion and command Yallop had over his men and the less-than-wholehearted response he was drawing from them. On the fourth day Hogg fielded, kept himself to himself, and we waited to see whether he would bowl.

Hurst and Carlson opened proceedings to Emburey and Taylor – whose first hundred loomed as the morning's potential sensation just as yesterday's was Tasmania's first-ever Sheffield Shield victory, an astonishing win over Western Australia brought about by a seventh-wicket stand of 172 between Woolley, 99 not out, and Jack Simmons (who else?), 78 not out.

There was no quick breakthrough, and after 25 minutes Yallop brought Higgs and then Yardley into the attack. They caused no discomfort to either batsman, and the sweep shot became the order of the day, bringing them both a steady stream of runs fine and square. At 17 Emburey was lucky, edging Yardley into and out of Border's hands as the fielder flung himself forward, but the 300 lead was soon up and then the 300 for the innings, in three minutes over ten hours. A Taylor boundary through mid-on took him to 83, and an Emburey sweep off Higgs brought the fifty stand, in 81 minutes. Yet another Taylor sweep off Yardley found the fence, taking him to 89, and a single raised his score to 90 and the nervous tension to something considerable. It increased further when the new ball became due, and Rodney Hogg marched up from the boundary, shoulders hunched, face expressionless.

Yallop made great show of talking with his chief striker, following him to the end of his run-up and discussing field-placings with him in an apparently cordial manner. Several times subsequently the captain went to Hogg and talked things over in such a way as to suggest that normal relations had been restored. It was a welcome development, ostentatious though it may have been.

Taylor, playing the innings of a lifetime, raced for another two as Yardley's throw hit the stumps, and further quick singles and a two took him to 97. A small, defiant figure under his helmet, with handkerchief at throat, Taylor stood waiting for Hogg, with lunch a few seconds away. It was the final ball of the over, and Hogg ran in off a short run. It was fast, starting to go down the leg side, and Taylor helped it on its way. But the touch was fine and Wright took the catch, mortifying the batsman, who had equalled his highest score (for the International Wanderers at Johannesburg, 1975-76), and arresting England's lead, which was surely now, in any case, well beyond Australia's range.

Bob Taylor, Derbyshire's 37-year-old model professional, had perished three runs from a momentous century, and was destined to think back a thousand times on the ball that got him. Always it would kiss the edge of his bat and always it would be swallowed by the 'keeper and always Taylor would wince at the memory. Of lasting importance, though, was the fact that this unexpected marathon of six hours had put England in an impregnable position after they had swayed on 132 for 6. Taylor had helped Miller take the score to 267 before the seventh wicket fell, and Emburey had helped Taylor add 69 before the eighth fell for 336. Lunch was immediately taken and an immediate anticlimax was thus avoided.

Emburey showed that *he* had no sore chest from diving into the pool after lemons. He hooked Hogg for four to reach 40. But Willis doubled up after Hogg hit him in the midriff, raising cheers, mostly from the juvenile section of the audience.

The cheers were universal when Emburey's innings was ended by a ball of full length from Hogg. He slapped his pad with disappointment, but his 42 was a most valuable contribution, and well above his previous Test best of 14. There followed only another slapstick tenth-wicket stand between Willis and Hendrick, the Warwickshire man creating most of the carnage, slashing Hurst over cover for four, hitting him to cover, where Wood collected a nasty blow in the mouth which necessitated two stitches, and skying Hogg to deep mid-on, where Darling missed a difficult catch. Willis's end came through a splendid if unspectacular catch by Wright, who clasped a very fast edge two-handed above his head, his feet still planted firmly. This final spell of 3 for 16 in 6.6 overs took Hogg to 40 wickets in the series, which left only Sydney Barnes, Jim Laker and Clarrie Grimmett ahead of him in the record book, and yet Australia's 1978-79 hero noticeably stood back to clap Alan Hurst in, in recognition of his fighting 37 overs which produced figures of 4 for 97.

So at last Australia's gruelling time was over. For 702 minutes they had been gunning England down, then fighting to deny them a recovery, then absorbing the disappointment of seeing their comeback invalidated and the eventual target inflated to a massive 366 (in an available 554 minutes). From 132 for 6, England had well-nigh trebled the score, and asserted yet again their basic superiority.

During the interval between innings we learned of Geoff Boycott's decision to continue to play for Yorkshire. He was to sign a two-year renewal, and at last we could abandon this painful saga and concentrate – if we were to be allowed – upon on-field matters.

Willis had an attack of no-ballitis at the start of the Australian innings, and the Wood-Darling stand progressed in bright fashion for 50 minutes, Wood's best stroke an off-drive for three off Hendrick, and Darling hooking as only he can for four off Willis. When Botham came on he cut him twice for two, once soundly and sweetly, once dangerously. Growing in confidence, he stepped inside a ball well up, flicked towards square leg, and lost his leg stump. Botham was ecstatic, Darling dejected, Australia one down for 31.

Hughes achieved something perhaps unique. He got five runs from his first ball. A three to third man was extended to five when Gooch's throw went over Taylor's head, and the crowd, well down on the three previous days, came alive again. There was further agitation when Wood aimed a glance at Botham and a monstrous shout by the fieldsmen and bowler for a catch behind was turned down by umpire Bailhache, leaving the Englishmen flabbergasted. Botham said a few things under his breath when he beat Wood with the next ball too.

And yet another incident followed. Hughes played forward to Miller, and the ball lobbed to slip, where Gooch fell and held it in his right hand. This time Randall was the most excited, dancing and tossing his sunhat high. But it was not out. Self-destruction was to bring the breakthrough when it came.

Wood pushed a ball to mid-on and sprinted off. Boycott fielded, took deliberate aim, and broke the wicket from side-on with Wood, having had to get past the large frame of Botham, about a yard short of his ground. Australia's openers both gone for 36, and Boycott mobbed like a Beatle at a stage-door.

Before tea there were two strokes of defiance from Hughes, a pull and a chesty drive/cut through cover, both for fours off Botham, and the break came at 44 for 2, most of the talk revolving around umpires, fielders' integrity, the absence of class batsmanship, and Wood's impulsive running between wickets.

It took Yallop some little time to break his 'pair', but he was steady, just as Hughes was measured and tough, pugnacious in stance and movement. The fifty came from yet another Willis no-ball, and a Hughes inside-edge for two was followed by a red-blooded pull for four by Yallop off Hendrick. A stand of 170, as these two achieved in Brisbane, would set Australia up, but it would need more than wishing on the part of this patient and slightly disillusioned crowd.

All through the third session Hughes and Yallop batted with the greatest circumspection. Pace gave way to spin, Miller from the Cathedral end, Emburey the other, and Yallop stretched or watched the ball pass while Hughes played well forward, using his feet athletically, often finishing with bat almost parallel to the ground. The fielders clustered around, except for a couple well out on the leg side – one even at straight midwicket on the fence – but this perfect pitch was offering up nothing to the bowlers, and the batsmen, for once, looked close to impregnable. The seagulls came to watch, sitting attentively in the outfield, and the ground looked quite as pretty as any in the world as the evening sun lit up the trees, the twin spires of St Peter's, and the distant hills. From tea till the close 38 runs were tacked on, and Australia stayed alive, 82 for 2, Hughes 30 in 143 minutes, Yallop 16 in 130. Emburey's six overs had cost two runs, Miller's 12 only 16 runs. Two hundred and eighty-four runs were still needed, no rain was in sight, and the last day presented itself as a stiff test for the much-maligned Australians.

Fifth day

A day that began in a mood of modest hope for Australia ended – not all that long after the start, at that – in the old gloom that had hung over four of the five Tests. Yallop and Hughes began soundly enough against the spin of Miller and Emburey, Yallop skipping down the pitch and thrashing Emburey to the midwicket fence, and Hughes putting his strong cover-drive to perfect use against Miller. When Hendrick came on, Yallop square-drove him for four, and if an acceleration could be achieved we could all have been on the edges of our seats five hours hence. But Hendrick put an end to any such speculation. In no more time than it takes to have a leisurely shower – and how I yearned for one in the rising Adelaide heat – he dismissed both of them.

Yallop, much as in the first innings, misjudged a ball that came at the stumps, flicking the pad-flap on the way as he held his bat clear: the action of a man who had lost his sense of confidence and certainty.

Hughes went in a wholly more dramatic way. He hit Hendrick very firmly to point, and Gower fell away and clasped the catch, much as he had done to catch Wood in the Melbourne Benson

& Hedges Cup match. Nor was he finished today, for the new batsman, Carlson, who now joined Border, was due to finish up in the Gower claws.

Before that, Border perished to the first ball from Willis, who suddenly began to look like the pre-Perth fast bowler. He ran in fast and with as much rhythm as his shuddering frame could summon, and the arm came over like a whip. Border offered only a limp forward stroke and was bowled through the gap. Drinks were taken as Yardley came in, but his stay was short. His second ball found the edge as he unleashed an ambitious drive against Willis, and Brearley took a fast, straightforward catch at first slip.

Carlson was over half an hour getting away from a 'pair', but he looked fairly sound, the last of the four Queensland players tried in the series. It was the newest Test cricketer who went next – Kevin Wright, who had made a favourable impression with the gloves and as a batsman in the first innings. Still to score, he went to a bat-pad catch by Botham off Miller, and five wickets had fallen for nine runs.

Hogg came in, carrying a helmet which he handed to the square-leg umpire. He told me he had once scored 150 in a Melbourne second-grade match, and the way he moved into his first ball supported credibility. A lofted drive off Miller had a touch of desperation about it, but brought him two runs, and showed that he would gladly have driven away the short-leg fielders who, in their helmets, looked like the cast of *Star Wars*. Alas, Miller spun one through his forward defence and bowled him. It was a lovely ball for Miller to relish all through lunch, taken at 131 for 8.

Soon after the interval the new ball was taken, and Hendrick picked up his third wicket when Carlson played him off his toes in the vicinity of square leg, where Gower took a lovely catch. There remained only two cover-driven boundaries off Willis by the ever-improving Hurst before a yorker did for him and settled England's match and series victory by 205 runs. It was the first time since the Bodyline series of 1932-33 that England had won four Tests in a rubber against Australia, an achievement that came toppling England's way so swiftly that the last eight wickets had fallen for 45 runs – and on a pitch without blemish. So many heads were hung in shame, so many expressions of disgust or bewilderment were uttered, so numb was the average spectator, that there was no desire to linger.

The presentations were marred by a breakdown in the public-address system, probably caused by Phil Ridings' suggestion that there was not a great deal between the two sides. He quickly moved on to the gracious remark that the cricketers from England were great ambassadors, and a credit to their country. Ian Botham was awarded the Man of the Match prize by a 3–2 majority over Bob Taylor.

The captains' interviews were going to be formalities; but we went, and asked the obvious questions, and had a brave response from Yallop and a modest, content, and analytical set of replies from Brearley.

Barely audible above the joyful noise of the England dressing-room, Brearley reasserted that greater batting and bowling depth had won the day. Was he surprised at Australia's collapse? asked the unstoppable Tom Prior. Weren't you? came back the retort, quick as an edge off Willis. He referred to the strain on fast bowlers in a six-Test series, and said that with five at his disposal it enabled him to utilise two or three at a time at full rate. He thought for a moment of Rodney Hogg, who had no such solid support: 'Poor Rodney Hogg; poor Australia! He's taken forty wickets.'

For Yallop, the same old resigned slouch, the same old loyalty to his players, the same parry to questions. These interviews must have been the worst part of his summer. 'Team morale is still high,' he said. 'They're all young, aren't they? We feel it more because we're young.' He was unhappy that the upsurge in fortunes in the second innings at Brisbane and in the Melbourne victory had not been maintained. There was, he said, a general lack of concentration and application.

There was little more to be said. The sun still shone; the surf still rolled in; the Australian dollar had strengthened; children played happily among the sprinklers in the city parks. There was no point in bemoaning the weaknesses in the Australian Test XI any further. The selectors were the men in focus again, and several sackings were tipped. Instead, they made one change only – NSW batsman and captain Andrew Hilditch into the twelve in place of Rick Darling, a surprising switch, since Darling, even if given to rashness, made a fairly convincing opening pair with Wood, and was invaluable in the field.

The ground was being watered as I walked across it, and the bas-reliefs on the Victor Richardson Gates, having opened to let out the cars and the subdued crowd of around 5000, stayed facing away from the scene of the debacle, as if to spare the memory of the great old sportsman.

The attendants were removing the wooden sign which had been propped forbiddingly outside the entrance to the outer ground. It read: Conveyance of intoxicating liquor into the Oval is prohibited. It might have been in Australia's interests if it had read: Loose concentration and reckless strokes forbidden under penalty of three months' imprisonment.

FIFTH TEST MATCH

Adelaide, January 27, 28, 29, 31, February 1

ENGLAND

			Mins	Fours			Mins	Fours
G. Boycott	c Wright b Hurst	**6**	21	0	c Hughes b Hurst	**49**	265	2
*J. M. Brearley	c Wright b Hogg	**2**	28	0	lbw b Carlson	**9**	82	0
D. W. Randall	c Carlson b Hurst	**4**	26	0	c Yardley b Hurst	**15**	59	2
G. A. Gooch	c Hughes b Hogg	**1**	10	0	b Carlson	**18**	85	2
D. I. Gower	lbw b Hurst	**9**	20	1	lbw b Higgs	**21**	76	3
I. T. Botham	c Wright b Higgs	**74**	159	6*	c Yardley b Hurst	**7**	34	1
G. Miller	lbw b Hogg	**31**	80	3	c Wright b Hurst	**64**	236	5
†R. W. Taylor	run out	**4**	29	0	c Wright b Hogg	**97**	361	6
J. E. Emburey	b Higgs	**4**	25	0	b Hogg	**42**	146	4
R. G. D. Willis	c Darling b Hogg	**24**	25	3†	c Wright b Hogg	**12**	35	1
M. Hendrick	not out	**0**	14	0	not out	**3**	17	0
Extras (1 b, 3 w, 2 nb, 4 lb)		**10**			(1 b, 16 lb, 2 w, 4 nb)	**23**		
		169	*plus 2 sixes †plus 1 six			**360**		

Fall: 10, 12, 16, 18, 27, 80, 112, 136, 147. 31, 57, 97, 106, 130, 132, 267, 336, 347.
Bowling: Hogg 10.4-1-26-4, Hurst 14-1-65-3, Carlson 9-1-34-0, Yardley 4-0-25-0, Higgs 3-1-9-2.
Second innings: Hogg 27.6-7-59-3, Hurst 37-9-97-4, Carlson 27-8-41-2, Yardley 20-6-60-0, Higgs 28-4-75-1, Border 3-2-5-0.

AUSTRALIA

			Mins	Fours			Mins	Fours
W. M. Darling	c Willis b Botham	**15**	39	1*	(2) b Botham	**18**	50	2
G. M. Wood	c Randall b Emburey	**35**	211	1	(1) run out	**9**	63	0
K. J. Hughes	c Emburey b Hendrick	**4**	7	1	c Gower b Hendrick	**46**	203	4*
*G. N. Yallop	b Hendrick	**0**	11	0	b Hendrick	**36**	178	3
A. R. Border	c Taylor b Botham	**11**	20	1	b Willis	**1**	31	0
P. H. Carlson	c Taylor b Botham	**0**	7	0	c Gower b Hendrick	**21**	72	2
B. Yardley	b Botham	**28**	81	4	c Brearley b Willis	**0**	4	0
†K. J. Wright	lbw b Emburey	**29**	76	3	c Emburey b Miller	**0**	17	0
R. M. Hogg	b Willis	**0**	4	0	b Miller	**2**	11	0
J. D. Higgs	run out	**16**	79	0	not out	**3**	28	0
A. G. Hurst	not out	**17**	46	1	b Willis	**13**	10	2
Extras (1 b, 3 lb, 5 nb)		**9**			(1 lb, 10 nb)	**11**		
		164	*plus 1 six			**160**	*plus 1 five	

Fall: 5, 10, 22, 24, 72, 94, 114, 116, 133. 31, 36, 115, 120, 121, 121, 124, 130, 147.
Bowling: Willis 11-1-55-1, Hendrick 19-1-45-2, Botham 11.4-0-42-4, Emburey 12-7-13-2.
Second innings: Willis 12-3-41-3, Hendrick 14-6-19-3, Botham 14-4-37-1, Miller 18-3-36-2, Emburey 9-5-16-0.
Toss won by Australia. Umpires: R. C. Bailhache & M. G. O'Connell.
*Captain †Wicketkeeper

ENGLAND WON BY 205 RUNS

11. AUSTRALIA'S ONE-DAY COMEBACK

Australia lacked heroes after the fifth-Test defeat, and my eyes lingered on the statue of aviator Sir Ross Smith as I left Adelaide Oval for the last time. At the airport, too, the Vickers Vimy is prominently displayed near the TAA maintenance hangar – the aircraft flown by the Smith brothers from England to Australia in November 1919, when a certain Keith Ross Miller was born in Melbourne. How wonderful it would have been for Australia if that great all-rounder had been born 35 years later.

The last newspaper placard I saw in Adelaide screamed: Test Star Axed. As I wondered if this was murder or death by misadventure, I discovered that it referred to the dropping of Rick Darling from the Australian team – apparently without the courtesy of a personal word from the selectors. His impetuosity had cost him his place, but there were many who hoped he would be back at some later stage.

The spectre of death walked twice into cricket's ranks during these few days. First came the shock news that Jim Burke, the dour but whimsical batsman of the 1950s, had been found with a shotgun by his side. He was 48 and had reached the depths of human endurance through causes yet to be made public. Just three weeks earlier I had asked him about a slow Test century he had made against India, checking if it had taken longer than Kim Hughes's apparently new record. The reply was as chirpy as might have been expected. I remembered listening to the radio description of his century in his first Test against England in 1951; I remember playing Sydney grade cricket against him, being an lbw victim of his in the first innings, struck on the hip-bone, caught nonchalantly at slip by him in the second off one of the fastest deliveries I'd ever known, fielding out to a painstaking century, and enjoying his jokes afterwards when he organised a nine-gallon keg of beer. Many players will recall his piano-playing and his Al Jolson impressions. The sadness of his death was with us for days and days.

News followed of the passing of Eddie Paynter, the high-scoring Lancashire and England batsman of the 1930s, who had brought the house down at the Centenary Test when, head barely above the level of the counter, he had pleaded for the barman to serve him a warm beer. Little Eddie, hero of the Brisbane Bodyline Test, maker of two double-centuries for England: gone to his rest, doubtless welcomed by Neville Cardus, who always loved a joker.

Then came news of some births – daughters to Ian Botham and to Alan Hurst, two of the combatants in the Benson & Hedges Cup match at Melbourne. Australia won, making 215 for 6 with ten balls to spare after Hughes had hit 50, Yallop 31, Toohey 54 not out (including the pleasure of the winning hit), Cosier a vital 28 (with an enormous six over long-on off Lever), and Laughlin a strong 15 not out to help clinch it, his six off Lever clearing the sightscreen. David Gower made an exquisite 101 not out, taking four through extra cover against a widely-spread field off the final ball, and winning the Man of the Match award – unanimously; I was not left on my own this time. The applause for his hundred was as warm and spontaneous as if it had been by one of their own.

There were some sour notes. There always seemed to be somehow. Willis was taunted by some of the crowd in the Southern Stand, and responded with the gorilla act – all fairly harmless – but the theft from the dressing-room of bats belonging to Boycott and Bairstow, Radley's helmet, and Miller's trousers and gloves was not easily overlooked. This and the invasion of the field by spectators, mostly children, towards the end of the one-day match at Geelong did little to endear a travel-weary English cricket team to Australia, even if it was a passing bitterness. Mike Brearley let his disgust show at the presentation ceremony a day later, after England had been beaten in the deciding Benson & Hedges Cup match.

This game was Australia's from the start. Put in to bat, Brearley having lost his tenth toss in thirteen in Tests, first-class matches and B & H matches, England were bundled out for 94 by Dymock, Hurst and Cosier, Brearley making a 46 which incorporated the run-out of Bairstow going for a sixth run after an overthrow on the fifth. Australia got a good start from Wood and Darling and ran to their target with little trouble, and the ground, indeed the country, was bathed in sweet relief. Their boys were capable of winning. In fact, they had won in a medium generally considered more difficult, since England were thought to be masters of the one-day game, with their five-prong pace attack (four here, Edmonds playing for Old) and their overall knowhow. Graham

Yallop had a euphoric look on his face as he took the golden trophy from Bob Parish on the presentation rostrum. Brearley, for his part, showed a reluctance to respond, and when baulked by beery noises, made some rather unworthy remarks that gave victory to the loud-mouths and created the impression that defeat was too much for him to handle. 'If you lot shut up ...' he began. 'If we'd won the toss ...' he tried again. 'I don't think I'll say anything more,' he said, as he stepped down. Many an England captain before has felt distaste towards Australian crowds. Stoddart felt hard done by in 1898. Jardine wasn't too happy in 1933. Dexter, Illingworth and Denness were glad to get home. But a bighearted man like Freddie Brown would have boomed back at the hecklers and Colin Cowdrey might have reasoned with them and won them over. Len Hutton would have ignored them. Whatever the reaction, it should not have been a blatant retreat.

In another sphere, the World XI had won the World Series $61,000 Supertest grand final at Sydney by five wickets in three days, Barry Richards taking the outsiders to victory with 101 not out and Tony Greig and Ian Chappell having another of their boring verbal punch-ups. Greg Chappell's withdrawal from the match – with a virus thought at one stage to be palsy – must have had some bearing on the outcome, but his presence in the side a week earlier was not enough to prevent WSC West Indies from winning the International Cup final. The WSC Australians thus missed out on the prizemoney both times, and must have started comparing winnings with their 'legitimate' brethren playing as Yallop's erstwhile losers.

There followed some rumblings in the World Series camp. On February 6 it was announced that managing director Andrew Caro had resigned. Then when Ian Davis was refused permission by his employers, the Commonwealth Bank, to take time off to tour West Indies, Kerry Packer ordered the transfer of the Murray Leisure Group and the Conpress Printing Ltd accounts to other banks.

At the same time, I was endeavouring to obtain a contract for Jeff Thomson with an English county for 1979. He had just won a World Series contest for the 'fastest and most accurate bowler in the world', and was rarin' to go. Surrey, Lancashire and Worcestershire showed early interest. The newspaper placards, reliable as ever, jumped the gun with 'Poms Grab Thommo' and other teasers. It sold papers. It sold cricket. Still my dream was to see the game reunified, for I would rather have seen Thommo – and several others for that matter – preparing for the World Cup in June. As it was, the Benson & Hedges Cup competition had given clues to the form of some of the Australian Test players, especially Gary Cosier, of the permed ginger hair. Here was a man now branded a one-day cricketer rather than a Test player. He might be seeing England again after all.

For myself, there was the melancholy experience of flying for the last time from one Australian city to another. It was another fine day as TAA lifted us out of Melbourne, headed for Sydney, with just enough small clouds floating by to suggest that the gods had been smoking their pipes as they deliberated on what to arrange for us next.

12. THE SIXTH TEST MATCH

SYDNEY, FEBRUARY 10, 11, 12, 14

First day

And so we came to the last contest, a Test match difficult to promote, with the series decided and the Australian public weary of keeping in touch with at least one important match each and every day of the summer – or so it seemed. The crowd was meagre as Yallop won his fifth toss out of six and chose to bat on a warm day getting warmer, with most of the celebrated 1948 Australian team in the members' enclosure, getting into the spirit of things before their reunion dinner that evening.

England fielded the same team as at Adelaide, with Lever again twelfth man, and Australia brought in Hilditch and Toohey for Darling and Border, the left-hand all-rounder having had the misfortune to follow his fine Sydney Test with an undistinguished game at Adelaide. The umpires, Tony Crafter and Don Weser, were both making their debuts in Tests.

The first over went decisively to Australia, Wood taking 11 runs, including hooked and cut fours, and Hilditch getting his first Test runs with a glance off his second ball. It may have been too early to say, but Willis looked lacklustre, the only bright aspect about him being the shiny soles of his new boots as he trotted in from the Noble Stand end. Hendrick restored that Test match feeling at the other with a maiden over.

In Hendrick's second over Australia's first wicket fell – in a heartbreaking manner. Hilditch, the 22-year-old Adelaide-born solicitor, played to slips, standing deep, and decided there was a run in it as the ball went through the cordon. But it did not go through; Gooch threw himself full length and somehow got the ball back to Emburey at the 'keeper's stumps with Hilditch having to return from halfway up the pitch. Despite a fumble, the wicket was broken and the batsman was narrowly run out. One down for 18, last man 3.

A run later Wood went, edging Hendrick almost safely wide of Botham, who hurled his bulk to his right and snapped up a wonderful one-handed catch. Yallop came in, looking like a colonel out for a stroll, and Botham remained in the game by taking over from Willis. Before long Yallop was showing who was boss by placing him for three fours in four balls backward of point to the foot of the rapidly-rising new grandstand.

Progress was slow, but no wickets fell, no chances were offered, no loose bowling intruded. Emburey came on for Hendrick and the fifty accrued in the 17th over, Hughes then sweeping Emburey for four. Twenty minutes before lunch Willis returned, and Hughes had just made it home when an underarm throw from the deadly Gower broke the bowler's wicket. As lunch approached, Miller was tried in place of Emburey. But the third wicket went down in the final over, when Hughes touched one from Willis and the eternal Botham dived like a goalkeeper to hold a two-handed catch low down. So on this brown and even pitch Australia had let slide another opportunity of getting a solid start, and England, having taken three wickets for 67, could consider it their morning.

The attendance and the temperature were both rising as play resumed, and with a sound from his bat like an artillery range, Yallop set about beating Botham to all parts of the field. He on-drove him to the fence in front of the Bradman Stand, and in one over took nine runs as he bowled around the wicket, square-driving him for four, hoicking his slower ball for two through square leg to raise his half-century (131 minutes, six fours), then putting up the century with a full-blooded square-drive for two.

Now a single exposed Toohey for the last ball, and Botham got his revenge. The batsman played forward with as much conviction as a learner-driver at a busy intersection, and Taylor took the edge with the same ease as most of his 15 previous catches in the series (surprisingly, he took none in the earlier Sydney Test).

Toohey, last season's hero, had now failed six times in nine Test innings to reach double figures, and half the Peter Toohey Stand banner fell down – or was torn – in mournful recognition.

There was time for another Yallop boundary, lofted off Emburey, before the fifth wicket fell, Carlson poking unclassically at a long-hop from Botham and giving Gooch a gully catch, and Yardley was in for a quarter of an hour, chopping Botham high over slips for four and slashing through cover for three before being bowled *past the left side of his pads* as he stretched across to the off against Emburey. Six down for 116; the old, old story.

Next to go was Wright (3), running down the pitch to Emburey and giving Taylor plenty of time to stump him, though he had to take the ball low down: 124 for 7. Wright lasted only ten minutes, but Hogg resisted stoutly for three-quarters of an hour, cutting Hendrick deftly through slips for four and presenting a straight bat to anything on the sticks.

Willis came back, but was to last only one over. Yallop hoisted a slower ball over midwicket off the front foot for four to reach 77, and did exactly the same to the next ball, persuading Brearley to transfer an extra man to the leg side, Randall guarding the midwicket boundary. Two backward of square helped the tally reach 13 off the over. Miller took over, making an all-spin attack with Emburey, who was hit for a couple of threes, Hogg's a steered stroke through the wide-open gully area, and when Yallop deemed it safe to remove his helmet, umpire Crafter found himself nursing two of them, short leg having cast his aside momentarily.

Tea was taken at 157 for 7 (Yallop 90), and Hogg fell soon afterwards, playing Miller to Emburey at close short leg. Yallop negotiated as much of the strike as he could while Higgs batted sensibly, and suddenly he was on 99. Miller bowled, well up, and the captain drove to cover, where Gooch misfielded, just as he had done at Brisbane when Yallop was 99. As at Brisbane, the batsmen were able to scramble a run and Yallop's third Test century, second of the series, was on the board, even a group of Australian Pressmen scarce forbearing to cheer. He had been in for four hours, all but a minute, and had hit ten boundaries, and not the least remarkable statistic was that he had made exactly two-thirds of the 150 runs scored since he came in at 19 for 2. It was a fine, bold innings, full of aggression blended with canny judgment, and all the more admirable for its isolation among so much failure.

Yallop's stand with Higgs was irritating for England. Higgs used to be regarded as the biggest mug in Australia when it came to batting, but he had put in some valiant efforts during the series, and now he supported Yallop in the drive for 200 and some respectability. Yallop thumped Emburey straight for four, and then gave England the long-awaited chance – which was spilt. When 105, he completely misjudged a ball from Miller and skied it to mid-off. Brearley scuttled after it, but was never in a good position to hold it. It bounced out of his hands and he fell chin-first as they ran two.

Four more through square leg off Emburey, and Yallop was exposed to the rare wiles of Geoff Boycott, who bowled one over, with his cap on, conceding two singles and a four to leg by Yallop, who looked as dangerous as at any stage of the summer.

Higgs stole a four between second and fourth slips, and then Yallop's superlative effort ended as he hit Botham straight to Gower forward of square leg. His 121 had come off 212 balls, 13 of which he hit for four, and he received a standing ovation as he walked off. In the face of all the numerous frustrations and condemnations that had followed him through the series, he had begun it and ended it with centuries, and established some kind of credibility as a Test batsman if not as a leader, though he was never going to be better than his material allowed.

We had the absurdity of drinks being brought out and Hurst being bowled first ball next ball, and it was time for assessment. Australia, bowled out for 198 by 5.02 pm on a slow wicket, taking gentle turn, was a great disappointment – if not a surprise – to the locals, and England at that point would have been favourites to march on to the threatened five-one series victory. But Hogg was chasing a record, and had had a reasonably long rest, and the side had a reputation to restore. England might have to fight, and they knew it.

Hogg's field for Boycott included a short point and short backward point, and at the other end Hurst had a more conventional layout. Boycott cover-drove Hurst for four after Brearley had broken his duck with a single, the wicketkeeper and slips standing in the elongated shadow of the floodlight pylon and the crowd of only 8601 threading its way out of the ground as if certain that there would be no further thrills. Both batsmen were sound and untroubled, and Hogg's quest for more wickets came to a breathless intermission as he bowled the last two balls off a few paces, Yallop giving him a paternal pat.

Yardley bothered Brearley in his first over, and had him missed by Hughes at slip, the ball flying low and fast to his left, the sort of catch an expert slips man would have scooped up. Brearley swept him fine for four with a venomous flash of the bat; some lively short deliveries from Hurst, sealed with a clever slow ball, brought no dividends. The final over, Yardley's, was expensive, Brearley taking three from a cheeky late cut and four from a sweep, and England were 24 without loss at the end, nicely poised perhaps for a tall first innings, or for nothing more than some kind of parity. Curiosity might just bring a few people through the gates tomorrow, Sunday.

Second day

Sunday brought greater heat, greater humidity, and a smaller crowd. If an England collapse had seemed likely, more would have come. But although the first hour was to bring two wickets, England were soundly placed at lunch with 98 on the board and no further loss.

The most exciting thing about the first half-hour, during which nine runs were made, was a mountainous bouncer from Hurst to Boycott. Then, after three-quarters of an hour, Boycott was out, failing to get behind Hurst and nicking to second slip, where Hilditch held the catch low down. Boycott was not satisfied. He pointed at the ground near the fieldsman, and doubtless expressed an opinion on the validity of the catch; but umpire Crafter indicated it was out, and that was that: 37 for 1, Boycott 19, his ninth score under 40 in 11 Test innings, and the first of two pre-lunch drinks were taken.

Randall tucked his first ball away for two, and when Hogg came back in place of Carlson, Brearley scored his first run of the day after 54 minutes, to knowing cheers. When Hogg dropped short, Randall swung him to the midwicket fence, and there were signs at last that some entertainment might be about to unfold.

But Randall, remembered so vividly for his ten-hour innings in the last Test here, was not to live long today. Hogg beat him with a full-length ball and he was leg-before, though he did not approve. He turned to scowl and natter several times on his way off. Gooch joined Brearley.

The fifty came with a sweet straight-drive for three by Brearley off Hogg, and it seemed time for Higgs's leg-spin. Instead, Yallop brought Yardley on at the Hill end, and there followed six overs from him of the most innocuous off-spin which Gooch enjoyed unashamedly and Brearley appreciated in a quiet sort of way. The captain late-cut him for three, and the big man, in one over, took boundaries to third man and cover and then a three to cover. After Brearley had removed his helmet, Gooch crashed another cover-drive to the fence to reach 29 out of 92, inspiring Brearley to strike his first four of the day, a drive off Carlson's medium pace, to raise the fifty stand in 57 minutes. Lunch came at 98 for 2, Brearley 41 (23 in the session and now the owner of a thousand Test runs, in his 45th innings), Gooch 29. Both were comfortably set, and when Higgs was eventually to be called up to bowl, he would not have the benefit of operating against newly-arrived batsmen. Yardley had played them in beautifully.

Yallop's plan became clear immediately after lunch. Higgs began from the Hill end, dropping infallibly into a length, and Hogg bowled from the other – as testing a combination as Australia could muster. The pitch encouraged neither, and so at ease were Brearley and Gooch that the latter wore a sunhat and Brearley alternated between cap and helmet.

The hundred appeared in the 35th over, and soon there was a very loud shout by Hogg and his fielders against Brearley (44) for lbw. Next over Gooch played a swatting kind of hook off him to the fence, an elementary reaction to a ball that might have presented problems; but it was a standard delivery at the other end that proved the undoing of his partner.

Brearley played some way from his body at a Higgs leg-break and lifted the ball to cover with sufficient carry to enable Toohey to fall forward and catch it. His 46 had taken 200 minutes, and it was only the second time in 11 innings in the series that he had passed 17. But, like his 53 in the previous Sydney Test, it was a most valuable innings.

Gower strolled out to the wicket, always a stimulating sight, and after Gooch had put a Hurst full-toss through square leg for four, Gower was down on his left knee sweeping Higgs for four, off-driving the next to the same effect, and the next for three. Gooch went to his first fifty against Australia with another four off Hurst, and Gower pulled casually for three just over midwicket's upraised arms. The biggest blow of all, though. came when Gooch went down the pitch and put all his weight into a straight-drive off Yardley that cleared the fence in front of the Bradman Stand and took him to 70, the stand reaching the half-century in only 43 minutes. A half-volley was sent whistling past Wood's face, at silly mid-on, and with his partner Gower, now capless, sweeping Higgs for four and surviving a sharp chance past Hughes's left hand at slip off the same bowler, the partnership was threatening to take the match firmly into England's command. Higgs's perseverance was then rewarded.

He bowled the perfect leg-break. It curved in late and spun away briskly. Gooch was down the pitch, beaten all ends up, and unable to get back before Wright completed a nifty piece of stumping. England 182 for 4, still 16 runs behind.

Botham might have been a novice for all the capacity he showed for handling the spin of Higgs, and he might have been angling for a World Series contract for all the tampering with his box. An untidy period followed. Gower fell over while sweeping Higgs, and Botham continued to be perplexed, and cut one over slip for three. To the sounds of approaching thunder, England went ahead with a sweep fine enough to pass within reach of Wright, only at an impossible velocity, by Botham, and further boundaries to him and his partner prompted estimates at England's target and needs – perhaps 350. By tea they were 216 for 4, Gower 47, Botham 17, the yield of 118 runs in the session being exceptional for the series, and now the storm decided to attack.

The thunderclaps were deafening, the rain torrential, obscuring view of anything beyond the far end of the ground, and some of the flags, including MCC's, were torn. The groundstaff battled to cover the square with the primitive tarpaulins as papers blew in upward spirals and women squealed in panic and exhilaration. Pieces of planking were dislodged from the scaffolding in the new stand by what might almost have been classed as a hurricane, and as it abated, several writers as well as half the crowd of 8187 left the ground, confident there would be no further play.

The sun came out, the youngsters ceased to frolic in the outfield, and the covers were carefully removed as half-past-four moved on towards five o'clock, the umpires inspecting the pitch and surrounds as they emerged from their protection. It looked like a 5.15 pm start or thereabouts, but there must have been more residual water out there than was apparent from our lofty perch, for the umpires called of play for the day just after 5 pm.

The main talking point that evening was whether Gooch had trodden on his off stump while playing a square-cut when in the twenties. The television playback threw no further light on the incident, but revived memories of a similar impasse involving Wally Grout during the Australia-West Indies series of 1960–61. The batsman survived there too, and it probably cost his opponents the game, but on-one was to blame, either time, for it is natural to watch the ball off the bat, and not to focus on the bails. It remained to be seen what bearing Gooch's escape – if it was that – would have on this contest as it moved slowly towards the halfway point.

Third day

'There's just no atmosphere here,' said the astronaut to his colleague as they walked out of a pub on the Moon. And so it was at the Sydney Cricket Ground on the third day of this final Test. The public voted with its feet. Although it was a Monday and although most of the holiday season was past, there would normally have been more than the hundred or so souls on the Hill as England resumed 18 runs ahead, six wickets in hand.

Carlson and Higgs opened the bowling, the new ball being due after seven overs, and Gower was soon to his fifty, only his second of the series, though he had got to the forties three other times. It seemed a century was there this time for the taking, so long as his casualness led him to no evil. When Yardley came on Gower played so freely that the ball seemed to be hit on purpose towards cover for catching practice, though luckily it was just to Hughes's left. They ran three.

Botham was the first to go, having looked hesitant against the slow stuff. He let go one of his booming off-drives off Yardley and Carlson took a headhigh catch with both hands, to his right: 233 for 6.

Miller was cramped and suspicious, and the runs were going to have to come from the other end. He on-drove a four off Yardley, whose spin and length were a little better today, but the flowing style of Gower was what mattered, and the day's value for spectators depended upon his survival. The bloom, however, was to die in early summer. A four through point off Higgs took him to 65, but next ball he played for more turn than was there and touched it through to Wright. Higgs's third wicket came in his 19th over, and England were 247 for 6, 49 ahead, still with plenty to do.

Taylor opened his score with a three to long leg – three runs he would have paid dearly for at Adelaide, where he fell for 97. Again, he batted in character, all caution, neatness and coolness.

Yallop tried his spinners to the 80-overs mark, and then called Hogg up for the new ball, taken at 265 for 6. Miller guided it to third man for four.

England's remorseless push had realised 54 runs and seemed to have cost only two wickets – major ones that they were – when Miller got out just as lunch beckoned. Hurst, who had bowled with great persistence, nipped one back at him and he was lbw for 18, sweated out in an hour and a half. So England went in at 270 for 7, and it was twenty minutes after the interval that the next wicket was won. Emburey still to score, thick-edged Hurst wide of Hilditch, who had time to launch himself to his right and trap the flying ball two-handed.

Taylor continued to keep command, but Willis stretched and edged and missed, as the crowd, and Bill O'Reilly, became restless and totally disgruntled. The 300 came up in the 99th over of the innings when Taylor swept Yardley for four under a diving Higgs, taking England's lead beyond 100, and Willis's innings extended beyond the hour, a worthy effort for someone with such severe restrictions as a batsman, though the amazing fact was that he was averaging almost three-quarters of an hour per innings during this series.

The advantage was growing and was not to be thrown away. So many sides – one thinks of some of the West Indies line-ups – would have gone helter-skelter and secured a narrow lead. This lead, which eventually rose to 110, was earned the hard way and by commodities so often identified as English specialties: patience and determination.

Willis was bowled at last by Higgs, in the leg-spinner's 30th over, and Yardley picked up his second wicket in finishing the innings by catching a hefty drive from Hendrick, leaving Taylor 36 not out in 162 minutes. It was only the fourth time in the series that England had passed 300, and only the second time that they had done so in the first innings. It also happened to be the first time since the second innings at Brisbane, in the opening Test, that Hogg had failed to take more than one wicket, and his chances of beating Grimmett's all-time Australian Test record of 44 wickets in a series seemed almost to have disappeared.

Tea was taken early, and Australia then embarked on yet another difficult voyage, seen off from the quayside by a nation that had almost rejected them during the past month. Trouble soon fell about them.

Wood began confidently, off-driving Willis for three in his first over and glancing fine for four in his second, but Hilditch, having made a single, was handed the second part of a disastrous debut double. He edged Hendrick and umpire Weser gave him out caught by Taylor, though the ball seemed to have fallen just short of the 'keeper. The batsman hesitated before leaving, chin on chest, a sad young man.

Hughes leapt into a pull stroke off Willis that thumped an advertising board noisily, and Wood straight-drove and glanced Hendrick for fours in one over before Brearley called up the men who were most likely to produce results, his off-spinners. Emburey took the Noble Stand end for the seventh over and Miller the other. Immediately it was apparent they were getting as much turn as they wished, even if the bite was relatively gentle at first.

Botham skinned his left elbow as he dived vainly for a catch at short leg off Hughes's bat, but Emburey's next ball was flicked to Gooch behind square and Australia were 28 for 2.

With 21 to his name, Wood played Emburey to Brearley at second slip, and the fieldsman claimed a catch, but the umpire was not interested and the reaction was somewhat petulant. It was obvious, though, that things were about to happen, for the ball was spinning, the close field clustered about like so much quicksand, and the bat was put only tentatively to the ball. Yallop top-edged Emburey and was almost caught by Gower, throwing himself at the cross-moving ball backward of point, and Wood swung into Miller and waited some time, as he ran, to learn his fate. Willis ran after the swirling ball from mid-off and held it, and Australia were 48 for 3.

Two more wickets toppled at that total, and the cornet-player on the east side of the almost-empty ground continued to drown out the Rod Stewart concert rehearsal at the Showground next door by playing a fading version of *Waltzing Matilda*, followed by a tender rendition of *The Last Post*. Toohey went for a duck, turning Emburey straight into Gooch's stomach at leg slip, and Carlson, also for a duck, was caught by Botham at short square leg off the same bowler. Three wickets had gone in nine balls for no runs, and Australians everywhere felt sick with shame.

The only sight to cause amusement was the several hundred seagulls which stood in the outfield, riveted to the play, without beer, without their cornet-player, but perhaps somehow sharing the shame, if their studied silence was to be interpreted.

Yardley came in and played some adventurous if inelegant shots, using his feet well and lifting his captain's spirits a little, but by the close the score had limped only as far as 70 for 5, and the match, with two full days left, was as good as over. Emburey had had another productive bowling spell on a pitch which Doug Insole was to describe as 'an English wicket', and everything in the garden was lovely for the touring team as they eyed their day of departure for home with a high degree of anticipation.

Fourth day

Australia's mood of prolonged mourning for its cricket shortcomings set the scene nicely for an evening with the 1948 Australian cricketers at a cocktail reception arranged by the Primary Club of Australia two nights after the reunion dinner. There was a likelihood that today's Test representatives would seem even more pigmy-like when the deeds of Bradman, Morris, Hassett, Lindwall, Miller, Johnston and Tallon were recalled, but the evening was less a wallow in nostalgia than a time for jokes about the alleged physical deterioration among the 'forty-eighters'. Memory glimpses attacked from all angles, especially when Ray Lindwall and Neil Harvey stood side by side, for they were the most lustrous of idols in the 1950s. The one now sells roses and carnations; the other has the misfortune to select losing Test elevens. They both live in the present, but how the glorious past must tug at their thoughts, especially at a time like this.

The weather was unsettled as play resumed after the rest day, but a start was made on time, and the spinners were on immediately, Emburey hurtling through his overs at the Noble Stand end, Miller at the Hill end. Yardley showed willing straightaway, hammering an off-drive to the fence in Emburey's second over, but Yallop had added only a single when he was beaten by Miller and caught as well as stumped by Taylor. It seemed to ensure a quick finish.

Yet Wright stayed for almost an hour, and Yardley survived by dint of initiative and courage and a little luck. He square-drove Emburey to the fence, and drove him to mid-on with an Errol Flynn type of rapier flourish, Brearley tripping over spectacularly as he fielded. He swept at Miller and gained three leg-byes, and then there were three byes as Taylor was unsighted. The ball was spinning sharply, and Wright allowed many deliveries to strike his front pad as he leaned forward. The sky was a mass of unbroken cloud, but it was high, and the air remained dry, the light poor.

Yardley brought up the hundred with a single to leg, and then his shirt was smeared with dirt as he dropped back into his crease as Hendrick fielded a hot sweep shot at short leg. At 105 for 6 Hendrick came on for Emburey, whose seven overs this morning had brought no wicket and 20 runs, and when Yardley swept Miller for a single to make Australia 110, England had to bat again.

An off-drive for four by Yardley off Hendrick was as good as any to be seen in this match, but Wright's sweep shot off Miller was misdirected and stayed in the air too long. Boycott caught it, and Australia were 114 for 7.

Hogg inside-edged his first ball for three, and after Emburey had come back for one over, Hendrick resumed, and Yardley got away with an ugly pull-drive off a good-length ball to make three for his fifty, which came in just over two hours.

Two more wickets fell before lunch, Hogg swinging at Miller and missing, Higgs giving Botham a bat-pad catch off Emburey, but Hurst hung on, even hitting an immaculate cover-drive for four off Emburey. But it came to a quiet and merciful end after lunch, when Emburey bowled a maiden to Yardley, who was left 61 not out, and Miller gratefully hugged a caught-and-bowled to his person as Hurst hit too soon. It was the first time he had captured five wickets in a Test innings, and for England's most improved player there could have been no more encouraging finale to the series.

England needed 34 to win, and Yallop banked on spin from the start to give his opponents a few shocks. Yardley took the Paddington end, Higgs the Randwick end, and operations began with a used ball after Brearley had disputed the matter with the umpires. Neither spinner caused concern, and Brearley was soon late-cutting Higgs whippily for four and matching Boycott's on-driven three with three runs of his own through mid-off. A cover-driven three to Boycott made them a dozen apiece, and three through extra cover off Yardley took Brearley ahead. It was a question of which of England's under-allocation batsmen of the series would have the honour of making the winning hit. With four runs needed, Brearley back cut, but got only a single as Carlson dived to cut it off. So he seemed to have lost his chance – especially as the next ball was short. Boycott wound himself up for the big shot through the covers, but spooned it to give Hughes the easiest of catches.

Randall strolled in, pretended to find a snake on the pitch (it was his own toy rubber one), and played two balls, and next over, at 2.40 pm, Brearley lifted the second ball to the pavilion fence to clinch the match by nine wickets and the series by the unprecedented margin (in England-Australia series) of five matches to one. It was a near-silent ending, willed for days beforehand, and bringing with it a sense of relief.

The presentations were made, England winning another Benson & Hedges $5000 winners' cheque which lifted their earnings from the series to $38,350, and Australia taking the losers' $2500, taking their earnings to $27,650. The Man of the Match award went deservedly to Graham Yallop, and for the last, weary time we trudged in to interview the patient skippers in the dressing-rooms.

Mike Brearley first spoke of the *contretemps* over the use of an old ball at the start of England's innings. The umpires had insisted it was all right, so there was little he could do apart from refer the matter in his match report. But here Doug Insole came in and said that he had told Messrs Crafter and Weser that they were wrong, but that he accepted that they were the sole arbiters of fair play.

Anyway, as Brearley pointed out, this was a storm in a teacup, raised during the last half-hour of a Test series which had lasted almost 150 hours.

He answered questions and volunteered views on many things. The one-day matches and country games had been better than expected, and they had got some good practice out of them on good pitches. On the Test pitches, every single one of them, the bowlers had received assistance from the surface. This one is Sydney had given help to the spinners early. 'We won the series five-one,' he said, 'so this isn't sour grapes.' Graham Yallop echoed this some minutes later, saying that when he made his Test debut three seasons ago the pitches were better.

Asked who was the most improved played in his side, Brearley said, without delay, that it was Geoff Miller, who had equalled the record for the number of wickets taken by an off-spinner for England in Australia. He referred also to the good performances by Boycott, Gower, Randall, Botham and Hendrick – who had kept fit all the way through this time, which, he offered, said something for the efforts of Bernard Thomas as physio. Turning to the Australians, he said he thought Wood and Darling had a lot of ability, and he was surprised to see the latter dropped. He thought Dymock unlucky too. 'He is a very good new-ball bowler.'

Already thoughts were moving to the World Cup, and, probed on the matter of the English players' attitudes towards World Series players taking part, he would say only that most of them seemed more concerned about any likely disruption than about making any stand on the issue. A Players' Association meeting was to be held shortly, when there would almost certainly be a variety of views expressed.

What did he think Australia could do to counter the general

despair that was felt by players and public? Australia, he said, must make their cricket enjoyable and better rewarded – attractive to them. They must keep their players together and get the best out of them. They could become a very good side. To have listened to people from all walks of life, as I had done, you would have thought that the most optimistic statement of the season. But the Australian sporting public usually drops its bundle when things go wrong. It lauds a successful young newcomer to the skies – but woe betide a failure.

Before moving back inside for the champagne, Brearley just had a word to say about bouncers. He felt there had been 'very few' in this series. 'But you don't want them when the ball is moving about off the seam.' How true. Could the answer to intimidatory bowling be to have these seamers' and spinners' pitches?

Yallop, wearing a white tracksuit and fiddling with his car keys as if he couldn't wait to get away, agreed that his batsmen did not employ very good techniques against the English off-spinners, and said that there would be a lot of talking before the two-Test series against Pakistan and the World Cup expedition. He would not agree that he should have been glad that this lop-sided series was at an end. 'I'm disappointed in our performances, and the series has been physically taxing. But I have enjoyed playing in it. Yes, I've enjoyed it.' Full marks for a big heart.

So on February 14, the day of the Chicago St Valentine's Day massacre, or of Captain Cook's death at Karakakoa Bay exactly two hundred years ago – one can take one's pick – the Australian flag was torn from the mast for the fifth time in two months. The noise of the tut-tutting had been deafening at times, and many of the local followers did anything but share Yallop's view that it was not a great relief that it was all over. England had leapt back to narrow the gap to 88 Australian victories to 79 since that first encounter at Melbourne in March 1877. There would be other confrontations between the two old antagonists, and Australia's state of hopelessness would be shoved into the past as fresh glories were played out in years to come. For the moment, it was apposite to look back at the swaying fortunes, and the individuals who had triumphed and failed.

SIXTH TEST MATCH

Sydney, February 10, 11, 12, 14

AUSTRALIA

			Mins	Fours			Mins	Fours
G. M. Wood	c Botham b Hendrick	15	31	2	c Willis b Miller	29	98	3
A. M. Hilditch	run out	3	18	0	c Taylor b Hendrick	1	20	0
K. J. Hughes	c Botham b Willis	16	101	2	c Gooch b Emburey	7	27	1
*G. N. Yallop	c Gower b Botham	121	266	13	c Taylor b Miller	17	110	0
P. M. Toohey	c Taylor b Botham	8	47	0	c Gooch b Emburey	0	3	0
P. H. Carlson	c Gooch b Botham	2	6	0	c Botham b Emburey	0	1	0
B. Yardley	b Emburey	7	15	1	not out	61	161	3
†K. J. Wright	st Taylor b Emburey	3	9	0	c Boycott b Miller	5	54	0
R. M. Hogg	c Emburey b Miller	9	45	0	b Miller	7	25	0
J. D. Higgs	not out	9	52	1	c Botham b Emburey	2	6	0
A. G. Hurst	b Botham	0	1	0	c & b Miller	4	16	0
Extras (3lb, 2nb)		5			(3b, 6lb, 1nb)	10		
		198				143		

Fall: 18, 19, 67, 101, 109, 116, 124, 159, 198. 8, 28, 48, 48, 48, 82, 114, 130, 136.
Bowling: Willis 11–4–48–1, Hendrick 12–2–21–1, Botham 9.7–1–57–4, Emburey 18–3–48–2, Miller 9–3–13–1, Boycott 1–0–6–0.
Second innings: Willis 3–0–15–0, Hendrick 7–3–22–1, Emburey 24–4–52–4, Miller 27.1–6–44–5.

ENGLAND

			Mins	Fours			Mins	Fours
G. Boycott	c Hilditch b Hurst	19	93	1	c Hughes b Higgs	13	35	0
*J. M. Brearley	c Toohey b Higgs	46	200	3	not out	20	40	2
D. W. Randall	lbw b Hogg	7	16	1	not out	0	3	0
G. A. Gooch	st Wright b Higgs	74	149	7*				
D. I. Gower	c Wright b Higgs	65	141	6				
I. T. Botham	c Carlson b Yardley	23	55	2				
G. Miller	lbw b Hurst	18	91	2				
†R. W. Taylor	not out	36	162	2				
J. E. Emburey	c Hilditch b Hurst	0	21	0				
R. G. D. Willis	b Higgs	10	70	0				
M. Hendrick	c & b Yardley	0	3	0				
Extras (3b, 5lb, 2nb)		10			(2nb)	2		
		308	*plus 1 six		1 wkt	35		

Fall: 37, 46, 115, 182, 233, 247, 270, 280, 306. 31.
Bowling: Hogg 18–6–42–1, Hurst 20–4–58–3, Yardley 25–2–105–2, Carlson 10–1–24–0, Higgs 30–8–69–4.
Second innings: Yardley 5.2–0–21–0, Higgs 5–1–12–1.
Toss won by Australia.

Umpires: A. R. Crafter & D. G. Weser.

ENGLAND WON BY 9 WICKETS

13. SACKCLOTH AND AFTERGLOW

The Qantas Jumbo-jet purred through the twenty-hour night like a spaceship. To the left was a sunset of rich orange and gold, wide as the horizon, and below it clouds, with all the light drained from them, clustered tip by tip like tall trees. The cricket tour was over, and we were chasing the sun westwards, towards loved ones – and snow, ice and industrial strife. The colourful towns of Australia were gone, as if forever. Ahead lay grey and white, gloom and exhaustion, waiting for the green buds of spring. Up on the flight deck, the thought expresses itself yet again: I'd settle for being a Qantas pilot. The Qantas pilot says he would like to be a cricket-writer. The computerised navigation and control system is most impressive. A brandy-and-soda in the Captain Cook Lounge dampens the emotions.

At the rear of the aircraft some of the journalists play cards. In the confines of twelve square feet of floor space huddle John Lever, Mike Hendrick, David Bairstow, Ian Botham and Ken Barrington, and the conversation is uninspired. The hostess brings some more Tooheys and we all brighten up. Derek Randall passes down the aisle and tries to scare us all by stating that the aircraft has woodworm. Botham goes back to reckoning out his Test figures. Bairstow gets his husky frame up and goes off for a shave. He comes back later bleeding at the throat, having achieved the near-impossible by nicking himself with an electric razor. Barrington reminds them that they are all to appear cleanshaven and properly dressed upon landing at Heathrow.

We glide onwards at almost 600 miles per hour, Gerry Rafferty's *Baker Street* and the Little River Band's *Reminiscing* passing through the earphones every forty minutes. The food is good, the wine is good. Sylvester Stallone 'acts' his way through the movie. Bob Taylor looks supremely happy by the side of his wife. Mike Hendrick looks brown enough to prompt special attention from the Immigration officials. David Gower gets off at Singapore, to get away from it all for a fortnight. The hours pass; fleeting visions return of the warm days of action, the crowd noises, the picturesque backdrops, the strained features of Australian and English cricketers.

How did the vast gulf open up between the two sides? Was the Packer invasion solely to blame? Would the full-strength Australian side, with the Chappells, Lillee and Thomson, have beaten England?

The fightback at Brisbane was worthy of recall, as was the Melbourne victory. It was at Sydney that the series moved England's way – because England made it do so – when Australia ought to have converted a first-innings lead of 142 into ultimate series-levelling victory. Here the difference between the sides showed most markedly, England's ringcraft, patience, resolution triumphing. Here Yallop's inexperience proved fatal. Something similar happened in the next Test, at Adelaide. And in the final Test the inadequacy of the home side – Yallop a glorious exception – was so marked that most people were wondering what possible point there could have been in having a sixth Test match.

The composition of the home team was often queried. Wood and Darling were always the best-looking, natural opening pair, yet Cosier was thrust in first at Brisbane and Darling was dropped almost as a scapegoat for the final Test. Toohey's pathetic form was unsettling as well as unexpected, and caused the selectors big headaches, as did Hughes's erratic form once he was appointed as the number three batsman. John Maclean's selection as wicketkeeper for the first four Tests proved to be an unprogressive move, and John Inverarity must have been a better choice as captain and middle-order batsman; but we shall never know now.

Australia's discoveries were Border, Hogg and Wright, and if Hogg stands a fair chance of being a one-series wonder, the other two should play a big part in Australian Test cricket in the 1980s. Hogg and Hurst took 66 wickets between them in the six Tests, eight more than Lillee and Thomson in the 1974-75 series, and Higgs took 19 at a noteworthy 2.38 runs per over. The next-highest wicket-takers for Australia took seven. In contrast, England had five bowlers with 16 or more wickets. The real anomaly came in the batting, where the side which lost so heavily recorded four centuries to England's two. Potentially, England's batting was no more distinguished than Australia's, but the two recurring qualities made the difference: experience and determination.

David Gower, compared with Denis Compton for his breezy attitude by Ken Barrington, was the only batsman on either side to pass 400 runs in the Tests, and went home content, even if he would have liked more runs still, just as Derek Randall would have liked to have added to his 385 aggregate, which included his best-ever innings, the 150 at Sydney which settled the destination of the Ashes.

Ian Botham provided very few sensations by his standards but constantly came home with important wickets and runs, as well as catches, finishing a maturer cricketer, just as Geoff Miller 'arrived' as a Test player, short now only of conviction as a batsman. It will not be enough for him simply to exist at the crease; he will have to take command.

Graham Gooch clung to his position in the side, happier by far when put down to number four, though there were times when one thought that better players must have missed out on an England cap. Just as Ken Barrington got to work – with positive results – on Gower's play outside off stump, so his attempts to get Gooch to keep his head down when driving began to pay off towards the end of the series.

One of the surprises of the tour was that Geoff Boycott would have lost his bet if he had backed his claim that he would make more runs than his captain. He made 533 to Brearley's 538, and the matter was settled, to the awareness of only a few spectators, during the last minutes of the last match. Boycott, of course, made a few more runs in the Tests, but at a deathly slow rate and poor average. His Test glories, it seems, are not due to stretch into his forties, as did Hobbs's, Hendren's and Woolley's.

Clive Radley's early disqualification by injury to eyebrow and confidence was one of those unpredictables, and the restriction to only one Test each for Chris Old, John Lever and Phil Edmonds could hardly have been foreseen back in November. The upshot was that nine men played in all six Tests, and this forged a cohesion worth a lot. John Emburey's introduction from the third Test gave the side a class off-spinner, superb close fielder and rapidly improving batsman, and Mike Hendrick, fit as never before and bowling a full, testing length, bowled meanly and had his best series ever, finishing as England's spearhead after Bob Willis showed signs of wilting.

The Willis decline was reversed for a while at Adelaide, but foot soreness and fatigue reduced his effectiveness materially. Had such misfortune overtaken Hogg, Australia's lucky bowler, the series would have been even more one-sided.

England were fortunate to have such a near-perfect wicketkeeper as Bob Taylor, with the bonus of his over-my-dead-body batting at number eight. There were times when a dose of Alan Knott's naughtiness with the bat would have been welcome, but even Knott cannot have kept as consistently well.

As for Mike Brearley, victorious captain in eight out of eleven Tests against Australia, with only one loss, no praise for his tactical and spiritual leadership could be too high. He is a lucky man to have been ready just when he was for his country's call after Tony Greig's demotion, for his playing ability would not have sustained him through those eleven Tests. His value as leader, though, was such that there can never have been any serious question of leaving him out of the side. It would have taken two defeats in succession to have raised the possibility, and when defeat threatened at Sydney it was Brearley himself who played a large part in turning the match round with a vital second-wicket stand of 111 with Randall. The softly-spoken, greying, dark-featured man with the little-boy manner in the field and the air of a philosopher off it never ceased to puzzle or infuriate Australians, and will not be forgotten, even if few of his deeds outside those of controller-in-chief will be remembered. History will show that the captain-batsman all-rounder did enough as captain to achieve immortality.

Bahrain came and went, and the Qantas flying hotel buffeted its way into a 200 kilometre-per-hour wind over Austria, still clothed in darkness. Bairstow had stopped bleeding, Randall had stopped sleeping, Botham had stopped talking. Outside the air was freezing cold and the ground, five or six miles below, was thick with snow and ice. The mission was now only a couple of hours from its end. The Ashes were retained, and the British public were happy, even if the victory had been somewhat hollow. The tour guarantee of $400,000 had been covered, with a quarter-million over to cover domestic outgoings. Total attendances were as low as 400,000, about half those of the last Ashes battle in Australia, when the home side trounced Mike Denness's side four-one.

The World Series figures for 1978-79 were $2 million and 700,000 spectators, with massive television advertising sales. There was therefore no doubting which brand of cricket, on the face of it, had won the day. Lynton Taylor, the new WSC managing director, told me the day his Australian team set off for their tour of West Indies that losses in the second year of operation had been cut back greatly, and that planning for the next few years had been confidently prepared. An arrangement for co-existence with the Australian Cricket Board was not a priority; they would be prepared to give nothing away; there might not even be a need for a settlement. Things were going well. 'Our prime strength is in marketing and promotion,' he said with significance.

So Australia's apologetic 1978-79 'official' team would shortly be setting off for the Prudential World Cup in England to face their tormentors again as well as a Pakistan side containing WSC players. In the other group would be a full-strength West Indies team, and the disruption caused by the split in world cricket would be more pointed than ever. Some of us continued to pray for a settlement so that the best from all countries could compete. But it still seemed a far-off likelihood. World Series Cricket had its audience, which seemed well-satisfied and loyal. Test cricket between England and Australia, as shown by public-interest figures, was sick. The medicine could only come from a restoration of the top talents – unless nature should surge back and take its course in maturing Yallop's battered young team.

So many questions still hung like icicles in the chill air. The Jumbo's mighty wheels touched down in the February dawn, and soon we were with our loved ones again, handing out presents, repeating stories first told in airletters and describing the warmth of the great south land and its people. Dozens of recollections fought for expression – the sultriness of Brisbane and the delights of the tropical fruit; the rude health of the inhabitants and Gower's century at Perth; the howl of the crowd at the Melbourne Supertest; the mosquitoes of Port Moresby; the yachts on the Derwent River; the stateliness of Melbourne; the elegance of Adelaide; the multiplicity of architecture and attitudes in Sydney; the joy of welcoming handshakes and the shaky timidity of farewell handshakes. Piles of luggage in hotel corridors; studies in facial expressions in dressing-rooms; rounds of drinks in lounges, with players' anxieties spilling out as only they can in informal settings; disciplines and humours of the Press box; one city to the next to the next to the next.

England had carried out her bombing raid over Australia, achieving submission. Buried in the rubble were some survivors, but the losses were great, especially among civilians. For the moment, there was a happier place: World Series Cricket, built by Kerry Packer, where colour and noise concealed any shortcomings and insecurities for those who wanted light entertainment. (In answer to the question, Is there such a thing as *heavy* entertainment? Perhaps Test cricket often falls into that category, to the gratification of so many over the years.)

By February, the optimists had expected a peace formula to have been drawn up, yet, if anything, peace between the Australian and English authorities on the one hand and World Series Cricket on the other seemed as far away as ever. All the palm-fronds were being sent to the Caribbean, Pakistan and India. The inherent dangers of this were too obvious to need spelling out. WSC was on its way to dividing and ruling. Ultimately, England and Australia could be left playing only against each other, before crowds only a fraction of the usual size. Not even the most ardent England-Australia Test fanatic would wish for that.

So the Test series of 1978-79 goes into the record book a species apart. I cannot bring myself to join the guttural chorus of condemnation towards the Australian players. They had limitations, and, on the whole, they failed to play beyond them. England were admirable, and will probably be broken up as a side before being put to a sterner test. When they had their opponents on the ropes they finished them off, and when they themselves were on the ropes they usually twisted out of trouble. It was a pleasure to watch their craftsmanship, even if it was not a universal pleasure.

As Douglas Jardine wrote at the end of his account of the Bodyline series:

The hooting mob of yesterday in silent awe return
To glean up the scattered ashes into history's golden urn.

TEST MATCH AVERAGES

Statistics by Andrew Thomas

AUSTRALIA

Batting

	M	I	N.O.	H.S.	Runs	Av.	Catches
A. R. Border	3	6	2	60*	146	36.50	3
G. N. Yallop	6	12	0	121	391	32.58	3
K. J. Hughes	6	12	0	129	345	28.75	5
G. M. Wood	6	12	0	100	344	28.67	6
W. M. Darling	4	8	0	91	221	27.63	4
B. Yardley	4	8	1	61*	148	21.14	4
P. M. Toohey	5	10	1	81*	149	16.56	5
J. A. Maclean	4	8	1	33*	79	11.29	18
R. M. Hogg	6	12	0	36	95	7.92	0
J. D. Higgs	5	10	4	16	46	7.67	0
G. Dymock	3	6	1	11	28	5.60	0
A. G. Hurst	6	12	2	17*	44	4.40	1

Played in fewer than three Tests:
G. J. Cosier 2 matches, 4 innings, 0 not out, 47 highest score, 52 runs, average 13.00 (2 catches). K. J. Wright 2-4-0-29-37-9.25 (7 catches, 1 stumping). P. H. Carlson 2-4-0-21-23-5.75 (2 catches). T. J. Laughlin 1-2-0-5-7-3.50 (2 catches). A. M. Hilditch 1-2-0-3-4-2.00 (2 catches).

Centuries:

Two –	G. N. Yallop	102	First Test, Brisbane
		121	Sixth Test, Sydney
One –	K. J. Hughes	129	First Test, Brisbane
	G. M. Wood	100	Third Test, Melbourne

Bowling

	O	M	R	W	Av.	Best
R. M. Hogg	217.4	60	527	41	12.85	6–74
A. G. Hurst	204.2	44	577	25	23.08	5–28
J. D. Higgs	196.6	47	468	19	24.63	5–148
G. Dymock	114.1	19	269	7	38.43	3–38
P. H. Carlson	46	10	99	2	49.50	2–41
A. R. Border	31	13	50	1	50.00	1–31
B. Yardley	113.2	12	389	7	55.57	3–41

Also bowled: G. J. Cosier 12–3–35–0. T. J. Laughlin 25–6–60–0.

ENGLAND

Batting

	M	I	N.O.	H.S.	Runs	Av.	Catches
D. I. Gower	6	11	1	102	420	42.00	4
D. W. Randall	6	12	2	150	385	38.50	4
I. T. Botham	6	10	0	74	291	29.10	11
R. W. Taylor	6	10	2	97	208	26.00	18 & 2 st
G. Miller	6	10	0	64	234	23.40	1
G. A. Gooch	6	11	0	74	246	22.36	9
G. Boycott	6	12	0	77	263	21.92	2
J. M. Brearley	6	12	1	53	184	16.73	5
J. E. Emburey	4	7	1	42	67	11.17	6
R. G. D. Willis	6	10	2	24	88	11.00	3
M. Hendrick	5	9	4	10	34	6.80	3

Played in one Test:
C. M. Old 29*. J. K. Lever 14, 10 (1 catch as sub). P. H. Edmonds 1 (1 catch).

Centuries:
One – D. I. Gower 102 Second Test, Perth
D. W. Randall 150 Fourth Test, Sydney

Bowling

	O	M	R	W	Av.	Best
G. Miller	177.1	54	346	23	15.04	5–44
M. Hendrick	145	30	299	19	15.74	3–19
J. E. Emburey	144.4	49	306	16	19.13	4–46
R. G. D. Willis	140.3	23	461	20	23.05	5–44
I. T. Botham	158.4	25	567	23	24.65	4–42

Also bowled: J. K. Lever 15.1–2–48–5. C. M. Old 26.7–2–84–4. G. Boycott 1–0–6–0. G. A. Gooch 6–1–15–0. P. H. Edmonds 13–2–27–0.

ENGLAND XI FIRST-CLASS TOUR AVERAGES

Batting

	M	I	N.O.	H.S.	Runs	Av.
D. W. Randall	10	18	2	150	763	47.69
R. W. Tolchard	3	5	1	72	142	35.50
J. M. Brearley	11	21	5	116*	538	33.63
D. I. Gower	12	20	1	102	623	32.79
G. Boycott	12	23	3	90*	533	26.65
G. Miller	11	18	3	68*	398	26.53
I. T. Botham	9	14	0	74	361	25.79
G. A. Gooch	13	23	1	74	514	23.36
R. W. Taylor	10	15	2	97	230	17.69
P. H. Edmonds	7	9	2	38*	115	16.43
C. M. Old	6	6	1	40	81	16.20
C. T. Radley	6	9	0	60	138	15.33
R. G. D. Willis	10	13	4	24	115	12.78
J. E. Emburey	9	12	2	42	101	10.10
J. K. Lever	6	7	0	28	67	9.57
M. Hendrick	8	12	4	20	68	8.50

D. L. Bairstow did not play in a first-class match.

Bowling

	O	M	R	W	Av.	Best
M. Hendrick	184.4	40	399	28	14.25	5–11
G. Miller	277.1	74	607	36	16.86	6–56
J. E. Emburey	261.1	73	563	31	18.16	5–67
I. T. Botham	239.3	44	848	44	19.27	5–51
R. G. D. Willis	210.3	34	696	34	20.47	5–44
C. M. Old	138	24	452	21	21.52	6–42
J. K. Lever	118.1	18	377	13	29.00	4–28
P. H. Edmonds	149	34	397	11	36.09	5–52
G. A. Gooch	26	2	80	1	80.00	1–16

Also bowled: C. T. Radley 1–0–4–0. D. W. Randall 2–0–9–0. G. Boycott 3–0–11–0.

TOUR SCORES

RENMARK

November 1

England XI 199 for 4 dec (C. T. Radley 64, G. A. Gooch 47); **South Australian Country XI** 137 for 6. **Match drawn.**

ADELAIDE

November 3, 4, 5, 6

SOUTH AUSTRALIA

J. E. Nash	lbw b Miller	124	st Taylor b Miller	33
W. M. Darling	c Miller b Willis	17	c Edmonds b Old	1
I. R. McLean	c Taylor b Edmonds	30	c sub (Randall) b Miller	52
B. L. Causby	c Brearley b Miller	20	c & b Edmonds	4
J. N. Langley	st Taylor b Edmonds	1	st Taylor b Edmonds	0
*R. K. Blewett	c Taylor b Willis	22	b Edmonds	12
P. R. Sleep	c Taylor b Lever	45	c Taylor b Edmonds	3
†T. J. Robertson	c Taylor b Willis	2	b Edmonds	24
R. M. Hogg	b Lever	11	run out	16
G. R. Attenborough	lbw b Miller	19	run out	3
A. T. Sincock	not out	14	not out	1
Extras (2 b, 2 lb, 2 nb)		6		0
		311		149

Fall: 31, 133, 195, 196, 200, 245, 261, 272, 281. 11, 55, 64, 64, 84, 90, 112, 144, 146.
Bowling: Willis 11–1–61–3, Lever 16–1–67–2, Old 18–2–78–0, Edmonds 21–5–53–2, Miller 18.4–5–41–3, Gooch 1–0–5–0.
Second innings: Old 5–1–20–1, Lever 9–0–40–0, Edmonds 21–3–52–5, Miller 16–2–37–2.

ENGLAND XI

G. Boycott	lbw b Hogg	62	lbw b Hogg	6
G. A. Gooch	c Robertson b Hogg	4	b Sleep	23
C. T. Radley	hit wkt b Hogg	4	c Sleep b Sincock	3
D. I. Gower	lbw b Attenborough	73	b Blewett b Sincock	50
*J. M. Brearley	b Sincock	27	run out	25
G. Miller	c Langley b Hogg	0	lbw b Sincock	5
†R. W. Taylor	c Blewett b Sleep	6	c Langley b Attenborough	4
P. H. Edmonds	not out	38	c Robertson b Attenborough	0
J. K. Lever	c & b Sleep	1	b Hogg	28
C. M. Old	c Darling b Sleep	4	c McLean b Sleep	40
R. G. D. Willis	absent hurt	—	not out	0
Extras (5 lb, 8 nb)		13	(4 b, 1 lb, 7 nb)	12
		232		196

Fall: 9, 15, 148, 148, 149, 179, 215, 222, 232. 19, 22, 67, 100, 108, 117, 117, 124, 192.
Bowling: Hogg 12–2–43–4, Sincock 9–0–42–1, Attenborough 15–1–49–1, Sleep 17.5–3–72–3, Blewett 10–4–13–0.
Second innings: Hogg 12.4–1–39–2, Sincock 10–2–28–3, Attenborough 11–2–49–2, Blewett 5–1–19–0, Sleep 12.5–1–49–2.
Toss won by South Australia. Umpires: R. A. French & M. G. O'Connell.

SOUTH AUSTRALIA WON BY 32 RUNS

LEONGATHA

November 8

England XI 130 for 8 dec. (C. Aitken 4 for 30); **Victorian Country XI** 59 (J. E. Emburey 5 for 10). **England XI won by 71 runs.**

MELBOURNE
(SIR ROBERT MENZIES MEMORIAL MATCH)

November 10, 11, 12, 13

VICTORIA

J. M. Wiener	c Edmonds b Lever	48	(2) not out	16
P. A. Hibbert	c Tolchard b Old	6	(1) not out	14
D. F. Whatmore	c Edmonds b Lever	27		
*G. N. Yallop	b Edmonds	10		
P. Melville	c Edmonds b Emburey	16		
J. K. Moss	c Emburey b Edmonds	73		
T. J. Laughlin	run out	37		
†I. L. Maddocks	c Radley b Edmonds	8		
I. W. Callen	c Tolchard b Emburey	8		
A. G. Hurst	b Emburey	1		
J. D. Higgs	not out	1		
Extras (15lb, 4nb)		19	(3nb)	3
		254	0 wkt	33

Fall: 11, 84, 93, 113, 129, 213, 239, 244, 249.
Bowling: Old 17-5-44-1, Lever 18-3-52-2, Hendrick 11-2-29-0, Edmonds 22-6-48-3, Emburey 26.5-5-56-3, Gooch 2-0-6-0.
Second innings: Lever 4-1-3-0, Emburey 5-0-11-0, Edmonds 2-0-3-0, Randall 2-0-9-0, Radley 1-0-4-0.

ENGLAND XI

*J. M. Brearley	not out	116
G. A. Gooch	lbw b Hurst	3
D. W. Randall	b Wiener	63
D. I. Gower	c & b Wiener	13
C. T. Radley	c & b Higgs	22
†R. W. Tolchard	c Whatmore b Higgs	0
P. H. Edmonds	c Melville b Higgs	5
C. M. Old	c Maddocks b Hurst	4
J. E. Emburey	c Higgs b Laughlin	5
Extras (3 lb, 2 w, 5 nb)		10
	8 wkts dec	241

Did not bat: J. K. Lever, M. Hendrick.

Fall: 7, 121, 145, 195, 199, 207, 225, 241.
Bowling: Hurst 17-4-44-2, Callen 16-4-44-0, Higgs 39-8-82-3, Laughlin 15.7-5-24-1, Wiener 13-3-31-2, Yallop 2-0-6-0.
Toss won by Victoria.

Umpires: R. C. Bailhache & K. J. Carmody.

MATCH DRAWN

CANBERRA

November 15

England XI 255 for 2 (40 overs) (G. Boycott 123*, R. W. Tolchard 108); **Australian Capital Territory & Districts** 76 (R. G. D. Willis 4 for 10). **England XI won by 179 runs.**

SYDNEY

November 17, 18, 19, 20

ENGLAND XI

G. Boycott	c Border b Lawson	14	not out	4
G. A. Gooch	c Rixon b Border	66	not out	0
D. W. Randall	c Hughes b Clews	110		
C. T. Radley	c Hughes b Border	13		
D. I. Gower	b Hourn	26		
G. Miller	st Rixon b Hourn	5		
I. T. Botham	c Toohey b Clews	56		
†R. W. Taylor	c Hilditch b Lawson	9		
J. E. Emburey	c Johnston b Lawson	0		
*R. G. D. Willis	not out	21		
M. Hendrick	b Border	20		
Extras (17 b, 6 lb, 2 w, 9 nb)		34		0
		374	0 wkt	4

Fall: 20, 145, 173, 250, 252, 276, 305, 313, 336.
Bowling: Lawson 17–5–39–3, Watson 18–2–61–0, Clews 13–1–88–2, Hourn 32–4–114–2, Border 12.1–2–38–3.
Second innings: Lawson 0.5–0–4–0.

NEW SOUTH WALES

J. Dyson	c Boycott b Miller	67	c Gooch b Willis	6
*A. M. Hilditch	c Taylor b Willis	4	b Botham	93
P. M. Toohey	c Gower b Hendrick	23	c Gooch b Botham	20
A. R. Border	c Taylor b Miller	11	c Taylor b Botham	12
D. A. H. Johnston	c Hendrick b Miller	16	c Gooch b Botham	3
G. C. Hughes	c Hendrick b Miller	27	b Emburey	11
M. L. Clews	st Taylor b Emburey	1	run out	5
†S. J. Rixon	c Hendrick b Miller	10	c Botham b Emburey	24
G. G. Watson	c Boycott b Emburey	2	not out	14
G. F. Lawson	not out	0	c Miller b Willis	7
D. W. Hourn	c Emburey b Miller	0	b Botham	0
Extras (1 lb, 3 nb)		4	(6 b, 4 lb, 1 w, 4 nb)	15
		165		210

Fall: 5, 47, 65, 107, 142, 146, 162, 165, 165. 18, 57, 82, 87, 119, 124, 173, 192, 209.
Bowling: Willis 8–3–16–1, Hendrick 12–2–33–1, Botham 9–2–41–0, Miller 18.4–3–56–6, Emburey 10–4–15–2.
Second innings: Willis 15–3–39–2, Botham 17.2–6–51–5, Hendrick 4–2–4–0, Emburey 22–5–44–2, Miller 24–6–56–0, Gooch 1–0–1–0.
Toss won by England XI. Umpires: T. F. Brooks & A. Drake.

ENGLAND XI WON BY 10 WICKETS

BUNDABERG

November 22

England XI 259 for 5 (35 overs) (R. W. Tolchard 74, J. M. Brearley 59); **Queensland Country XI** 127 (31.6 overs) (K. Maher 47, J. K. Lever 4 for 17). **England XI won by 132 runs.**

BRISBANE

November 24, 25, 26, 27

QUEENSLAND

M. J. Walters	c Gower b Willis	0	(2) retired hurt	4
W. R. Broad	c Taylor b Old	41	(1) lbw b Willis	0
A. D. Ogilvie	retired hurt	43	(7) c Gower b Willis	45
G. J. Cosier	c Taylor b Botham	32	(3) b Willis	0
P. H. Carlson	c Miller b Old	1	(4) b Botham	37
T. V. Hohns	c Taylor b Willis	3	(5) c Old b Botham	43
*†J. A. Maclean	c Boycott b Botham	1	(8) c Gooch b Old	94
G. K. Whyte	c Brearley b Old	10	(6) b Botham	0
G. Dymock	c Brearley b Botham	13	c Taylor b Botham	16
L. F. Balcam	not out	10	b Botham	21
G. W. Brabon	lbw b Old	2	not out	2
Extras (16 nb)		16	(4 b, 2 lb, 21 nb)	27
		172		289

Fall: 4, 90, 97, 100, 129, 135, 158, 159, 172. — 0, 0, 83, 83, 121, 169, 214, 268, 289.

Bowling: Willis 11–1–40–2, Old 14.7–4–33–4, Botham 12–1–66–3, Gooch 3–0–11–0, Edmonds 5–2–6–0.

Second innings: Willis 11–1–46–3, Old 14.2–3–63–1, Botham 20–3–70–5, Miller 11–1–40–0, Edmonds 8–1–35–0, Gooch 1–0–8–0.

ENGLAND XI

G. Boycott	c Cosier b Brabon	6	c Maclean b Balcam	60
G. A. Gooch	c Brabon b Dymock	34	c Ogilvie b Carlson	22
D. W. Randall	c Maclean b Balcam	66	b Whyte	47
†R. W. Taylor	c Maclean b Dymock	2		
*J. M. Brearley	not out	75	(4) not out	38
D. I. Gower	b Balcam	6	(5) c Cosier b Hohns	1
G. Miller	c Maclean b Dymock	18	(6) not out	22
I. T. Botham	c Maclean b Dymock	6		
C. M. Old	lbw b Balcam	2		
P. H. Edmonds	c Maclean b Cosier	14		
R. G. D. Willis	b Brabon	6		
Extras (1 b, 3 lb, 1 w, 14 nb)		19	(7 b, 2 lb, 9 nb)	18
		254	4 wkts	208

Fall: 14, 75, 90, 129, 148, 188, 201, 208, 241. — 42, 117, 165, 168.

Bowling: Balcam 13–1–56–3, Brabon 10.1–1–45–2, Carlson 14–1–48–0, Dymock 19–3–46–4, Hohns 2–0–3–0, Cosier 4–0–19–1, Whyte 7–3–18–0.

Second innings: Balcam 12–2–25–1, Brabon 5–0–31–0, Carlson 9.3–1–29–1, Dymock 17–5–38–0, Cosier 5–2–10–0, Whyte 15–3–44–1, Hohns 8–5–13–1.

Toss won by Queensland — Umpires: C. E. Harvey & M. W. Johnson.

ENGLAND XI WON BY 6 WICKETS

BRISBANE

December 1, 2, 3, 5, 6

FIRST TEST MATCH – England won by 7 wickets.

PERTH

December 9, 10, 11

ENGLAND XI

G. Boycott	lbw b Clark	4	c Marsh b Yardley	13
G. A. Gooch	c Wright b Alderman	3	c Wright b Porter	15
C. T. Radley	b Alderman	2	c Marsh b Yardley	18
*J. M. Brearley	c Wright b Porter	11	b Yardley	18
D. I. Gower	c Wright b Alderman	0	c Wright b Porter	4
†R. W. Tolchard	not out	61	b Yardley	3
I. T. Botham	c Charlesworth b Porter	4	c Marsh b Yardley	4
P. H. Edmonds	lbw b Porter	21	c Wright b Alderman	27
J. E. Emburey	c Wright b Clark	22	not out	7
J. K. Lever	c Wright b Mann	2	b Alderman	1
M. Hendrick	c Charlesworth b Mann	6	b Clark	8
Extras (1 b, 2 lb, 1 w, 4 nb)		8	(7 b, 1 nb)	8
		144		126

Fall: 7, 7, 13, 17, 25, 31, 69, 115, 121. 23, 41, 58, 63, 69, 73, 98, 115, 117.

Bowling: Alderman 12–4–18–3, Clark 16–4–50–2, Porter 17–4–37–3, Yardley 2–0–7–0, Mann 8.3–2–24–2.

Second innings: Alderman 9–2–26–2, Clark 12–2–22–1, Porter 16–9–16–2, Yardley 13–1–54–5.

WESTERN AUSTRALIA

G. M. Wood	b Lever	2	(2) lbw b Botham	15
R. I. Charlesworth	c Tolchard b Botham	3	(1) lbw b Lever	6
K. J. Hughes	b Botham	8	lbw b Botham	1
G. R. Marsh	c Tolchard b Botham	0	c Tolchard b Hendrick	9
*R. J. Inverarity	c Tolchard b Hendrick	9	lbw b Botham	2
A. L. Mann	c Botham b Hendrick	3	c Tolchard b Botham	0
G. D. Porter	c Brearley b Hendrick	8	c Tolchard b Hendrick	2
B. Yardley	c Tolchard b Hendrick	8	not out	38
†K. J. Wright	c Brearley b Botham	0	b Hendrick	0
W. M. Clark	not out	2	run out	1
T. M. Alderman	c Botham b Hendrick	1	run out	2
Extras (3 lb, 1 w, 4 nb)		8	(2 lb)	2
		52		78

Fall: 4, 6, 10, 16, 28, 39, 48, 49, 49. 22, 22, 28, 32, 32, 35, 48, 64, 69.

Bowling: Lever 8–3–10–1, Botham 9–3–16–4, Hendrick 5.4–2–11–5, Gooch 2–0–7–0.

Second innings: Lever 7–3–16–1, Botham 13.5–4–37–4, Hendrick 7–2–23–3.

Toss won by England XI. Umpires: D. Hawks & D. G. Weser.

ENGLAND XI WON BY 140 RUNS

ALBANY

December 13

England XI 208 for 4 (40 overs) (G. A. Gooch 112); **Western Australian Country XI** 139 (B. Miguel 53, P. H. Edmonds 6 for 53, G. Miller 4 for 68). **England XI won by 69 runs.**

PERTH

December 15, 16, 17, 19, 20

SECOND TEST MATCH – England won by 166 runs.

ADELAIDE

December 22, 23, 24

SOUTH AUSTRALIA

J. E. Nash	c Tolchard b Old	10	lbw b Emburey	25
W. M. Darling	c Tolchard b Old	19	(7) not out	41
I. R. McLean	c Tolchard b Gooch	7	(2) c & b Emburey	25
B. L. Causby	b Old	87	(3) c Randall b Emburey	7
R. J. Parker	c & b Edmonds	51	(4) c Randall b Emburey	42
*R. K. Blewett	c Old b Emburey	19	c Brearley b Emburey	51
P. R. Sleep	not out	31	(5) c Tolchard b Old	18
†S. R. Gentle	lbw b Lever	1	not out	21
A. T. Sincock	not out	12	did not bat	
Extras (3 lb, 1 nb)		4	(1 lb)	1
	7 wkts dec	241	6 wkts dec	231

Did not bat: G. R. Attenborough, D. A. Johnston.

Fall: 25, 36, 38, 129, 174, 220, 221. 45, 57, 58, 96, 140, 184.

Bowling: Lever 16–1–63–1, Old 18–2–55–3, Gooch 6–1–16–1, Emburey 17–3–48–1, Edmonds 17–3–55–1.

Second innings: Lever 10–1–33–0, Gooch 4–0–11–0, Emburey 26–3–67–5, Edmonds 28–9–91–0, Miller 4–1–6–0, Old 5–0–21–1, Boycott 1–0–1–0.

ENGLAND XI

G. Boycott	c Gentle b Sincock	4	(11) not out	7
G. A. Gooch	st Gentle b Causby	20	(5) st Gentle b Blewett	64
C. T. Radley	c Gentle b Attenborough	60	lbw b Attenborough	1
†R. W. Tolchard	run out	72	lbw b Johnston	6
D. W. Randall	c Gentle b Attenborough	47	(2) c Blewett b Johnston	45
*J. M. Brearley	not out	18	(1) c Parker b Johnston	26
G. Miller	not out	2	(6) not out	68
C. M. Old	did not bat		(7) b Attenborough	2
P. H. Edmonds	did not bat		(8) lbw b Blewett	2
J. E. Emburey	did not bat		(9) b Blewett	0
J. K. Lever	did not bat		(10) c Darling b Attenborough	11
Extras (3 b, 4 lb, 4 nb)		11	(1 b, 2 lb, 3 nb)	6
	5 wkts dec	234	9 wkts	238

Fall: 26, 32, 138, 186, 231. 65, 68, 74, 91, 180, 187, 196, 202, 223.

Bowling: Attenborough 13–5–41–2, Johnston 8–2–21–0, Sincock 5–0–27–1, Causby 6–0–34–1, Sleep 12–1–58–0, Blewett 8–1–41–0, Nash 1–0–1–0.
Second innings: Sincock 5–0–39–0, Attenborough 16–1–92–3, Johnston 7–0–44–3, Sleep 2–0–22–0, Blewett 7–0–35–3.

Toss won by South Australia. Umpires: R. A. French & M. G. O'Connell.

MATCH DRAWN

MELBOURNE

December 26

First **Benson & Hedges Cup** one-day international – match abandoned without a ball bowled. Match rescheduled for February 4.

MELBOURNE

December 29, 30, January 1, 2, 3

THIRD TEST MATCH – Australia won by 103 runs.

SYDNEY

January 6, 7, 8, 10, 11

FOURTH TEST MATCH – England won by 93 runs.

SYDNEY

First Benson & Hedges Cup match (40 overs)

January 13

AUSTRALIA

G. M. Wood	c Tolchard b Old	6
W. M. Darling	not out	7
K. J. Hughes	not out	0
Extras (4 lb)		4
	1 wkt	17

Did not bat: *G. N. Yallop, P. M. Toohey, A. R. Border, G. J. Cosier, P. H. Carlson, †J. A. Maclean, G. Dymock, A. G. Hurst.

Fall: 17.
Bowling: Lever 3–0–8–0, Old 3.2–1–5–1, Hendrick 1–1–0–0.

ENGLAND

G. Boycott, *J. M. Brearley, D. W. Randall, G. A. Gooch, D. I. Gower, †R. W. Tolchard, I. T. Botham, C. M. Old, P. H. Edmonds, J. K. Lever, M. Hendrick.

Toss won by England. Umpires: A. R. Crafter & C. E. Harvey

Match abandoned – rain.

NEWCASTLE

January 14, 15, 16

Northern NSW Country XI 223 for 9 dec (C. Beatty 62, J. Gardener 59) and 166 (C. Evans 64, R. Neal 44, C. M. Old 4 for 30); **England XI** 163 (J. M. Brearley 66, R. Holland 4 for 60) and 230 for 1 (G. Boycott 117*, C. T. Radley 55*, J. M. Brearley 50). **England XI won by 9 wickets.**

LAUNCESTON

January 18

England XI 240 for 8 (40 overs) (I. T. Botham 61, D. W. Randall 60, C. T. Radley 44); **Tasmania** 77 (34.4 overs). **England XI won by 163 runs.**

HOBART

January 19, 20, 21

TASMANIA

M. J. Norman	c Taylor b Old	13	b Emburey	43
G. W. Goodman	c Taylor b Old	1	c Taylor b Willis	1
S. J. Howard	c Taylor b Old	13	b Lever	20
J. H. Hampshire	c Taylor b Old	0	not out	46
†R. D. Woolley	b Old	4	c Radley b Miller	0
T. W. Docking	b Emburey	39	not out	2
*J. Simmons	c Miller b Old	1		
D. J. Gatenby	b Willis	1		
G. J. Cowmeadow	c Edmonds b Willis	10		
M. B. Scholes	b Miller	10		
G. R. Whitney	not out	0		
Extras (5 b, 3 lb, 5 nb)		13	(2 b, 1 lb, 3 nb)	6
		105	4 wkts	118

Fall: 6, 20, 20, 36, 47, 60, 61, 75, 105. 3, 34, 102, 107.

Bowling: Willis 10–1–24–2, Old 14–3–42–6, Lever 7–3–18–0, Emburey 4–3–1–1, Miller 3–1–7–1.

Second innings: Willis 4–1–9–1, Old 5–2–12–0, Lever 8–0–27–1, Edmonds 12–3–27–0, Emburey 6–1–15–1, Miller 5–1–18–1, Boycott 1–0–4–0.

ENGLAND XI

G. Boycott	not out	90
G. A. Gooch	c Goodman b Whitney	14
C. T. Radley	c Woolley b Cowmeadow	15
D. I. Gower	b Gatenby	30
†R. W. Taylor	b Whitney	1
G. Miller	b Gatenby	44
P. H. Edmonds	not out	7
Extras (4 b, 2 lb, 3 nb)		9
	5 wkts dec	210

Did not bat: C. M. Old, J. E. Emburey, J. K. Lever, *R. G. D. Willis.

Fall: 30, 54, 99, 102, 187.

Bowling: Cowmeadow 16–2–64–1, Whitney 26–3–73–2, Scholes 10–4–40–0, Gatenby 5–1–22–2, Simmons 1–0–2–0.

Toss won by England XI. Umpires: K. Connor & A. Edsall.

Match drawn.

MELBOURNE

Second Benson & Hedges Cup match (40 overs)

January 24

AUSTRALIA

G. M. Wood	c Gower b Edmonds	28
A. M. Hilditch	c Bairstow b Botham	10
A. R. Border	c Willis b Hendrick	11
*G. N. Yallop	run out	9
K. J. Hughes	lbw b Hendrick	0
P. H. Carlson	c Randall b Willis	11
T. J. Laughlin	c Willis b Hendrick	6
†J. A. Maclean	c Edmonds b Botham	11
R. M. Hogg	c Botham b Hendrick	4
G. Dymock	c & b Botham	1
A. G. Hurst	not out	0
Extras (4 b, 2 lb, 4 nb)		10
		101

Fall: 27, 52, 54, 55, 76, 78, 94, 99, 101.

Bowling:		
	Willis	8–4–15–1
	Lever	5–2–7–0
	Hendrick	8–1–25–4
	Botham	4.5–2–16–3
	Edmonds	7–0–26–1
	Gooch	1–0–2–0

ENGLAND

G. Boycott	not out	39
*J. M. Brearley	b Hogg	0
D. W. Randall	c Yallop b Dymock	12
G. A. Gooch	b Carlson	23
D. I. Gower	not out	19
I. T. Botham	did not bat	
†D. L. Bairstow	did not bat	
P. H. Edmonds	did not bat	
J. K. Lever	did not bat	
R. G. D. Willis	did not bat	
M. Hendrick	did not bat	
Extras (5 lb, 4 nb)		9
	3 wkts	102

7, 29, 69.

Hogg	6–1–20–1
Dymock	6–1–16–1
Laughlin	5–1–13–0
Carlson	5–0–21–1
Hurst	5.2–1–14–0
Border	1–0–9–0

Toss won by Australia.
Man of the Match: M. Hendrick.
England won by 7 wickets.

Umpires: A. R. Crafter & C. E. Harvey.

ADELAIDE

January 27, 28, 29, 31, February 1

FIFTH TEST MATCH – England won by 205 runs.

MELBOURNE

February 3

Tasmania (Gillette Cup winners) 131 for 6 (48 overs); **England XI** 134 for 7 (43.3 overs).
England XI won by 3 wickets.

MELBOURNE

Third Benson & Hedges Cup match (40 overs)

February 4

ENGLAND

G. Boycott	lbw b Laughlin	33
*J. M. Brearley	c Wright b Dymock	0
D. W. Randall	lbw b Dymock	4
G. A. Gooch	c Hurst b Carlson	19
D. I. Gower	not out	101
I. T. Botham	c Wood b Hurst	31
†D. L. Bairstow	run out	1
C. M. Old	not out	16
Extras (3 b, 3 lb, 1 nb)		7
	6 wkts	212

Did not bat: J. K. Lever, R. G. D. Willis, M. Hendrick.

Fall: 0, 7, 50, 89, 153, 158.

AUSTRALIA

G. M. Wood	b Old	23
W. M. Darling	c Old b Willis	7
K. J. Hughes	c Boycott b Lever	50
*G. N. Yallop	c Gower b Hendrick	31
P. M. Toohey	not out	54
G. J. Cosier	b Lever	28
P. H. Carlson	c Brearley b Lever	0
T. J. Laughlin	not out	15
Extras (6 lb, 1 nb)		7
	6 wkts	215

Did not bat: K. J. Wright, G. Dymock, A. G. Hurst.

7, 55, 90, 145, 185, 185.

Bowling:	Hurst	8-1-36-1	Willis	8-1-21-1
	Dymock	8-1-31-2	Lever	7-1-51-3
	Carlson	8-1-27-1	Hendrick	8-0-47-1
	Cosier	8-0-48-0	Old	8-1-31-1
	Laughlin	8-0-63-1	Botham	7.6-0-58-0

Toss won by Australia.
Man of the Match: D. I. Gower.

Umpires: R. C. Bailhache & D. G. Weser.

AUSTRALIA WON BY 4 WICKETS.

GEELONG

February 6

England XI 165 for 9 (40 overs); **Geelong & Districts XI** 100 for 9 (38.6 overs). **England XI won by 48 runs** (match awarded to England XI on relative scores at 38.6 overs after pitch had been invaded by spectators).

MELBOURNE

February 7

Fourth (deciding) Benson & Hedges Cup match (40 overs)

ENGLAND

G. Boycott	c Cosier b Dymock	2
*J. M. Brearley	c Wright b Cosier	46
D. W. Randall	c Hughes b Dymock	0
G. A. Gooch	c Hughes b Hurst	4
D. I. Gower	c Wood b Hurst	3
I. T. Botham	b Cosier	13
†D. L. Bairstow	run out	3
P. H. Edmonds	lbw b Laughlin	15
J. K. Lever	b Laughlin	1
R. G. D. Willis	c Wright b Cosier	2
M. Hendrick	not out	0
Extras (2 lb, 3 nb)		5
		94

Fall: 10, 10, 17, 22, 42, 56, 91, 91, 94.

AUSTRALIA

G. M. Wood	c Bairstow b Botham	30
W. M. Darling	c Brearley b Willis	14
K. J. Hughes	c Brearley b Willis	0
*G. N. Yallop	b Lever	25
P. M. Toohey	not out	16
G. J. Cosier	not out	8
P. H. Carlson	did not bat	
T. J. Laughlin	did not bat	
†K. J. Wright	did not bat	
G. Dymock	did not bat	
A. G. Hurst	did not bat	
Extras (2 nb)		2
	4 wkts	95

Fall: 29, 37, 54, 87.

Bowling:	Hurst	5-3-7-2	Willis	5-2-16-2
	Dymock	6-1-21-2	Hendrick	6-0-32-0
	Carlson	8-2-22-0	Botham	5.5-0-30-1
	Cosier	7-1-22-3	Lever	5-0-15-1
	Laughlin	5.7-0-17-2		

Toss won by Australia.
Man of the Match: G. Dymock.

Umpires: R. C. Bailhache & D. G. Weser.

AUSTRALIA WON BY 6 WICKETS

SYDNEY

February 10, 11, 12, 14

SIXTH TEST MATCH – England won by 9 wickets.